African Women's Histories in European Narratives
The Afropolitan Krio Fernandino Diaspora (1850–1996)

African Women's Histories in European Narratives

The Afropolitan Krio Fernandino Diaspora (1850–1996)

Yolanda Aixelà-Cabré

LEUVEN UNIVERSITY PRESS

This work was supported by the projects "Africans, Maghrebis and Latins (1808–1975)" (BLACK SPAIN) (PID2022-138689NB-I00), "Africans and Maghrebis in the Iberian Peninsula (1850–1975)" (AFRO-IBERIA) (PID2019-108397GB-I00/AEI/10.13039/501100011033), both funded by MCIN/AEI/10.13039/501100011033 and "FEDER Una manera de hacer Europa", and by the project "Música, patrimoni i societat" (SGR 2021 00499) funded by AGAUR-Generalitat de Catalunya.

Original title: Africanas en África y Europa (1850–1966), published by Bellaterra Edicions, 2022

© 2025 Leuven University press / Presses Universitaires de Louvain/Universitaire Pers Leuven. Minderbroedersstraat 4, B-3000 Leuven.

All TDM (Text and Data Mining) rights are reserved.

This book will be made open access under a CC-BY-NC-ND Licence within three years of publication thanks to Path to Open, a program developed in partnership between JSTOR, the American Council of Learned Societies (ACLS), University of Michigan Press, and The University of North Carolina Press to bring about equitable access and impact for the entire scholarly community, including authors, researchers, libraries, and university presses around the world. Learn more at https://about.jstor.org/path-to-open/.

As of 2028, attribution to this book should include the CC-licence and read as follows: Yolanda Aixelà-Cabré, *African Women's Histories in European Narratives: The Afropolitan Krio Fernandino Diaspora (1850–1996)*. Leuven: Leuven University Press, 2028. (CC BY-NC-ND 4.0)

ISBN 978 94 6270 461 9 (paperback)
eISBN 978 94 6166 664 2 (ePDF)
eISBN 978 94 6166 665 9 (ePUB)
https://doi.org/10.11116/9789461666642
D/2025/1869/17
NUR: 680
Typesetting: Crius Group
Cover design: Daniel Benneworth-Gray
Cover image: Mabel Barleycorn Beckley, daughter of Napoleon William and niece of Amelia in a plantation of Equatorial Guinea. (© Amalia Barleycorn and Sally Fenaux Barleycorn)

To my mother, Evelina Cabré Enclusa (1934-2022)

Table of Contents

Chapter 1. African women's histories in European narratives – Introduction — 13
    1.1. Premise — 18
    1.2. Hypothesis — 21
    1.3. Academic aims and state of the art — 22
    1.4. Methodology — 37

Chapter 2. Fernandino women in colonial Santa Isabel and independent Malabo — 49
    2.1. The African context and Europe: English and Spanish presence in Fernando Poo and Santa Isabel — 50
    2.2. The Krio Fernandino community and Amelia Barleycorn de Vivour — 55
    2.3. Everyday life in Santa Isabel — 75
    2.4. Tensions and conflicts: surviving under colonial repression — 94
    2.5. The connection between Malabo and Barcelona since 1968: Equatorial Guinean exile — 110
    2.6. Conclusions — 114

Chapter 3. The Fernandino in Barcelona during colonisation and post-independence — 119
    3.1. Barcelona and Santa Isabel — 120
    3.2. Amelia Barleycorn heading to Europe — 129
    3.3. Life in Barcelona — 146
    3.4. The Krio Fernandino: trade, health and social life — 157
    3.5. Barcelona, missionary actions and student intake aimed at Equatorial Guineans — 169
    3.6. Krio Fernandino intersectionality: class, gender and race — 174
    3.7. Spain's collective amnesia post-1968 and the onset of racism during the 1990s — 180
    3.8. Conclusions — 186

Chapter 4. Decolonising the African past from a gender perspective — 189

- 4.1. *Amelia Barleycorn de Vivour v. Spanish Government* (1911): marriage, nationality, gender and religion — 189
- 4.2. Fernandino women: between bourgeois elitism and colonial power — 200
- 4.3. The domestic service used by the Krio Fernandino community or how to (de)racialise class from intersectionality — 210
- 4.4. The status and social presentation of the body as a formula of distinction Fernandino — 218
- 4.5. Fernandino women mixing cultures and continents (Africa, America and Europe) — 224
- 4.6. The impact of Spanish colonialism and Fernandino decline — 233
- 4.7. Conclusion — 240

Chapter 5. A past forged in the present: the collective memory of Krio Fernandino women – Closing notes — 243

Notes — 249

Primary and secondary sources — 253
- Primary sources — 253
- Secondary sources — 255

Index — 267

List of Figures

Figure 1. Settlers and *braceros* climbing on the trunk of a ceiba tree.   30
Figure 2. Passport of Alicia Lucy Barleycorn, owned by Amalia Barleycorn, who showed me the document.   43
Figure 3. Aerial image of the Club Fernandino, Santa Isabel, 5 October 1963.   72
Figure 4. Aristocratic wedding, Fernando Poo. Undated (likely 1910s).   92
Figure 5. Report on the Tribute to Mr Alfredo Jones Níger together with Susana Dougan in the Ritz Hotel in 1963.   166
Figure 6. Letter of safe passage for Juana Elena Collins Jones.   228

List of Tables

Table 1. Population of Santa Isabel and Barcelona. Census of 1877	40
Table 2. Population of Santa Isabel and Barcelona. Census of 1950	41
Table 3. Population breakdown for Santa Isabel, 1856	77
Table 4. Population of Santa Isabel. Census of 1862	78
Table 5. *White population* in Fernando Poo, 1942 and 1950	80
Table 6. *Coloured race* population of Santa Isabel, 1942, by nationality	81
Table 7. Prices of staples in Santa Isabel, 1871	82
Table 8. Prices of main European staples in Santa Isabel, 1946–1947	84
Table 9. Prices of basic services in Santa Isabel, fourth quarter 1941 (in pesetas)	85
Table 10. Indigenous Equatorial Guinean and Spanish monthly salaries on a 1959 coffee plantation (in pesetas)	85
Table 11. Santa Isabel Mixed School (European pupils), 1942	89
Table 12. Monthly teaching salaries in Spanish Guinea, 1930 and 1933	89
Table 13. Causes of death in the Spanish Territories in the Gulf of Guinea, 1942	91
Table 14. Arrests made in Santa Isabel, 1946	95
Table 15. Crimes in Santa Isabel, second semester 1941	96
Table 16. Colonial Guard workforce in the Spanish Territories in the Gulf of Guinea 1946	102
Table 17. Equatorial Guineans in Spain, 1961–1996	113
Table 18. African tourists in Spain, 1970–1973	113
Table 19. Selection of products exported from Barcelona to Santa Isabel, October 1915	127
Table 20. Movement of passengers by sea through ports of origin and destination Santa Isabel, 1942	128
Table 21. Residence and travel permits in Santa Isabel in 1941, 1942 and 1943	130
Table 22. Selection of Krio Fernandino members who travelled between 1950 and 1960	140
Table 23. Selection of Equatorial Guineans who travelled between 1950 and 1960	142
Table 24. Annual public salaries by profession in Barcelona, 1914	152

Table 25. Main prices of consumer items in the markets of
   Barcelona, 1914   153
Table 26. Causes of mortality in Barcelona in December 1920   155
Table 27. Annual study expenses of an Equatorial Guinean girl in
   the Sagrada Familia College in Barcelona, 1921 (in pesetas)   173
Table 28. Total population of Barcelona, Catalonia and Spain and
   proportion of resident foreigners, 1996   184
Table 29. Foreigners residing in Barcelona, Catalonia and Spain by
   nationality, 1996   185
Table 30. Largest Spanish populations in Santa Isabel. Census of 1942   236

CHAPTER 1

African women's histories in European narratives – Introduction

This book reveals a story of African women in Africa and Europe from the onset of Krio Fernandino women's participation in trade, cultural and social matters in Santa Isabel (now Malabo), Equatorial Guinea and Barcelona (Catalonia), Spain.[1] My general aims are twofold. Firstly, to accept Walsh's decolonial challenge (2018) of turning extended *histories* (the stories about him) into *herstories* (stories about her). Secondly, in turn, to foster an emotional geography between continents that takes into account the fact that Europe's history is similar to that of its colonies (Aixelà-Cabré, 2022b) along with their migrations (Sassen, 2013).

I set out to achieve these goals using research by studying colonial archives and oral sources from one of the standout reference points in Equatorial Guinean economy, Amelia Barleycorn, Vivour's widow.[2] Her case sheds light on a hitherto-unknown family, community and nation-based story, as it allows for studying the standing and involvement of African peoples in Spain's peripheral and overseas territories from the middle of the nineteenth century to the end of the twentieth (Aixelà-Cabré, 2023a).

The comparative perspective that I offer in this book is inspired by the work of Fradera (2015, p. 1) from Havana and Barcelona, where he proposed studying the cities and countries that exercised an official or informal capital as "they were linked by long economic, social and cultural relations, in essence human."[3] To this end, two chapters have been included that compare life in Santa Isabel and Barcelona, highlighting the hall of mirrors that living in both cities entailed, with the survival of certain racial colonialities as a socio-political and employment framework.

The Krio Fernandino were a rich African group of multi-ethnic origin formed in Fernando Poo (ancient Spanish Guinea) from 1827. They received both African and European socio-cultural influences during their multilocal and multi-sited residences. It is also likely that some of their customs and activities maintained certain similarities between their settlements in Santa Isabel and Barcelona, which allowed them to live on both continents with relative ease. These simultaneities required comparing the two localities to delve into the social dynamics and individual and collective daily life there, since a more generic approach would have prevented us from detailing the experiences and responsibilities of the people living in those two cities.

The study shows how relations between the Spanish and the Equatorial Guineans were determined by Spanish colonial experiences in Africa. As a result, African communities in Spain were disadvantaged by coloniality in terms of race and gender, a form a discrimination that was particularly widespread throughout colonial times, and which was transposed to the post-independence phases, even affecting the Krio Fernandino community, on whom this research focuses.

The study is a considerable challenge given that more attention has been paid to the arrival of Africans in Europe in the Early Modern period than in the Late Modern period, which went more unnoticed until the explosion in transnational migrations in the 1960s. Indeed, until the eighteenth century, works focused on portraying the figure of the slave, as this was the most common status in the black population. As Ares Queija and Stella (2000, p. 15) observe, the social reality of Africans in Europe that I study here was shaped by "legal constraints, individual strategies and social opportunities."

It is worth stressing that the historical framework of this volume encompasses the period of the effective colonisation of the African colonies, that is, 1850 until the end of the 1990s, also comprising the final decolonisation ventures in the 1970s. The search for coloniality in the postcolonial period entailed studying the phenomenon of the upsurge in racist violence aimed at Africans at the end of the 1980s, taking as a benchmark the aggression suffered by the descendants of an eminent Fernandino family in Barcelona in 1992.

Curtailing the account in 1968 would have weakened my decolonial proposal of creating awareness of the extent to which the colonialities of power (Quijano, 2014) and the rejection of African otherness (Mbembe, 2021) acted as domination processes that worsened the post-independence period, when supposedly the collectives whom the European powers had colonized had been given the reins to their own fate and a chance to tell their own stories – testimonies of the past that looked to the future with optimism, which should have led to hitherto unseen times.

The increase of African communities in Spain, combined with Spain's failure to assume accountability vis-à-vis its colonial past, had as its result a rise in racism that coincided with the enactment of the Immigration Law in 1985 and the increase in migration in the 1990s, with the consequent expulsions and migratory regularisation of the state in 1996. The ill-will toward migrants alongside the legislative changes led to shifts in the treatment and consideration they received, to which, as will be seen, the wealthy Krio Fernandino minority that is studied in particular detail in this work had been accustomed. The Krio Fernandino community was characterised by their enjoyment of a series of economic and legal privileges that made them an elite group, though also by their transnational multilocality, their multi-sited residence, their factual intersectionality and a kind of African cosmopolitan that was Afropolitan.[4] Indeed, as proposed by Mbembe (2007, p. 28), the Afropolitan mindset entails a pluralism of African cultures sharing a geographical space, which brings to the fore the idea that borders and spaces forming the "new" African identities are a cultural mixture comprising interwoven worlds, conditions that migrants carry with them following centuries of intercontinental history. This Afropolitanism based on mixing and weaving worlds will be hugely useful in explaining the specific nature of the Krio Fernandino community. In the case of Amelia Barleycorn, this means not forgetting or overlooking her African pluri-ethnic roots and instead combining them with other cultural experiences.

The findings allow for the background and presence of this African community on the Iberian Peninsula[5] to produce a Euro-African historical re-enactment vis-à-vis gender, which will enrich the basis for studies, showing the European imprints of multi-regional, transcontinental and Afropolitan women. As will be seen, Amelia Barleycorn constitutes an exception to the normal status of black women in Spanish Guinea and the Barcelona of the early years of the twentieth century, as her wealth and power conferred upon her a series of privileges that *a priori* were denied to African women.

I would also mention that this book does not study the link between the Catalan bourgeoisie who made their fortune in Spanish Guinea and the Catalan fortunes amassed in Cuba, nor does it suggest parallelisms between the impact of slavery and the onset of capitalism with its elites, in relation to the effect of Fernandino participation in the turning of colonial capitalist cogs that would catapult them into the African elite bourgeoisie.

To conclude, I set out the structure of this book, which is composed of five main chapters.

The first chapter proposes the premise, main hypotheses, research goals and theoretical framework, and concludes with a description of the methodology used in the research.

The second chapter tackles the social reality of Krio Fernandino women and other Equatorial Guinean female groups in the city of Santa Isabel, providing a historical reconstruction of what Fernando Poo and everyday life in the city against the backdrop of European and Spanish colonialism was like, as the cities shifted from being markedly English in their outlook to undergoing a process of Hispanisation, from the mid-nineteenth century onwards. This chapter reviews the Krio Fernandino community, taking as a starting point Amelia Barleycorn de Vivour and other influential families, namely the Joneses, Dougans, Kinsons, Collinses and Balboas. Next, a sketch is given of what life was like in Santa Isabel in terms of population, cost of living and services in the colony. The final sections are devoted to explaining the tensions and conflicts that would emerge as part of the cohabitation between Africans and Spaniards, which was characterised by colonial repression and in which there were tell-tale signs of impunity, abuse of women and young girls, and armed struggles with the indigenous Colonial Guards, along with the expulsion of Spanish Africans from the colony. The chapter concludes with a reconstruction of the connection between Barcelona and Malabo, from the declaration of independence in 1968 onwards, with the onset of Equatorial Guinean political exile.

The third chapter studies the Fernandino diaspora in Barcelona. For this reason, the connections and similarities between Santa Isabel and Barcelona in terms of population, cost of living and services are detailed to give a better idea of the journeys made by Amelia Barleycorn de Vivour and other Krio Fernandino and Equatorial Guinean women to Barcelona. A section is devoted to setting out the relationship between missionary actions in Barcelona and the intake of students, laying the foundations for an analysis of feminine intersectionality in terms of class, gender and race. The chapter concludes by describing the Spanish colonial reluctance to remember its colonial past and the upsurge of racism in the 1990s.

The fourth chapter provides elements that can be used to decolonise the African past through gender categorisation. It begins with the request lodged by Amelia Barleycorn to the Spanish government in 1911, which granted her and all Equatorial Guineans the right to follow Protestantism while also facilitating the obtaining of nationality for the Krio community as a whole. The chapter continues by analysing the transversal aspects of Fernandino women, namely what powers and authority they held and the first demonstrations. It then discusses how domestic servitude in the Fernandino community could (de)racialise the class divisions and to what extent the social unmasking of the bodies of Fernandino women had a bearing on Spanish colonies of Krio Fernandino descent.

The fifth and final chapter brings together the most relevant conclusions from this work.

Finally, I would not wish to finish this brief introduction without expressing my gratitude to various people. First and foremost, I would like to thank Amalia Barleycorn and Sally Fenaux Barleycorn for their patient kindness and the warm welcome I was given to the complex world of Barleycorn genealogy. I am indebted to them, as their agreement to help me was the basis of the most prized asset for any anthropologist. Amalia's smile and Sally's words of encouragement will be forever etched in my memory. I would also like to thank Jeremy Crump for the information regarding the existing documentation on the Barleycorns stored at the School of Oriental and African Studies archive in London. I am grateful to my dear friend and colleague Elisa Rizo (Iowa State University) for her patience and thorough reading of this book, which was pivotal in readdressing the content and structure, thus bolstering the argumentation. To Remei Sipi, a loyal friend of many years and also a prolific writer and activist, I offer thanks for her unwavering support on a personal level, and her generosity in sharing her expert knowledge of the Bubis for this work, as her sagacious comments on the legacy of Fernandino women gave this book additional depth from the very moment she kindly agreed to assess it. Similarly, my thanks go to the GRIMSE Research Group, and particularly to Albert García Balañà and Teresa Segura (UPF), for inviting me to join their seminar circle, where I received first-rate suggestions on the subject matter of this book. Likewise, I would like to acknowledge the support of my editor of Leuven University Press, Mirjam Truwant, as well as José Luís Ponce from Edicions Bellaterra in Spain.

I also want to extend my special thanks to all my team members in the Afro-Iberian and Black Spain R&D projects. They have been a source of support for my analysis, both in the quarterly meetings and at our

International Afro-Iberia / Black Spain Seminars (2021, 2024) and the Afro-Iberia International Conference (2022). They are: Ana Lúcia Sá (ICSTE-IUL), Jordi Moreras (URV), Jessica Falconi (CEAD-Universidade de Lisboa), Elisa Rizo (Iowa State University), Diana Arbaiza (Universiteit Antwerpen), Nuria Fernández-Moreno (UNED), Mar García (UAB), Eduardo Costa Dias (ICSTE-IUL) and JM. Persánch (Lakeland University).

Also worthy of a special mention is Juan Tomás Ávila Laurel, who accepted the challenge of writing a novel inspired by the accounts given in this book, entitled *Dientes blancos, piel negra* (*White Teeth, Black Skin*, 2022). This text documents my research and includes my mother's life experiences, Evelina Cabré Enclusa, who thrilled us in heated postprandial conversations on the lifestyle of the Catalan bourgeoisie in the first half of the twentieth century, accounts that would prove vital in creating a historical framework for the arrival in Barcelona of the novel's main character, Valerina Diana Vivour.

1.1. Premise

This work is grounded on the premise that the Fernandino people were a multilocal, transnational, transcontinental and Afropolitan community that lived between Africa and Europe.[6] My aim is to decolonise the past by collaborating in the circulation of other knowledge, and cultures, experiences and rhetoric of African otherness in Europe.

The work by Rosenhaft and Aitken (2013, p. 1) has been a source of major inspiration for this research work. It has provided proof of its feasibility in relation to how mobility between continents altered the imagined construct between Africa and Europe. Similarly helpful has been the work by Northrup (2014) dealing with the active roles that Africans played in the encounters with Europeans between 1450 and 1850, and that of Oualdi (2020) on the reconstruction of the transimperial and transnational life of a slave at the end of the nineteenth century.

However, the academic challenge was complicated by the relative lack of studies on the Krio Fernandino. The excellent previous works by Sundiata (1974, 1976, 1996), Clarence-Smith (1994) and Aranzadi (2016), and by Yakpo (2010) from a linguistic standpoint, should be highlighted, as well as the work undertaken also by other researchers such as Bolekia (2019), Ndongo (1977), Sant (2015, 2017) and Armengol (2015). The relative scarcity of previous studies led me to an extensive consultation of some thousands of texts and documents, data that have provided a solid foundation of clues to give a well-founded description of what life was like for the Krio Fernandino in Santa Isabel and in Barcelona.

The book is similarly based on the premise that it is necessary to reverse African invisibility on the Iberian Peninsula and in Spain specifically. For this reason, a historical reconstruction of the Equatorial Guinean settlement in Santa Isabel and Barcelona is offered, paying special attention to the Krio Fernandino diaspora and to one of its major reference points, Amelia Barleycorn, the widow of W. Vivour. By contrasting the Krio Fernandino case with that of other African groups, it is shown that they did not always suffer processes of minoritisation, racialisation and subalternisation, which were so markedly widespread between the late nineteenth and early twentieth centuries, both in the metropolis and in the colonies.

The Krio Fernandino: between black colonisers and racial liminality

The collaboration of the Krio Fernandino with European colonisation was controversial for the rest of the Equatorial Guinean population. It is relevant that their European commercial intermediation not only enriched them, but also gave them the much sought-after letter of emancipation that placed them on a level footing rights-wise to the Spaniards, while the rest of Equatorial Guineans remained classified as unemancipated. Therefore, the Equatorial Guinean historian Iyanga Pendi (2021, p. 42) has concluded that "their *distinguished* social class" came from being "intermediaries between Europeans and Africans", which had turned them into "black colonisers".

This image of black colonisers is particularly striking yet somewhat imperfect. It makes the Krio Fernandino an exception, on the one hand, because they were also a colonised black community whose rights were equal to those of white Europeans, and on the other hand because the image equated the Krio Fernandino with the colonisers, who would no longer be solely white, but rather also black African. This label of "black coloniser" to define the Krio Fernandino is dotted throughout this book.

It should be noted that during Spanish colonialism, cases of mistreatment by Krio Fernandino landowners of labourers were proven, including on Amelia Barleycorn's estate, an abusive practice that also happened on those owned by Catalans and Spaniards. However, in favour of the Krio Fernandino it can be said, for example, that they leaped to the defence of other Equatorial Guineans when they thought it timely, an attitude that differentiated them from the Spanish colonists and aligned them with the Africans, even though their wealth and lifestyle were closer to their European colonisers than the colonised Africans.

For all these reasons, it is interesting to apply the notion of racial liminality to define the status of the Krio Fernandino, understanding "liminality" as the transition from one state to another (Van Gennep, 2008), and "racial liminality" as the existence of people unclassifiable through their skin colour due to their physical appearance, background or identity (Pekarofski, 2021).[7]

It is evident that at the height of the Fernandinos' powers, they were characterised by a light and shade that related to their participation in the colonial inner workings, to their racialisation, to a classism that required distinguishing themselves from their black African workers, and to their racial liminality between the European colonial power and the Equatorial Guinean society that welcomed them and was subjected to oppression.

Racial liminality allows us to overcome the difficulty of classifying the Krio Fernandino, throughout the colonisation process, simply as Equatorial Guineans or as settlers. Moreover, for the Equatorial Guineans, the Krio Fernandino were not originally from Fernando Poo, and they treated other Africans unfairly. For Iyanga Pendi (2021, p. 41), they were eternal foreigners. This reaction does not consider that they have been installed in what is now Equatorial Guinea for more than 150 years, as well as in other countries and continents. The Krio Fernandino have provided an excellent example of the melting pot of cultures and Afropolitan insertion. For the Spanish settlers, their existence in Santa Isabel strained the seams of race rhetoric – as a cultured and elegant black African elite – which did not mean that they could not participate in some of the same social activites in Santa Isabel. The Catalan bourgeoisie took a more nuanced view of the Krio Fernandino, as they had already amassed their own experiences in colonial Cuba (Yañez, 2006, p. 679), but with white Cuban elites. Catalans did not view commitment in maintaining a certain degree of public sociability in Santa Isabel and Barcelona in the first third of the twentieth century, since the relationship need not entail the establishment of mixed marriages with the Krio Fernandino that would have brought controversy since such unions were highly frowned upon (Rubiés, 2001, p. 50; 2017).

It would seem that at the height of the Fernandinos' powers the community had a liminal status, not so much by its own choice but rather because of its lack of full acceptance by the Catalans and Spaniards on the one hand and by the Equatorial Guineans themselves on the other. The former saw the full acceptance of the Krio Fernandino as conditioned by the colour of their skin. At the same time, the Equatorial Guineans considered them to be African colonisers, a status that researchers like Pardue (2020) also gave them, but without the connotations of Iyanga Pendi (2021).

The liminality of the Fernandinos ended with their loss of economic power in the final years of the colonial period. Their decline diluted them with other Krios of Santa Isabel and the Equatorial Guinean population in terms of status, while at the same time that it dragged them to be considered again eternal foreigners, since they were Africans without history. As a result, it was forgotten that the Afropolitan status of the Krio Fernandino had taken root in the city at the end of the nineteenth century.

1.2. Hypothesis

The central hypothesis of this book is that the colonial framework conditioned the arrival and establishment of African women in Europe, as it entailed legal inequalities that would lead to a reduction of their rights, a status of inferiority with respect to other citizens and major socio-cultural rejection on the grounds of their skin colour that responded to the process of colonial racialisation. These colonialities promoted by the logic of European colonisation were neutralised for decades for the Krio Fernandino from Spanish Guinea in Barcelona, as they constituted a transnational, transcontinental, multilocal and Afropolitan elite. Their case was an exception that had effects on Fernandino women, since their economic capacity and socio-political influence was beyond than that of many European women from the middle and upper social classes. Applying the intersectional perspective of Crenshaw (1995) and Stolcke (1995), it is observed that these women successfully overcame the inequalities suffered by other Equatorial Guinean and Spanish men and women. This demonstrates that discrimination on the basis of African and black women's status was neutralised by their belonging to an upper social class, as will be seen from the study of the figure of Amelia Barleycorn de Vivour.

1.3. Academic aims and state of the art

Below, the five aims of this research are listed with an explanation of their respective states of the art.

Krio Fernandino women and Amelia Barleycorn de Vivour

African women are not part of Europe's androcentric history, nor of the European countries in which they settled. There is no emotional geography that connects Africa and Europe.

This book studies a European past with African roots in terms of gender, through the study of the figure of Amelia Barleycorn (1860? Santa Isabel–1920 Barcelona), widow of W. Vivour, a black African woman from Spanish Guinea who belonged to the Krio Fernandino community. The Krio were an African group of multi-ethnic origin formed in Fernando Poo from 1827 with the arrival of slaves freed by the British, and then of Africans brought from Sierra Leone, Liberia and Nigeria. The Fernandino community was clearly aware that it had escaped from the slave trade, which for Northrup (2006, p. 1) had conditioned its African identity.

The first aim of the book is therefore to use the case study of the Krio Fernandino citizen Amelia Barleycorn to reverse the Eurocentric imagery that has hidden African footprints in Europe, as researchers like Small (2019), Pitts (2019) and Fraiture (2022) have decried.

I have approached this challenge from the perspective of postcolonial and decolonial studies, which encourage this type of analysis as their lenses focus and amplify marginal realities. In particular, the proposal regarding the epistemologies of the south that aims to recover other experiences and cultural knowledge is particularly useful and provides the grounding for a chapter of this book that reconstructs Fernandino social dynamics in Santa Isabel, since it is based on the theory that academic knowledge has socio-political coordinates (Sousa & Meneses, 2014) that can condition the analytical gaze.[8] In this regard, a historical reconstruction of these Africans' traces, who, as will be seen, held Spanish nationality, will create the scenario to promote an emotional geography that builds bridges between past and present, between Spain and its colonies.

Thus, Amelia will act as our figurehead to illustrate the gradual settlement of an African elite in Europe. For her part, following several trips to English cities (such as London and Liverpool), she ultimately settled in Barcelona at the end of the nineteenth century. My study concludes in the 1990s, when the press began to report on the existing racist violence, a fact that reveals not only the lack of empathy with Africans in Barcelona and Spain but also the deep-rooted ignorance of the Fernandino past.

The foregoing forms the narrative put forward by the Equatorial Guinean writer Ávila Laurel (2022) in his novel inspired by the family of Amelia Barleycorn de Vivour, a challenge that he accepted within the framework of the Afro-Iberian and Black Spain R&D projects of which this book is part. Ávila Laurel constructs an excellent biographical story of a Vivour descendant that, flitting between fiction and historical novel, allows us to trace a path that begins with her birth in Santa Isabel and her journey to Barcelona in the 1930s, and ends with the racist aggression against a Fernandino subject published in the press in 1992.

The case study into Amelia Barleycorn in Barcelona reveals how wealthy and highly educated Africans settled in European countries, thus demonstrating that the African presence did not abruptly come to an end between the end of the Early Modern period and the beginning of the Late Modern, but rather that some them also forged a new homeland in European cities.

The powerful Krio Fernandino elite transited betwixt two worlds, sharing certain Eurocentric rhetorical bases with colonial structures. However, the Fernandinos were also characterised by their transnationality (Vertovec, 1999), as they had ties that went beyond the territorial borders of the colony; by their multilocality of multi-sited residence (Marcus, 1995),[9] as observed in their families being scattered across different countries; by their Afropolitanism (Mbembe, 2007), with a way of viewing the cosmopolitan world while not betraying their strong African roots; by their transculturality (Ortiz, 2002) and mixing (Stolcke, 2010; Ventura, 2010), as a mixed and border category; and even by their glocalisation (Robertson, 1997; Roudometof, 2021), since their local African elitism, centred in Santa Isabel, passed on globally to other regions and countries of the world.[10]

The transnational mobility of Krio Fernandino women was particularly noteworthy. These were self-employed women who travelled alone or with other relatives or Fernandino friends, as can be ascertained from the lists of passengers who embarked with different destinations or in the news items that, beyond the anecdotal, synthesised a way of being and participating in the world. Furthermore, this aspect was also significant because it should be remembered that European androcentrism, which had seen the denial of rights and visibility to European women, as reported by Beauvoir (1949) in general and by Nash (1983) in particular in the case of Spain, was even more radical with regard to African women due to their status as black women.

Nor should we overlook the fact that the dominant socio-political framework was that in which the colonial inequalities promoted by European instances against African populations justified the diminution of rights based on a racialisation adhering to skin colour, without ever tackling the "indigenous demands in matters of civic rights and racial equality" (Mbembe, 2021, p. 89).

This reality in colonial rhetoric and practices was an example of the contempt that many African women had to endure in the colonies and in the metropolises, an androcentrism that, as an ideology, left women in a situation of subordination to men. This male-focused logic was transferred from Europe to Africa, constituting a powerful colonial legacy in terms of gender (Amadiume, 2018), which continued in the postcolonial period in the so-called colonialities of power (Mignolo, 2004; Quijano, 2014; Walsh, 2018), according to which European societies were superior to African ones because the treatment of women in Europe was supposedly better. Here I understand gender as the variable that allows sex to be considered as an analytical category, the framework in which relationships between men/women are built and recreated, and the factor that allows us to analyse the socio-cultural construct of the sexes from the ideological level as a result of a set of social, cultural and historical factors (Aixelà-Cabré, 2005). It is indeed the construction of gender which conditions people in their daily lives, since it can impose a sexual hierarchy which subordinates women to men, in other words resulting in clear androcentrism.

However, noting the European colonial bias, it is similarly worth bearing in mind that part of the Equatorial Guinean population also had an androcentric bias that took power and authority away from women. In other words, androcentrism was not a solely European phenomenon, since the privileges of the women of the Krio Fernandino elite were not present in other Equatorial Guinean ethnicities. However, this is not to overlook the detrimental androcentric effect of the Spanish missions or that Equatorial Guinean women were considered mere sexual objects by white men, as will be reviewed in due course.

From Euro-African to Afro-European: from political identities to cultural identities

Women and men of African descent received an effective but limited European citizenship in Africa. Those who settled in Europe were subsumed by the colonialities that emanated from the colonial regime, a circumstance that finally also extended to the Fernandinos when they lost their privileges.

The terms Euro-African and Afro-European enable us to ponder the mutual legacies of contact between the two continents: Euro-African places greater emphasis on European imprints than on African ones, and Afro-European prioritises African footprints over European ones (Aixelà-Cabré, 2021, p. 2). The use of this terminology is intended to facilitate the study of synergies and exchanges between the two continents. One of the effects of the constitution of the colonies was the granting of European nationalities to the African populations, which legally meant they became Euro-African. Euro-African is used herein to define the European character of the nationality they received and which legally prevailed among Africans who resided in both Europe and Africa during the colonial period and until independence. Conversely, the Afro-European concept is used to define the African nationality that would legally prevail during residence in Europe after the postcolonial period.

The Euro-African concept has recently been used to study exchanges between Europe and Africa in the migratory and identity sphere (Marazziti & Riccardi, 2005; Rosenhaft & Aitken, 2013), in international relations (Oloruntoba, 2016) and in colonial memories (Aixelà-Cabré, 2020b). The Afro-European concept, in contrast, appears more linked to literary studies (López, 2008; Innes & Stein, 2008; Brancato, 2009, 2011; Thomas, 2014), to identity and migration issues (Clark Hine et al., 2009; Otele, 2020) and to academic networks and social movements (for example, *Afroeuropeans* and *Afroféminas*). The research efforts to explain the terms Euro-African and Afro-European have not proliferated in Europe to define the numerous relations that were historically established between the two continents, particularly when considering how widely used the prefix "Afro" has been to determine the relations between the continents of Africa and the Americas, as well as between Africa and different countries of the American continent. Perhaps an initial conclusion on the disinterest by these concepts would suggest European states' intent, and likewise that of the Spanish state regarding the history of black Spain, to deny their African imprints, since this could definitively draw a veil over an uncomfortable colonial past, avoiding reparations, skirting the recognition of European debts and denying African roots as a cultural basis of numerous European countries.

This lack of visibility and social recognition of Africans in Europe and specifically black Spain (Aixelà-Cabré, 2020a, 2023b; Garrido-Castellano & Leitão, 2022; Aixelà-Cabré & Rizo, 2023; Arbaiza, 2023, 2024; Falconi, 2023a, 2023b; Raposo & Garrido Castellano, 2023; García, 2024; Grau et al., 2024; Moreras, 2024; Persánch, 2024; Rizo, 2024) has fostered the fight for recognition of the Afro-European collective that, far from seeking protection in its Euro-African imprint, demands rights in postcolonial times: these are Africans in Europe who defend and claim the equality, recognition and mutual respect they deserve after playing a role in a shared past (Borst & Gallo-González, 2019; Aixelà-Cabré, 2020b).

It is of the utmost importance to stress that the granting of European nationalities in Africa by colonial governments only sought to identify the inhabitants of the overseas empires as attached to their territories, as if they were another property, rather than to make them equal in rights and duties to Europeans in Europe, since such recognition of these European nationalities did not bring with it citizenship rights.

This *de facto* nationality granted by different European countries to African populations was complemented by the exceptional granting of full citizenship since most of the population had to be placed under guardianship. Establishing a colony often required the recognition of a certain degree of emancipation of a small African minority that collaborated with the colonial powers. I also start my discussion from the fact that the emancipated status of a large part of this minority, granted at the time of colonisation, guaranteed a certain equality of rights with Spanish nationals, as evidenced by the revised documentation of Amelia Barleycorn and other Krio Fernandino individuals.

Thus, throughout this book I will use the Euro-African concept with the intention of defining the legal nationality of Africans in colonial times, not their identity or cultural affiliation. I do so because I believe that this legal antecedent could also be used today by descendants of those Africans who settled in Europe to prove that their European status dates back more than 150 years.

The arrival of Africans who settled in Europe from newly African independent states would illustrate the transition from Euro-African to

Afro-European *experienced by* those Africans who settled in the European continent. In fact, the claim in Spain of being Afro-Spanish, no longer from a legal point of view, but from that of identity, was made from the late 1990s, with some precedents, such as those identified by Nfubea (2021): the Afro-European claim, or, in our case, Afro-Spanish, was formulated in post-independence times as a form of rejection of the colonialities that continue to transit between Africa and Europe.

It is important to note that in the documentation of Spanish Guinea – namely, decrees, ordinances, complaints or judgments against the Equatorial Guineans, to give just a few examples of the extensive documentation consulted – the "nationals" of Spanish Guinea were usually classified as "subjects" or "indigenous" Spaniards, as if the adjective reflected a different and lower level than that of the Spaniards of the cities. However, the words "subjects" or "indigenous" were not stated on their birth certificates, visas, safe-conducts, passports or other identification issued during the colonisation period, because they were for all intents and purposes Spanish.

The historical and political backdrop was marked by European colonial empires that were interested in promoting inequality on both continents by diminishing Africans' rights. It should be remembered that the emancipated status that some of the Krio in Spanish Guinea came from their ability to demonstrate loyalty to and unwavering faith in the colonial system, a status that could be reversed had their efforts been deemed lacking. Thus, with few exceptions, until the end of the 1920s only the Krio Fernandino minority would attain the status of emancipation: this right was the result of the enormous economic and social power that they had accumulated in the last third of the nineteenth century during the British occupation.

Raising the idea that during colonial times Africans were also Europeans and, therefore, Euro-Africans allows us to become aware of the existence of political, cultural, social and economic legacies resulting from their coexistence, not only in Africa, but also in Europe. García Balañà (2019) notes that France and Great Britain incorporated thousands of indigenous soldiers into their ranks during the First World War, which brought with it certain colonialities, something similar to what happened on the side of the rebels against Franco during the Spanish Civil War (Madariaga, 2002). Plus, the African presence in Europe during the first half of the twentieth century was evident thanks to the organisation of human zoos that began in the last third of the nineteenth century (Pardo-Tomas et al., 2019), as well as to particular channels such as missions or the military (Atlan & Jézéquel, 2002). However, it is very important to highlight that the amount of influence these Africans settled in Europe had was, with exceptions, highly limited, especially if compared to the power of the European minorities that settled in Africa, who, thanks to the military and civil deployment, managed to transfer to the continent their way of seeing the world (Stoler, 1991; Cooper & Stoler, 1997), leaving their postcolonial imprint on the political construction of their states and in the configuration of their national identities (Aixelà-Cabré, 2022a), as well as in the social construction of the African sexes (Amadiume, 2018). In Europe, the Euro-African condition of those with great wealth and public renown de-racialised their blackness and African origin, entering a stage of racial liminality. However, from a gender perspective, European androcentrism and Christianity conflicted with the female power and authority of African mother-focused matricentric families.

The subsumption of the African into the European that I propose to study from the legal perspective of nationality lasted until independence from colonial rule was declared.

The interest in the use of the Euro-African concept lies therefore in the desire to make visible the statutory link to various European countries that, for more than a century, many Africans enjoyed. In my view, if we trace this contemporary historical story of disconnection between continents, there would have been greater incentives to write a shared history that did not turn its back on the legacies of the African continent in Europe. Indeed, this awareness of the closely linked past between Africa and Europe would have made it difficult, for example, for the European Union authorities to erase the few benefits that the colonised territories maintained in relation to their former metropolises after independence from colonial rule, such as easily receiving a travel visa. This advantage has been rejected in recent years in the promoted amnesia of the European Union, as Rizo (2012) found in the Spanish case.

In fact, the European amnesia of its colonial past, denying its historical debts, was exacerbated after the accession of countries such as Spain to the European Union in 1986 and the signing of the Schengen Agreement in 1991, as it marked the beginning of the "Schengenisation" of the borders and policies of EU countries like Spain (Ferrer-Gallardo, 2008; Aris, 2021). The so-called "Fortress Europe" emerged, a concept studied by Carr (2012) and Tsianos and Karakayali (2010), that for Mbembe (2006) ended up becoming the expression of his necropolitics.

The impact of intersectionality: class, gender and race from a multilocal transnational perspective

Intersectionality allows us to discern the different impact that class, gender and race variables had on the Equatorial Guinean collective in Santa Isabel and Barcelona. Wealthy Krio women subverted the sexual abuse of the Spaniards in the colony that was unavoidable for all other Equatorial Guinean women, while during their European stays they maintained privileges highly similar to those of upper- and upper-middle-class Catalan women.

The reasons behind African invisibility may have been multicausal, yet would remain very similar to the racism that Stoler (1995, p. 116) detected between the Dutch and the population coming from their colonies: the requirements to acquire the equivalent status of European, with relevant aspects such as the use of the Dutch language, schooling, dress or church membership, were rarely sufficient because there always emerged "a basic and disturbing symmetry that subscribed to its racial grammar [...] native sensitivities could not be extracted from an Indian child as native blood circulated through its veins" (Stoler, 1995, p. 116). The racism to which Stoler referred (1995) is what Rubiés (2017, p. 33) deftly defined for the Early Modern period – also applicable to the Late Modern era – as: "the justification of ethnic discrimination based on a concept of race that implies natural criteria."

As Mbembe (1999), and earlier Césaire (2006 [1950]), concluded, blackness was part of the European colonial socio-cultural hierarchy, while the capitalist system has continually detracted from the value of the same races, as well as the same social classes and the same sex.

Therefore, despite the differences in how the European countries constructed race,[11] the viewing of colonial hierarchies always concluded by activating a racialisation process that denigrated "the black", since, as Mbembe (1999, p. 22) pointed out, race had always been present in discrimination in terms of "imagining the inhumanity of foreign peoples and the domination that must be exercised over them."

Stoler (1991, 1995) linked race, gender and class in order to show the underlying discourses of European colonial practices as they filtered a way of thinking about otherness and women. For Stoler (1991, p. 51), "having studied how the colonisers have viewed the indigenous Other, we are beginning

Figure 1. Settlers and *braceros* climbing on the trunk of a ceiba tree. General Archive of the Administration, box 81/0680, envelope.

to resolve how the Europeans of the colonies imagined themselves and how they built communities built on asymmetries of race, class and gender." In her analysis, Stoler projected the racist and androcentric European gaze that had promoted the racialisation, minoritisation and subalternisation of Africans, topics that Spivak's subaltern studies (1988) had also looked at.

Crenshaw (1995), like Stolcke (1995), developed the intersectional perspective to demonstrate that women's experiences and circumstances vary greatly according to their social class, gender and race. These perspectives allow us to analyse with greater certainty the case of Amelia Barleycorn, since the intersectionality she exemplified reproduced the variables of race, gender and class, both in Santa Isabel and in Barcelona, since her power and authority was equal to that of the Spanish and European white men in her same social class. These recalls must recover the accurate of Alcoff (2007, p. 256) about the importance of always balancing "class and race".

In the Spanish case, the race ideology was used to support the supposed Spanish colonial civilising work of the late nineteenth and early twentieth centuries. With rhetoric on the brotherhood of the "Hispanic race" that relativised the significance of geographical origin or skin colour, it finally justified an annulment or significant limitation of the rights of local populations, with unforgivable arbitrariness of all kinds involving expropriations or workplace and sexual abuse.

For Ugarte (2009), the transfer made by Spanish structures of the notion of the Hispanic race to Equatorial Guinea was evident. Thus, it is relevant to note that this racialisation of the existing populations in the African colonies was also transferred to Spain, where it was perpetuated in the postcolonial period and extended to other cultural groups. As Martín Díaz, Cuberos and Castellani (2012) have shown, blackness also impacted the Latin American population settled in Spain; despite sharing the Spanish language with Spaniards, just as Equatorial Guinean Africans did, Latin American immigrant women and African women received the same treatment.

African women in Barcelona: from an Afropolitan bourgeois elite to racism and racialised migrations

The Fernandino elitism of the late nineteenth century weakened until it fell into oblivion in the twenty-first century. The Krio Fernandino diaspora, like other Equatorial Guinean groups, ended up suffering the racialisation of migrations, as happened with other Africans who arrived on the Iberian Peninsula.

It should be noted that the available literature on the population of Equatorial Guineans in Spain is limited.[12] Highlights include Fons (2002), Bolekia (2003), Aixelà-Cabré (2011, 2012, 2020a), Doppelbauer and Fleischmann (2012), Porzio (2014), Iliescu and Bosaho (2015), Iliescu (2017), Stucki (2016, 2019) and Schlumpf-Thurnherr (2022).

Bela-Lobedde (2018), of Bubi heritage, offers an account based on her biographical experiences as the daughter of an Equatorial Guinean migrant, continuing a reflection begun years ago on African migrations by Vi-Makome (2000) and Sipi (2004, 2010). Other works on Equatorial Guinean migration in Spain have focused on literature and blogs, such as Ugarte (2009), Riochí-Siafá (2018), and Borst and Gallo-González (2019), among others. Mbare Ngom (1996), Lewis (2009, 2017), Rizo (2012), Otabela and Onomo-Abena (2009) and Okenve (2014) have analysed the traces of Equatorial Guinean memory through the literary work of Ndongo (1987, 1997, 2015), Ávila Laurel (1999, 2000, 2006, 2009), Boturu (2010) and J. Mbomio (2016).

Africans' invisibility in Spain is common to that in other European countries. Small (2018, p. 1185) has detailed how the difficulties in promoting black Europe are due to its deep precariousness: "black people are over-concentrated and hyper-visible at the lower ranks of every major political, economic and social hierarchy, from political representation, in business, educational and medical occupations, in the non-profit sector, and in the illicit activities of sex work." This is certainly the case of Equatorial Guineans in Spain. There is no doubt that the African diaspora[13] has low socio-political visibility, in spite of the fact that their skin colour makes them highly visible in a phenotypically white majority, an effect of the racialisation of migrations and of the colonialities inherent in the socio-cultural construction activated in Spain and other European countries. The few exceptions to this invisibility, such as Bosaho, Ávila Laurel, Ndongo, L. Mbomio, Bela-Lobedde and other Equatorial Guineans, do not compensate for the minorisation that the collective suffers.

For all these reasons, this book accepts Small's (2018) premise that the black community in Europe is invisible to European countries. My aim is to reverse this situation by undertaking a study of the presence of the Equatorial Guinean community, especially the Krio Fernandino in Barcelona, though without entering into the study of the self-definition of the identities of Equatorial Guineans in the present with respect to their Afro-European or Euro-African affiliation.

This issue is key because, as Small (2019, p. 2) states, "[t]here is very little talk about black people, especially black citizens, even though the vast majority of black people in Europe are citizens and legal residents." African populations are part of twenty-first-century Europe, as is clearly evidenced by the growing number of immigrants who have settled permanently on the continent: in 2017, of the 673,000 third-country nationals residing in an EU Member State who acquired EU citizenship – 27% – were from Africa.¹⁴ In Spain there were 1,218,691 foreign residents of African origin in 2018 (the total number of foreigners was 4,663,726), within a total population of 47,007,367.¹⁵

My outlook is inspired by the work of Adeleke (2009, p. 22), *The Case Against Afrocentrism*, where he suggests that the "[Black Atlantic] approach acknowledges the complexity of the black Diaspora experience, arguing that a monolithic, racialized, and conflict-driven paradigm could not adequately represent the gamut of the African and black Diaspora experiences."¹⁶ According to his general framework on how to study the diaspora, my interest is focused on studying the socio-cultural contact of the Fernandino and Equatorial Guinean Krio community with Catalans, Spaniards and other Equatorial Guineans. My stance is that this issue should be researched to give more prominence to the dilemmas of Afro-descendants in Spain, given that this African community has barely been studied, with no research at all tackling this particular point.

Gilroy's (1993) book *The Black Atlantic* is also of some interest since, beyond the current criticisms surrounding the usefulness of the notion of the "Black Atlantic", his work has been useful in connecting local and global networks whose epicentre is blackness, given Gilroy's desire to transcend both the structures of the nation-state and the limitations of ethnicity and national particularity. My work presents some differences with Gilroy's starting point, since mine focuses on the Euro-African connection.¹⁷ My interest is thus in studying the local and global connections of transnational networks between Africa and Europe, not on what he calls the "transatlantic world". This need to connect multilocal networks, and multi-sited, transnational, transcontinental and global residences is particularly relevant in the case of Equatorial Guineans, whose diaspora has spread across several continents (Aixelà-Cabré, 2011).¹⁸

My research also adheres to the proposal of Balakrishnan (2017) to prefer the concept of Afropolitanism to African cosmopolitanism, following Mbembe's (2007) argument that Afropolitanism unites Africa and the world.¹⁹ In my case, I am interested in examining whether the centrality of African pluralism is part of the global Krio Fernandino identity practices as a multi-ethnic and highly Afropolitan group at its heart, appearing as one of the possible obstacles to building a community of the Equatorial Guinean black diaspora, since in previous works I have already pointed out the difficulties of constituting a Equatorial Guinean community in Spain due to the pressures of this African dictatorial system abroad.

Finally, Ugarte's book (2009) *Africans in Europe* offers a valuable approach to the feelings and disappointments of Equatorial Guineans in Europe that helps to understand from their exiles – the internal exiles– the scarce recognition obtained in contexts such as the Spanish context referring to their status as eternal foreigners (Iliescu, 2017). In this sense, it is very relevant to observe how racism was unmasked and became more aggressive with the gradual arrival of Africans. In this sense, Essed and Hoving's (2014, p. 9) work on Dutch racism is highly inspiring, noting that "it has its own legacy in the Netherlands and the (former) colonies, operates in and beyond the national borders, is shaped by European and global influences, and intersects with other systems of domination." And this book is pieced together from elements of the arrival and establishment of Africans, many of whom could not avoid racism in Catalonia and Spain because it was the socio-cultural and normative framework dominated by racialised discourses that undervalued the African community (Aixelà-Cabré, 2012).

Urban Iberian colonialities: from the twilight of the Spanish empire to a Catalan metropolis on the margins

Iberian colonialities reveal how the Spanish empire in Spanish Guinea was in decline, and that the Catalan–Fernandino connection between Santa Isabel and Barcelona resembled that maintained by an overseas colony with its metropolitan capital. In addition, it was this contact that allowed for the social encounters between the Fernandino and Catalan bourgeoisie in Barcelona in the first third of the twentieth century.

Although this book focuses on two cities, Santa Isabel and Barcelona, it is particularly relevant to note that life there was could not have been more dissimilar in terms of the people who circulated between them, who offered their ways of seeing the world, of relating, of dressing, of living. These experiences would form part of Mbembe's (2007) analysis of Afropolitanism: Africans interweaving worlds.

Both cities were rich, although Barcelona was a European city of major historical significance compared to Santa Isabel, which was nascent and undergoing development. Both localities were cosmopolitan, although Barcelona was highly visible in many areas, including the arts, sciences and thought, between the late 1880s and the end of the 1920s (Hochadel

& Nieto-Galán, 2016). Fradera (2015, p. 3) also highlights the spectacular urban growth that Barcelona experienced between the eighteenth and nineteenth centuries, which would turn it into a genuine metropolis. Therefore, it is easy to venture that the vacuum left by the loss of Cuba in the Barcelona trade that Fradera (2015, p. 4) identified was filled by Spanish Guinea.

For its part, Santa Isabel was a city in which the Krio Fernandino bourgeois elite, which was engaged in cocoa production, was very powerful, visible and socially active, unlike in Bata, the second city of the colony, located on the continent, which was highly segregated. The economic potential of the Krio Fernandino led Sundiata (1996, p. 115) to classify them as an example of black capitalism. In fact, their profoundly intersectional character has allowed us to observe how Krio Fernandino women enjoyed positions of power, travelled to Europe and settled in Barcelona, perfectly aware of their autonomy, prestige and authority.

I must point out that, in this book, Resina's (2009) perspective of "Iberian cultures" prevails over Campoy-Cubillo and Sampedro's (2019) enveloping formulation of "global Hispanophone", since Resina's conception is about avoiding the standardisation of the Catalan colonial specificities to the Spanish majority, also defended by Vilaró (2011) or Gargallo and Sant (2021), since such specificities would have been blurred under the Spanish assimilationist tendency and the hierarchical subsumption of the Catalan under the Hispanic, without even entering into debate on the nuances of whether the Catalan efforts in Spanish Guinea were to extend Spanish colonialism and linguistic and cultural Hispanisation.

A revisionist work has been published on the Catalan presence in Spanish Guinea. García Ramon et al. (2008) showed how Catalans promoted colonialism as an Africanist movement by actively encouraging public and private bodies to influence politically, economically and culturally in Africa. For them, the Catalan bourgeoisie in the process of economic expansion and cultural renaissance and nourished by a geopolitical conception sought to intervene and expand Barcelona's power beyond its borders (García Ramon et al., 2008, p. 365). The authors expressly cite the Comillas Group through the Compañía Trasatlántica[20] that linked the peninsula and Barcelona with the Gulf of Guinea via the transport of people and goods, as well as the organisations Societat de Geografia Comercial (Commercial Geographical Society, 1884), Societat Geogràfica de Barcelona (Barcelona Geographical Society, 1895) and Societat Geogràfica

Comercial de Barcelona (Commercial Geographical Society of Barcelona, 1909). Gargallo and Sant (2021) have written about the greater presence of Catalans in Equatorial Guinea compared to settlers from other parts of Spain, and Antebi et al. (2017) have studied the close connection between Barcelona and Spanish Guinea from the perspective of animal trafficking to the Barcelona Zoo.

These works reveal how Catalans spearheaded the colonisation process in the Gulf of Guinea. That said, the presence of colonisers from the Canary Islands, Madrid and other Spanish regions should not be overlooked. The first were attracted by the supposed similarity between the two island territories; the second because Madrid was the capital of the Kingdom of Spain and there were concerns about the influential Catalan presence.

In any case, the above studies agree that the Catalan presence was very significant in Spanish Guinea until the 1930s. The data, however, become less clear after the consolidation of Spanish colonialism against the Catalan influence on the island at the end of the 1930s, coinciding with the recentralisation of the Delegation of the Cámara Agrícola de Barcelona (Agricultural Chamber of Barcelona), which moved from Barcelona to Madrid. The population from Madrid surpassed that from Catalonia in Santa Isabel in 1942 (see Table 30). This change occurred after the Spanish Civil War and was made possible by the incentives and aid that were launched by the Franco government to create business opportunities for investors from Madrid and other cities. Alongside the above, at the end of the 1910s Madrid businessmen had begun to obtain help covering travel and other expenses for trips to Spanish Guinea, after seeing the business that the Catalans were carrying out on the island of Fernando Poo, with the city of Barcelona informally acting as the capital of mainland Spain from the margins of the Spanish empire, which was in its twilight.

It is likely that one of the elements that facilitated the arrival and gradual settlement of Krio Fernandino people in Barcelona was the historical relationship that Santa Isabel maintained with the city through the Catalan settlers who came to the island and acquired agricultural plantations. In its favour, Barcelona was a coastal city, which was clearly appealing for the islanders. The cross-settlement coincided over time, becoming especially intense between 1900 and 1930, which would explain why both Santa Isabel and Barcelona were cities of migratory reference for both groups. Indeed, the Fernandino people of that time constituted a true African bourgeoisie, as they were highly enterprising, hence why it seems more appropriate to refer to them as "bourgeoisie" rather than "aristocrats". This aspect connected them to the Catalan bourgeoisie and also explains the warm reception the latter gave to the Krio Fernandino community when they travelled to or settled in Barcelona.

Lang (2017, pp. 105–106) observes the rhetoric according to which Catalan nationalism was detached from a

> decadent Spanish state and enemy of European progress [...] Catalan re-generationism creates a virtual border between civilisation and the barbarism of another non-European [...] From this border, Catalonia creates its own civilising mission by conquering the deserted lands of a supposed "black Spain".

This other colonialism of the imagined colonial war of Catalan imperialism is articulated not only as a socio-political battle, but also as a battle of literary references. For Lang (2017, p. 106), Catalonia aligned itself with the Europe of enlightenment and the triumph of secularism, and rejected "absolutist and arch-Catholic Spain". Lang (2017, p. 110) believes that it was about escaping the usual mapping and denying the reproach of "periphery" since "Catalonia reconstructs the borders around it". As the privileged code of European imperialism, the colonial perspective serves as a model for Catalan self-affirmation. In his opinion, Spain maintained an intermediate place between Said's claim that Spain was an "unchallenged centrality" of Europe (1991, p. 7) and Martín Márquez's view that Spain "is a nation that is at once Orientalised and Orientalising" (2008, p. 9). Lang (2017, p. 108), for his part, concludes that:

> if 1900s Spain tries to integrate into the European paradigm through colonial activity in Africa and compensate for its image of a failed colonial empire, the impression of cultural hybridism between Africa and Europe is present in the colonialist discourse itself.

1.4. Methodology

The research has combined different methodologies, some related to cultural anthropology and oral history, and others based on historical anthropology and history.

Methodological basis: oral and written sources

This research is grounded on a methodology based on primary sources, both oral and written. For the written sources I have located and analysed different types of documents in order to understand the social dynamics between Africans and Spaniards. Extensive documentation of various kinds has been analysed both physically and online (for the details of the materials and archives consulted, see chapter 6), following the relevant requirements in the reproduction licences. The endeavour proved substantial since there has been no previous academic work on the Krio Fernandino community that also studied their footprints in Europe. This led me to propose a historical and cultural reconstruction that combined archival sources with information printed in colonial magazines, in the Barcelona press and from oral sources that I will also set out below.

The sum of hundreds of small pieces of information provided a global perspective on the figure of Amelia Barleycorn and the Krio Fernandino community in the colony and in the mainland.

The primary most important sources came from the African Funds of the Archivo General de la Administración de Alcalá de Henares, the Biblioteca Nacional de España, the Resúmenes Estadísticos de los Territorios Españoles del Golfo de Guinea, the Gaceta Municipal de Barcelona, the Boletín Oficial de los Territorios Españoles en el Golfo de Guinea, the Population Census of the Gobierno de España, the Cementiris de Barcelona-Les Corts, and the Registro Civil de Barcelona. Photographic materials were found in the Archivo General de la Administración, the Biblioteca Nacional de España, the Biblioteca Nacional Digital de España, the Archivo Histórico Nacional, the Arxiu Fotogràfic de Barcelona, and the Arxiu del Gran Teatre del Liceu. Other archives consulted were the Arxiu Històric de la Ciutat de Barcelona, the Arxiu Municipal Contemporani de Barcelona, the Arxiu Municipal Sarrià-Sant Gervasi, the Biblioteca de la AECID, the Institut Estadístic de Barcelona, the Instituto Nacional de Estadística, the Fondo Giménez Ferrer of the IMF-CSIC, and Open Source Guinea.

Likewise, Barcelona press, digital press and articles published in electronic magazines and on internet blogs were consulted.

I carried out a thorough 100-year survey of the Barcelona newspaper *La Vanguardia*, in tandem with two colleagues at the newspaper *Hemeroteca*, covering the years 1900 to 1999 (see details in section 6.1.). Between us we pored over the newspaper page by page, taking note of all the articles items in which news was given of the arrival of foreigners and migrants in the city of Barcelona throughout the entire twentieth century.

In terms of information contained in magazines, *La Guinea Española* and *La Voz de Fernando Poo* were consulted systematically, and others, such as *Africa. Journal of Colonial Troops and Spanish News*, as required (sources detailed in section 6.1.).

As will be noted, a great effort has also been made to facilitate an understanding of the socio-economic and population frameworks of Santa Isabel and Barcelona, with the preparation of 30 tables. To draw these up, various data were collected from the two localities in order to promote a comparative perspective between what life was like in the Spanish overseas colony and on the mainland. To this end, statistical sources have been consulted to compile data on population, health, education, standard of living, etc. These data facilitate an understanding of the challenges and difficulties that the Fernandino and Equatorial Guinean communities faced in both contexts, as indicated in Tables 1 and 2, which set out the population of the two cities at different moments in time. In all the tables, it was considered necessary to maintain the nomenclature used in each historical period to classify human groups, with the aim of demonstrating the extensive use of concepts such as "race", "black population", "white population" and "coloured population".

It is worth noting that there is a stigmatising bias in the Spanish press and reports from the archives consulted, which can also be perceived in the narratives about women and their autonomy. It is also evident in the court trials regarding the African population and, of course, in the promulgation of norms and the requirement of documents to regularise the status of the inhabitants of Spanish Guinea, which, as we will see, Amelia Barleycorn herself challenged.

Regarding the oral sources, these have been divided into "lived memories" and "narrated memories" (Aixelà-Cabré, 2022a, pp. 22–24). The lived memories were collected in semi-structured interviews and use the life history format to extrapolate biographical experiences in a specific time and space. The narrated memories were compiled from documentary materials written by the protagonists, documents that allow us to recover their voices in the first person, with the limitation that their thoughts cannot be verified with interviews, since they are missing persons. Fieldwork was based on a multi-sited ethnography (Marcus, 1995). The

Table 1. Population of Santa Isabel and Barcelona. Census of 1877

Santa Isabel	Inhabitants			
	Men	Women	Total	Percentage
Santa Isabel, Spaniards*	635	176	811	73%
Santa Isabel, foreigners	159	138	297	27%
Total	794	314	1,108	100%
Barcelona	Inhabitants			
	Men	Women	Total	Percentage
Barcelona, residents	110,512	123,319	233,831	94%
Barcelona, temporary residents**	9,751	5,361	15,112	6%
Total	120,263	128,680	248,943	100%

Source: Compiled by the author. Fondo Documental del Instituto Nacional de Estadística. Census of 1877 (1877, pp. 76, 706). *This figure includes the national Equatorial Guinean population from Spain, who were considered Spanish. **The concept of "temporary resident" is how statistics referred to the foreign population.

lived memories were compiled following the approach of Thompson (1988) and Jelin (2002), since the objective was to recover life stories that allowed for the reconstruction of different historical periods based on the respondents' experiences.

To reconstruct the migrations of Equatorial Guineans to Barcelona and other cities on the Iberian Peninsula, I used the ethnographic materials collected in different periods and contexts, with plural and diverse voices that include Equatorial Guineans and Spaniards. My trips to Equatorial Guinea took place between 2004–2012 and 2023–2024. Almost every year I travelled and took the opportunity to gather substantial ethnographic materials and conduct interviews on different themes. I have also used interviews with Equatorial Guineans living in Barcelona and other cities on the peninsula that I began collecting in 2005, as well as in African countries such as Cameroon and South Africa, and other European countries, such as Great Britain, Switzerland and the Netherlands, although the data from the latter did not provide significant information for this book. Taking all this into account, the ethnographic work of gathering

Table 2. Population of Santa Isabel and Barcelona. Census of 1950

Santa Isabel	White Race			Black Race			Total inhabitants	Percentage
	Men	Women	Total	Men	Women	Total		
Residents	1,352	720	2,072	9,616	7,760	17,376	19,448	64%
Temporary residents*	213	18	231	9,475	1,167	10,642	10,873	36%
Total	1,565	738	2,303	19,091	8,927	28,018	30,321	100%

Barcelona	Inhabitants		Total inhabitants	Percentage
	Men	Women		
Residents	568,953	704,722	1,273,675	99.1%
Temporary residents*	10,188	1,819	12,007	0.9%
Total	579,141	706,541	1,285,682	100%

Source: Compiled by the author. Fondo Documental del Instituto Nacional de Estadística. Territorios españoles del Golfo de Guinea (1950, p. 331). Instituto Nacional de Estadística. Barcelona 1950 generals (1950, p. 40). *The concept of "temporary resident" is how statistics referred to the foreign population.

interviews spans from 2004 to the present. In the final list of respondents, I only recorded the ones who are cited in this work.

The oral sources used in this book are subject to the ethical commitments by which all researchers in general, and anthropologists in particular, are bound, prioritising the anonymity of the informant and the safeguarding of his/her identity, unless expressly waived. All the participants were informed of my research interests, and I only interviewed people who freely decided to participate because they considered their life story a collective good.

Decolonial methodologies in the recovery of African women's stories

The oral and documentary material gathered on the specificities and experiences of the Krio Fernandino community, with special attention paid to the reconstruction of African women's stories in Santa Isabel and Barcelona from the end of the nineteenth century to the end of the twentieth century, has constituted an enormous academic challenge (see chapter 4).

The information to be collected had to be varied in nature and was scattered throughout institutional and personal archives, as well as in magazines and newspapers, and it was important to include oral testimony from the main figure in this study, Amelia Barleycorn.

It should be noted that historical reconstruction requires the compilation of data from various sources, in addition to a careful reading because often the testimonies and experiences of women constitute nothing more than marginal notes or mere anecdotes in documents that focus on news related to men.

Of the Africans studied in this book little is known, because they have not had a voice to articulate their past. Sources have ignored their voices, something that this book seeks to redress using a combination of documentary and oral sources from historical anthropology and cultural anthropology, framed in a theoretical perspective of postcolonial and decolonial studies.

Postcolonial studies have provided the theoretical-methodological tool necessary to understand Euro-African hybridisations in Europe and the processes of European racialisation. Decolonial studies have made it possible to study Euro-African footprints in Spain and Equatorial Guinea, explaining how the Spanish colonial identity was projected onto the Fernandino community specifically and Equatorial Guineans in general, both in the overseas territory and on the Iberian Peninsula.

These two theoretical frameworks have allowed me using solid historical data to delve into how the past and experiences of African women have been distorted or how they have permeated transnational and transcultural identities. During research, biases emerge, as voices are clearly marked by an otherness that is historically constructed, minoritised and undervalued by Spaniards and Europeans, as pointed out by Mudimbe (1988, p. xi), Castro-Gómez and Grosfoguel (2007, p. 31), and Mignolo (2018, p. 106).

It should be noted that writing an unknown story about the Krio Fernandino diaspora between Africa and Europe has led me to the realisation that these voices were not collected and that the oral memories contain quite a few errors. Most misunderstandings are due to the fact that it has been very common to repeat the names of ancestors in subsequent generations, which has led family members and researchers to confuse people and activities many decades apart. That said, the remembrance

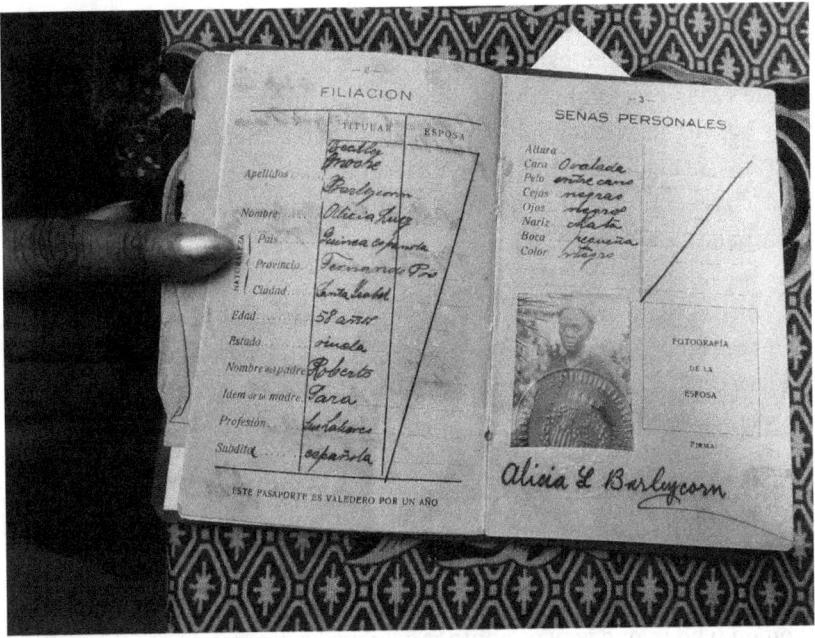

Figure 2. Passport of Alicia Lucy Barleycorn, owned by Amalia Barleycorn, who showed me the document. Photograph: Yolanda Aixelà-Cabré, May 2021.

of family members through repeating names undoubtedly shows the importance of bloodlines and the remembering of former glories.

For this research, the descendants of the main protagonist, Amelia Barleycorn de Vivour, have been located. Due to COVID-19 pandemic restrictions, the first meetings were held remotely and by telephone until conditions allowed a meeting with Amalia Barleycorn, arranged by her daughter, Sally Fenaux Barleycorn, referred to in the text respectively as Amalia and Sally. I hope that this book will redress the silences and oblivions around the extraordinary figure of her ancestor.

It must also be stressed that while there are some details of Amelia's life that remain unknown, they can be abstracted from the experiences of other women of the same Krio Fernandino group. As interviewee Amalia Barleycorn (2021) pointed out, "In terms of how they travelled – we are focusing on one person, but I know her from her time and how that person lived. But if we take it out of its context, I couldn't give you concrete information about it."

Unfortunately, at the time of writing, no image of Amelia Barleycorn had yet been found, except for her signature, although photographs of her female descendants, male relatives and husband have come to light. This has not prevented her descendants from remembering her for generations, using her first name to name their daughters. For this reason, it was of great importance that Amalia Barleycorn agreed to be interviewed. As Amalia (2021) explained:

> Amelia lives in everyone's memory [...] There are no photos, but she is in our imagination. There we roam. An imagination of the period in which she lived, how people dressed, until no more could be known, but more or less all of them were somewhat equal.

Amelia Barleycorn, like other Krio Fernandino women, became almost invisible in documentary sources, which is why significant efforts have had to be made to feminise Krio history and that of her descendants, highlighting certain other women from influential Krio Fernandino families, women who in one way or another achieved a reputation for themselves or for the activities they undertook in Santa Isabel or Barcelona.

Regarding the voices and their dynamics, it is especially striking to see how the Fernandino Daniel Jones Mathama (1962) represented himself and the Krio Fernandino. In Jones Mathama's book *Una lanza por el boabí*, he explained that the Fernandinos were descendants of slaves freed by the British mixed with free men of colour. He described how they had a Westernised lifestyle, with a high economic level, that they used to speak Spanish and English, and that they were emancipated. In reality, his narration and gaze aligned closely with the interpretation that the Spanish missionaries made of the Krio Fernandino, which is why Bolekia (2019, p. 232) concluded that Jones "accepts European influence raising cultural levels and ending situations of domination grounded on magic or superstition."

Against documentary androcentrism and Eurocentrism

Colonial Eurocentrism was accompanied by a marked documentary androcentrism, the effect of which was that the history of the Krio Fernandino in Spanish Guinea was written from a masculine, not feminine, standpoint. Despite this, fortunately, the family's oral memory has preserved the role of some Fernandino women such as Amelia Barleycorn.

Proof of the preservation of the role of women is found in the fact that despite the death of his only daughter and being left without offspring, Amelia's brother Napoleon established the recovery of her name through his descendants, something that has persisted through the three generations that have since had children. As Amalia Barleycorn (2021) recalled, the name was not a mere mechanical fact; there were oral histories that explained how this great woman must persist in the family's memory.

Within this Eurocentric and androcentric Spanish colonial framework, which was especially contrary to the rights of African women, influential Fernandino women like Amelia Barleycorn become almost invisible in sources. This does not reflect the power they wielded during their lifetimes, but does prove the limits of intersectionality with respect to gender within the documentary framework, which especially corrosive when referring to the collective memory of women and the gathering of historical data concerning them.

Thus, in the following paragraphs, some of the strengths and clear limitations of the journals used for the historical reconstruction of the Fernandino community will be presented.

La Guinea Española was a fortnightly magazine produced by Catalan Claretian missionaries. It was set up in 1903 and published its last issue after independence, in 1969. An extensive research of this source was carried out for this study because of its wide circulation among Fernando Poo's community of Spaniards, as well as within the European and African communities in the colony and Santa Isabel. It has been a vital source for retracing the stories of the Krio Fernandino community because it echoed social, cultural, commercial, economic, political and associative concerns. Finally, it is worth stating that the volume of the data found in *La Guinea Española* related to the Fernandinos after 1915 reduced, probably due to the Spanish presence gaining standing in the colony while the Krio were losing influence.

I would also claim that the arrival and settling of Spaniards on the mainland can be easily identified from the lists of passengers published in *La Guinea Española*, which for decades included not only the full names of passengers, but also their profession and any family links with other persons listed (wife, cousin, child, etc.), as they similarly did with European travellers. For years, the only Equatorial Guineans who gave their full names when travelling were Krio Fernandino passengers, as the rest of the Africans were grouped under the simple heading of *morenos* (coloured people, literally "browns").[21] Detailed lists of the Spanish passengers were made until the number of passengers exceeded fifty, after which some names were kept but the complete list was not always included, nor the activities of each traveller, as in previous years. Although at first in some cases only selected passengers were listed, *La Guinea Española* accustomed to detailing the Spaniards, Europeans and Fernandinos, continuing with the custom of stating the overall figures for the *braceros* who were returning to their countries of origin. A research of the documentation has also allowed us to see how Spanish travellers were initially from the armed forces, civil servants, public sector or missioners, and how, over time, a larger number of varied professions and a greater percentage of women arrived, changes that were noticeable from 1910 onwards. The passenger lists also afford us the possibility of observing the arrival of workers from Central and Western Africa, first named *jornaleros* (day labourers) and then *braceros* and *krumanes*. As will be seen, in certain cases only their first names were provided, as they lacked surnames to distinguish them, a practice also widespread in the colonial documentation of plantations, detainees, migrants, etc.: their origin and their family identity were anonymised. It is worth clarifying that on the odd occasion, those who "made the Africas" without a fixed job were classified as "emigrants", emulating the Spaniards who in previous centuries "had founded the Americas", almost always men rather than women. Furthermore, in the case of visas, the verification of departures and arrivals of African Spaniards was done by analysing the lists in the magazine until the 1940s. From that date onwards, I went through the exit and entry records of the Government Police of Santa Isabel by consulting the documentation available in the Archivo General de la Administración.

Certain aspects of the magazine are very important because, although they seem like anecdotes, they actually reflected a way of thinking about and building the colony. For example, it is of the utmost significance to point out that *La Guinea Española* tended to include the professions of travellers, and that after the names of Amelia Barleycorn and Isabel Vivour (mother and daughter) the abbreviation "s.c." was added, which would mean "housewife", or in the Spanish form, *ama de casa*. This is somewhat surprising in the case of Amelia Barleycorn, who could not be further removed from this status, and certainly it would have been the simple fact that she was labelled thus as a woman, bearing in mind this was the year 1917 and by then all and sundry knew of her immense fortune.

For its part, the fortnightly magazine *La Voz de Fernando Poo* was published entirely in Barcelona, and was a key publication on trade issues between Barcelona and Spanish Guinea. The magazine was founded in 1910 (Sant, 2015, p. 203). It has recorded news of meetings or initiatives in both Santa Isabel and Barcelona, social life, announcements, etc. Some articles have special relevance because they use colonial rhetoric, as well as indicating the hopes and interests in the territory. The magazine also gave an account of daily life, news of powerful people, etc.

Finally, I will add a selection of brief comments on the photographic material consulted in the funds of the Archivo General de la Administración. It must be stressed that the images of Spanish Guinea were enormously androcentric, featuring for the most part only men. Equatorial Guinean women were relegated, with exceptions, to illustrating their motherhood, choirs, dances, ballets, posing, cooking, queens of the party, childrearing or at school, which, although they are interesting images, do not have too broad a spectrum.[22] Likewise, the Krio Fernandino community was represented through the influential men of their families, not through their women, who, when they appear, are not identified. To counteract this fact, I found the exit and entry cards to the country useful, as well as various passports, because in this way I was able to obtain the images of some women of influence in Santa Isabel and Barcelona.

CHAPTER 2

Fernandino women in colonial Santa Isabel and independent Malabo

The island of Fernando Poo formed part of the Spanish Overseas Territories in the Gulf of Guinea (*Territorios Españoles del Golfo de Guinea*) along with the areas on the mainland and other Atlantic islands such as Annobon, Elobey Chico and Elobey Grande and Corisco, thereby being the sole Hispanised region in all of sub-Saharan Africa. The overseas colony was also named Spanish Guinea (*Guinea Española*) and its capital, Santa Isabel, was where the genuine hub of economic, political, social and cultural of the territory was located, thus monopolising all researcher interest above the rest of the Equatorial Guinean territories.

The cultural make-up of the Spanish Territories in the Gulf of Guinea was indeed fairly diverse. Its inhabitants were drawn from the Bubi, Fang, Ndowe, Annobon, Bissio and Krio peoples. The Krio group was formed from a Creole community that came into being following the colonisation of the island of Fernando Poo, from within whose number a small minority would emerge, the Krio Fernandino. While these groups learnt and used Spanish from colonisation onwards, on the island of Fernando Poo some also spoke English and the Pichi language (Pidgin English), which would ultimately be deemed the colloquial lingua franca (Sundiata, 1996, p. 147; Yakpo, 2010; Castillo, 2016). Vernacular languages in Spanish Guinea were the Fang, Bubi, Ndowe, Fa d'Ambô and Bissio tongues. It is worth stressing that the percentage of the population making up the diverse groups in colonial times is unknown, although the figures probably resembled the present ones. In 2019, it was estimated that the Fang majority accounted for 85.7%, Bubi 6.5%, Ndowe 3.6%, Annobonese 1.6%, Bissio 1.1%, and Krio 0.3% (Aixelà-Cabré, 2022a, p. 35).

The Krio Fernandino group was eminently urban and chose as its main base the city of Santa Isabel, plus, to a lesser extent, San Carlos (modern-day Malabo and Luba respectively). They had received their schooling under the British syllabus in Western Africa, though select Krio Fernandino alumni studied in English universities. The Krio Fernandino was the first Equatorial Guinean community to travel to the Iberian Peninsula,[23] specifically to Barcelona. As will be seen, they embarked upon a fluid multilocality characterised by multi-sited residence alongside transnational and transcontinental mobility.

From here on in, I will present the Krio Fernandino of Santa Isabel as they were from the mid-nineteenth century until the proclamation of independence, making special mention of the focal point of this essay, Amelia Barleycorn de Vivour. The aim is to analyse the role the city had in bolstering the Krio Fernandino elite and their Afropolitan nature, as well as to assess the significance of the city as an overseas colony forming part of the African territories. What life was like in Santa Isabel will be studied in terms of population, cost of living and services, while at the same time reviewing the tensions and conflicts that emerged in the Equatorial Guineans daily lives, proving the impunity of the Spanish in relation to the Equatorial Guinean collectives, including on certain occasions the Krio Fernandino. Finally, the connection that existed between Barcelona and Malabo upon independence because of Equatorial Guinean exile is also highlighted.

2.1. The African context and Europe: English and Spanish presence in Fernando Poo and Santa Isabel

Fernando Poo and Santa Isabel remained caught between European colonial pressures exerted by the Spanish and the British, along with Christian conversion to the British Protestant and Spanish Catholic faiths, two key aspects that make abundantly clear the European footprint and influence to which the Krio Fernandino community was subjected.

The island of Fernando Poo, modern-day Bioko, was declared a Spanish overseas colony following the Treaty of El Pardo in 1777–1778, after an agreement with Portugal. However, after years without being formally occupied by the Spanish, the British took a foothold at the beginning of the nineteenth century. Thus, although the island went from being Portuguese to being Spanish, the impact of the British presence in the first half of the nineteenth century would be felt until well into the twentieth century.

From Port Clarence to Santa Isabel: the Hispanisation of an Anglicised island

The city of Port Clarence was founded in 1827 by the British, who remained there for decades exerting their influence.[24] The effective colonisation by the English meant certain missionary and trade exchanges, which established Protestantism as the religion of choice and fostered the export of raw materials to Great Britain, above all palm oil. Yet Port Clarence had another English-founded city as a rival, Freetown, which had been created in 1787 in Sierra Leone (Sundiata, 1996, p. 65), a factor which led the British to leave Fernando Poo once Spanish colonial pressure became evident.

As Unzueta recalled (1947, p. 273), referring to the Krio, the city was already formed by the British and by Africans who, "due to their language, customs, trade and even their name considered themselves British." The replacement of the English way of life with the Spanish one, as well as the implementation of new legislative measures with the employment of colonial civil servants, was notably gradual.

The British–Spanish struggle for control of the island, its agricultural output and trade worked in the Krio Fernandino community's favour, as the possibility of growing and trading palm oil or cocoa landed at their doorstep until the beginning of the twentieth century, as the applications from Spaniards to colonise the territory were scant and these arrived very sporadically to the island at this time. An example of how the Spanish authorities wished to settle can be seen in the Royal Decree for the Organisation of the Consejo de Vecinos (Residents' Council, a body equivalent to the city hall) on 18 November 1904, which ruled it mandatory in an addendum that "representatives must read and write in Spanish" (AGA, box 81/06356). It is stated therein that members of the council had to be Spanish or Spanish subjects (Article 1) and have been in the vicinity for two years (Article 2), and explicitly said that under no circumstances could foreigners, paid civil servants, people who had been arrested or those in debt to the treasury be elected to the council. The English would therefore be excluded from the new organisational structures and Hispanisation became an absolute priority for the colonial authorities.

Despite this, the impact of the British presence was appreciable in the widespread use of English and the Pichi language amongst the Krio peoples and other colonisers of the renamed Santa Isabel and throughout Fernando Poo.

The English influence continued throughout the twentieth century, as there were constant articles in magazines and the Spanish press that reported for decades on the reluctance and idleness on the part of the colonised population to speak Spanish, highlighting major difficulties in spreading the language.

It must also be added that, despite the significant British influence, those born in the colony were to all intents and purposes African Spanish subjects. This was legislated for in royal decrees and orders, in which it was clearly stated that the skin colour of the population always had to be collected in the census, thereby demonstrating the clear racialisation of colonial practices, despite the fact that the African inhabitants were classified as part of the Spanish population.

This aspect is highly relevant since it allows us to understand that "being Spanish" could mean different things during the colonial period. The changes were undeniable when migrations of Spanish colonists began to arrive in Fernando Poo from the early years of the twentieth century onwards. In previous statistics and documents, "Spanish" referred to those born in the colony (see Tables 3 and 4), yet afterward a distinction began to be made between Spaniards belonging to the "white population" and those belonging to the "black population" or "coloured race" (see Tables 5 and 6).

This divergence in what it meant to "be Spanish" also made itself felt depending on the context, as the mobility afforded by the status of Spanish subject in the colony or in mainland Spain was wholly different depending on whether the citizen was white and had been born in Spain or was of black origin from the African territory. Thus, 'racialisation was not solely used to subordinate parts of the population due to their skin colour, it was also a variable extensively used to set legal distinctions in relation to the rights inherent in Spanish nationality. However, an exception to the foregoing was a large part of the Krio Fernandino collective, who would only suffer the same rejection and discourtesy if their garments and mannerisms did not impress their interlocutor, providing undoubted proof of the relevance of the intersectionality in place in terms of class and race, as well as between race, class and gender, as in the case of wealthy and well-endowed Krio Fernandino women such as Amelia Barleycorn, who undertook trips to Barcelona.

It is worth mentioning that Catalan missionary endeavours through schools were vital for the conversion to Catholicism and for the subsequent

Hispanisation of the colony (Vilaró, 2011). Therefore, added to the tension over the persistence of the English language was the Catholic–Protestant rivalry.

Afropolitan Santa Isabel

The change of colonial power from the British to the Spanish led the capital of Fernando Poo to change its name from Port Clarence to Santa Isabel in 1843, which symbolised the process of substitution of the British presence for the Spanish one. As will be explored below, this ended up indirectly benefiting an Anglophile Krio Fernandino community.

But what was Santa Isabel like in the nineteenth and early twentieth centuries?

The urban organisation of Santa Isabel inherited the British layout. For Guillemar de Aragón (1852, pp. 60–62), "it is necessary to admire the order and equality of spacious streets and houses drawn by the intelligent hand of the English." Guillemar de Aragón (1852, p. 59) also recalled that the city had a building to house "the governor of Fernando Poo, the church and the school of the missionaries [...] and some houses for blacks and that of a Dutchman [...] All the rest is uninhabited." The "houses for blacks" corresponded to the residences of the Fernandino population. The presence of the Fernandinos in Santa Isabel, with their elevated social status, had the effect of partially neutralising in Santa Isabel the deep racial segregationism that would be found in Bata exhibit a century later.

Amelia's descendant, Amalia Barleycorn (2021), recalled that "they lived in English fashion, speaking *Pichi*, something that to this day has had a bearing on us in some way." Amalia (2021) added:

> This small community or colony – we were not autochthonous, and were the ones who founded the city that today called Malabo with the English – had a peculiar, different way of life', because these people [Fernandinos], owing to their origins, came from contact with the English way of living.

For Enyegue (2014, p. 487) a selection of news articles, such as those by Muñoz y Gaviria (1871a, p. 15), also insisted on the English character of the customs and languages of Santa Isabel in the last third of the nineteenth century: "Santa Isabel is still an English town, where English is spoken, all customs are English and fashion is English."

Now, although the English influence and the Protestant religion made their presence felt, as the Spanish language and the Catholic religion would later be, whites were always in a minority in Santa Isabel since the population was mostly African. Guillemar de Aragón (1852, pp. 60–62) explained that in the mid-1850s

> the population of Clarens amounted to around 900 civilised blacks and only 15 Europeans. Marrying according to the Protestant rite, they refer to themselves as English, and they all speak English. It is, then, an English colony.

Thus, for the incoming Spanish colonists, overcoming Anglicisation was not without its challenges, nor was imposing Hispanisation straightforward. Balsameda (1869, pp. 185–186) noted that shortly after 250 Cubans arrived on the island of Fernando Poo in the 1860s, the Presbyterian father with whom he had spoken told him that he had only converted sixty people, mainly children. In fact, the first ship carrying Cubans, who were brought over to promote Hispanisation and provide a workforce, was registered in the Royal Order of 5 April 1861, approving the sending of "200 emancipated Cubans to Fernando Poo" (Miranda Junco, 1945, p. 31). It was said that the Queen had been so satisfied with the results of sending the Cubans that she proposed the arrival of 200 more in 1862 (Miranda Junco, 1945, p. 37).

The presence of the Spanish population can be easily tracked in the passenger lists provided by the magazine *La Guinea Española*. At first these lists were complete due to the low number of people arriving in or leaving the colony, but later they only included the most significant African names and also the Spanish and European population that travelled. The research carried out of the lists allows us to see the wide variety of professions of the Catalans and Spaniards who came to Fernando Poo, especially post 1910, since their occupations were detailed. Many declared that they were engaged in commerce, but there were also some national or European diplomats, estate administrators, interns, cooks, plumbers, farmers, industrialists, pilots, attorneys, recruiting agents, machinists, telephone operators, employees of private companies like the Compañia Trasatlántica, masons, pharmacists, doctors and other medical practitioners, among many others.

The lists also included the arrival and departure of African labourers to work on the cocoa and coffee plantations. Access to African labourers was key for the development of the colony (Martino, 2012). Large numbers of *braceros* were hired by many of the Krio Fernandino families that we will review in the next section, namely the Barleycorns, the Collinses, the Dougans and the Kinsons.

It is highly significant that the majority of Fernandinos were Protestants during the nineteenth century, so much so that Hall (1874, p. 144) explained the reasons for this in 1868. He also noted the tension in which the Krio Fernandino lived between the Methodist Baptist missions of Protestantism and the ecclesiastical missions of Catholicism.

The diverse cultural and national backgrounds of Santa Isabel's population, with an African majority, are relevant to understanding that it was an enormously diverse city in which, in addition to Europeans and Equatorial Guineans, there lived numerous African ethnic groups brought or arriving from different places. Its cosmopolitan nature, with an African majority, gave it an Afropolitan tone from its foundation onwards.

In any event, the Afropolitan condition of Santa Isabel was also down to the Krio Fernandino, who, due to their status and means, were able to travel to different European countries to maintain their businesses and consolidate their family, economic and commercial ties, with Liberia, Sierra Leone and Nigeria being the countries that saw the greatest exchange. As we will see, the Krio Fernandino community was multilocal, transnational and transcontinental.

2.2. The Krio Fernandino community and Amelia Barleycorn de Vivour

African empowerment in Santa Isabel became a reality after the formation of the Krio Fernandino community. The Fernandinos' very existence called into question the Spanish civilising colonial rhetoric that classified Equatorial Guineans as savages and lacking in culture because of their skin colour (Aixelà-Cabré, 2017). And it is the case that the extraordinary wealth, excellent education and exquisite tastes of the Krio Fernandino community, typical of any European high bourgeoisie, not only overcame the androcentric vision of the sexes in Spain at the time, but also questioned the deep foundations on which the racial and class barriers imposed by Spanish colonialism had been erected to minorise, devalue, denigrate and infantilise the colonised African populations.

A selection of the main characteristics of the Krio Fernandino are reviewed below, especially focusing on the case of Amelia Barleycorn de Vivour. For the rest of the families, I have provided a brief and less thorough approach, though always highlighting some other outstanding woman with the aim of feminising a story that, until now, has basically been formulated in the masculine.

The Krio Fernandino community

The founding of the city of Port Clarence in 1827 was accompanied by the Slavery Abolition Law of 1833 that allowed slavery to be legally eradicated. The city was established as one of the locations to free slaves from ships captured on other islands and African coasts. As I explained above, these freed blacks, together with other Africans who arrived in the city, constituted the Krio, among who the small and select group of the Krio Fernandino would stand out. Their name is an extension of the name of the island Fernando Poo.

Therefore, at the end of the first third of the nineteenth century, the Krio Fernandino formed a Creole community of African origin to which, decades later, a Latin American ancestry would be added that came from their marriage with members of the Cuban community, and exceptionally with some West Indian and Jamaican ancestors of Sierra Leonean origin (Granda, 1988, pp. 215–220). It took several decades for the mixing with the Cubans to happen because they arrived empty-handed as the chronicles explain.

Although the Krio community was quite large, the Krio Fernandino were characterised by being a very small community and by its endogamy. Starting in the first half of the twentieth century, they also entered into some marriages with Bubis.

The Nigerian, Sierra Leonean and Liberian origin of the Krio Fernandino is essential to understanding their frequent trips to Freetown, Lagos and Monrovia because, in addition to trading, they visited relatives. This aspect, combined with the close cultural and commercial contact of the Fernandinos with the English and later with the Catalans, led them to also travel to Liverpool, Manchester, London and Barcelona. I will analyse this transnational, multilocal dimension of multi-sited and transcontinental residence of the Krio Fernandino in the third chapter.

The diversity of origins of the Fernandino group paints a complex picture of this community. Those Fernandinos from Sierra Leone had been more Anglicised, since they were school-educated freedmen who had received considerable colonial support. Some of them had even been able to travel to Great Britain to study or receive and healthcare. The picture was more varied in the case of the Liberian and Nigerian Krio, as not all had received the same support and schooling, which for some made them appear more "African".

The place occupied by the Krio Fernandino in the socio-cultural and colonial pyramid of the island of Fernando Poo until the final third of the nineteenth century was notably lofty. The Bubis were native Equatorial Guineans and were stranded at the base of the pyramid with their rights curtailed, as they were pressured to work for the plantations (like Fangs, Ndowes and Annoboneses). Non-Equatorial Guinean Africans who had other origins and who worked as artisans or other professions in Santa Isabel, some of them Krio, or who had been brought to the island to work as labourers in the plantations, were in the middle of the pyramid, as some of them were hired, received a salary or had certain rights that the Equatorial Guineans lacked (Sepa, 2011, p. 247). The Krio Fernandino collective would remain at the top of the pyramid, thanks to their collaboration with English and later Catalan and Spanish trade, which allowed them to gain power and visibility. The Bubis were the first ones who received serious punishments and violent incursions on their lands by the Spaniards, who did not seek anything other than to force them to work on the plantations.

The definition of full or limited emancipated and unemancipated status would finally lead to the drawing of distinctions between the Equatorial Guinean groups. At the end of the colonisation period, the social pyramid would become gradually less rigid, and would come to include a minority of Bubis, Fangs, Ndowes and Annoboneses, who would eventually be granted different degrees of emancipation over time (full or limited).

It should be noted that different legislative measures were passed in the colony to regulate the rights and duties corresponding to the African subordinated. On 11 July 1904, the Patronato de Indígenas (Indigenous Council) was responsible for the legal status of the Africans (Miranda Junco, 1945, p. 142). As explained by Sá (2015, p. 96), in 1911 "the 'indigenous peoples' were considered unemancipated and subject to the guardianship of the colonial agents." Those not granted emancipation were governed by harsh legislation in socio-employment matters named *prestación personal*. The so-called *prestación personal* was nothing other than forced labor (Aixelà-Cabré 2022a).

The Patronato de Indígenas granted emancipation to certain Equatorial Guineans, mainly Fernandinos, which allowed them to maintain comprehensive self-rule in their status as full citizens. Meanwhile, the unemancipated, forming the large part of the population, continued to be bound by the Patronato de Indígenas (Sá, 2015, p. 96; Ndongo, 1977, pp. 37–38).

The Decree of 29 September 1938 approved legislative measures that maintained the foregoing distinction between the emancipated and non-emancipated indigenous population and was under control of the recently created Tribunales de Raza (Race Tribunals). These measures would have the effect of legitimising the existing racial segregation in the colony that the population was forced to withstand on a daily basis, both in the workplace and on a personal and socio-political level. The Tribunales de Raza purpose was to safeguard the rights held by the European minority over the autochthonous majority in all Spanish territories in the Gulf of Guinea. This had limited consequences for the emancipated Krio Fernandino minority, but not for the rest of the population, which this indigenous legislation would bind.

Thus, Spain had to establish its civilising rhetoric from within an island on which skin colour was not the determining factor in a person's rights and duties – although as the decades passed this was the reality that was finally embedded. It could be seen in the colonisation of the continental lands where rights and duties were set in line with skin colour, and from the 1930s onwards on the island of Fernando Poo with the dwindling of the Fernandino power base and the commencement of the Tribunales de Raza.

The fact the Fernandino people were of African descent did not make a major difference to how their properties were managed compared to those run by European or Spanish owners. The same was the case with labour. In the documentation consulted, various complaints lodged against Fernandino owners were found. The significance of class also meant that the weight of race was sidelined in how the Krio Fernandino dealt with the Spanish, with the former being the only group excluded from racialisation to a certain extent over the decades.

The issue of class also arose between the Krio Fernandino and the rest of the Africans, as there were Fernandinos who tackled and aimed to reverse injustices or difficult situations faced by other Equatorial Guineans or people of African origin. Particularly prominent here was Maximiliano C. Jones, who often played the role of a mediator. In general terms, however, the possible solidarity that might be found between other Krio groups, Africans and black labourers was notably limited. Fernandino abuse of labourers on their properties is also mentioned by Sundiata (1996, p. 137).

Thus, the collaboration between the Krio Fernandino, Catalans and Spaniards was very intense from 1920 onwards. I would similarly highlight that the Krio Fernandino collaborated closely amongst themselves, which allowed them to bolster their status as a powerful elite, in order to prevent the withdrawal of their privileges.

Amelia Barleycorn, widow de Vivour

Amelia Barleycorn was born in Santa Isabel around the year 1860 and died in Barcelona in 1920. She had married William Allen Vivour. She was an influential and tireless woman lived her life in a racialised and male-centred world in which the highest-ranking Protestant ecclesiastical figures, along with those who oversaw trading and controlled palm oil and cocoa production, were almost exclusively men.

Reconstructing her character has not been an easy task. To this male-based ideological, socio-political, economic and cultural framework, the androcentric gaze of European writing in newspapers and magazines, often missionaries, must also be added, with the latler acting to overshadow her, overlooking the testimonies that might have brought to the fore her standing and that of other admittedly less relevant Fernandino women of the period. It is for this reason that this reconstruction of the Barleycorn bloodline includes more information on men than women from the family or on Amelia herself. It is also noteworthy to add that sadly, thus far, Amelia Barleycorn not yet been the subject of documentary study, despite the fact that her importance and influence exceeded that of her brother William Napoleon Barleycorn, who has been widely studied. Fortunately, Equatorial Guinean literature has indeed endowed us with two excellent novels that have generously defended her legacy: the work of fiction by Bolekia (2016) and the historical novel by Ávila Laurel (2022).

In the next section, I will reconstruct the Barleycorn bloodline, as a large part of its power and authority are explained through the pre-eminence of one woman: Amelia Barleycorn de Vivour.

The Barleycorn bloodline was one of the foundational Fernandino families of greatest importance in the nineteenth century. It was a Nigerian family of Igbo origin (Sundiata, 1996, p. 149). The roots of the Barleycorn family in Fernando Poo date back to the birth of Napoleon Barleycorn, who settled on the island as a Methodist minister. Of Napoleon Barleycorn's offspring, Amelia Barleycorn and William Napoleon Barleycorn deserve special mention.

William Napoleon Barleycorn (1848–1925), Amelia's brother, was born in Santa Isabel. His wife was Dorcas Fanny de Barleycorn (Santa Isabel, 1851–1889), with whom he had two children. William Napoleon Barleycorn studied in Quinton, Barcelona, Victoria and Cameroon, and penned the first Bubi grammar guide with the missionary William B. Luddington, a document that can be accessed in the SOAS archives. He attained the status of Presbyterian minister in Port Clarence. He became a highly visible figure in the Krio Fernandino community in the 1890s. This also coincided with the widowhood of his sister Amelia Barleycorn de Vivour, which made her the richest person in Fernando Poo and the owner of the most extensive plantations.

That said, despite the highly important role that Amelia had in the island's development, the monument that would be raised in the Protestant cemetery close to what would later be Port Clarence was in honour of her brother William Napoleon, further proof of the overriding androcentrism at work. The social importance of William Napoleon Barleycorn explains why his sister was wed to Vivour.

As I have mentioned, William Napoleon Barleycorn had a daughter and a son with his first wife Dorcas Fanny, who were called Julia and Harry. After Dorcas Fanny's death, he took as his second wife the grandmother of my interviewee, Amalia Barleycorn, who was called Alice, and who gave birth to Mabel, Irene, Sara, Robert, Guillermo, Daniel and George; they also adopted a youth named Balaam Aba. The rest of Amelia and William's brothers and sisters also had children whose descendants have reused their names as a means of commemorating their ancestors. The documentation consulted provides details of William Napoleon (second generation), Rolando, Eva, Mariana, Edward, Edward's sons Emilio and John (referred to in the Spanish documentation as being named Juan) offspring of Edward, Juliana and Jeremías, with greater information available on Rolando, Edward and John. Rolando Barleycorn was a landowner and exporter of products in Equatorial Guinea, and other Barleycorn descendants also called Rolando appear to honour his legacy, including one of the children of Trinidad Collins Jones who was married to Rolando Barleycorn. This couple also had a daughter named María Raquel Barleycorn. It appears from the AGA documentation and the press clippings that Rolando was the closest protégé of Amelia Barleycorn, as under her auspices he would sit on the Consejo de Vecinos in Santa Isabel with two other Fernandinos who were board members, along with some Spaniards. It is likely that it would have been Amelia Barleycorn herself who held this spot on the Consejo de Vecinos, despite the Spanish colonial authorities and policies not allowing for women to sit on such bodies – although not so much because the law prohibited this, but rather because it had never even been contemplated.

John Barleycorn managed to acquire a relatively large plantation in Santa Isabel, in the second-ranked group in terms of size behind the largest ones in the possession of the Vivours and La Vigatana (Sundiata, 1996, p. 93). His father, Edward Barleycorn (1891–1978), was well known because he travelled as a delegate to Liberia in 1927 to act as a signatory to one of the numerous major labourers' agreements from this country to cover the plantation employment market in Santa Isabel (Clarence-Smith, 1994, p. 197; Sundiata, 1996, p. 114). With regard to Eva and Julia Barleycorn, it is known that they founded an association named Constancia (see chapter 4). It is similarly known that Ricardo Barleycorn Macfoy, son of Rolando Barleycorn and his wife Isabel Macfoy, completed his studies in Barcelona, there obtaining his high school leaver's certificate from the Salmerón Secondary School in 1934, and that he received a medal in 1964, awarded by Pilar Primo de Rivera. Indeed, new reports also mention that Rolando Barleycorn Macfoy, a descendant of Ricardo, was awarded the Order of Africa in October 1964. This fact cannot be disregarded as there is no doubt that the large part of the Krio Fernandino community adhered to the Franco dictatorship in order not to lose their power and influence, bearing in mind the social, economic and political consequences that they would have faced had they been viewed as rebels, communists or unsupportive of the Spanish dictatorial regime.

However, we return to the figure of Amelia Barleycorn following this brief journey through the history of her relatives and descendants. There can be no doubt that Amelia was a powerful figure. Amalia (2021) described her as being an independent woman who was energetic and forthright. Unfortunately, despite her ingenuity and renown, the information available regarding her life is scant in comparison to that for male members of her household, a fact that this book aims to redress by overcoming documentary androcentrism, even through the use of oral sources.

Considering the above, the visibility and power held by Amelia Barleycorn were exceptional. It must be borne closely in mind that the Spanish colonial framework put African women in a disadvantaged position in Fernando Poo in general. The same was true in other European contexts as a result of European influences, since the rights of the colonised population were drastically reduced, particularly in the case of women – although it must be emphasised that not even in nineteenth century Spain was there any attempt to ensure both sexes enjoyed equal rights (Nash, 1983). Thus, the legal, social and political Spanish context fostered male progress and gave Equatorial Guinean women a very low standing, although markedly worse for those African women who, because they were maids or the wives of labourers, came to the island from neighbouring countries. Spanish androcentrism did not sit well with the African paradigm of Bubi women, whose family and political structure had prioritised a matrilineal kinship that recognised female primacy and power in the identity of the family bloodline, in the worship of their forefathers and the holding of public positions. Nonetheless, androcentrism left a mark on the Bubi kinship structure following decades of missionary endeavours to minimise women's social influence (Fernández-Moreno, 2018).

In spite of these conflicts brought about by the rise of androcentrism in the gender construct of African women, Amelia Barleycorn (like other Fernandino women) safeguarded her independence and authority as a powerful and rich Protestant widow who spent her time between Santa Isabel and Barcelona, interspersed frequent visits to England. While Amelia made donations to the Catholic missionaries, a group of whom publicly acknowledged her in letters thanking her for her generosity, she was not the sort of woman who liked the Claretian Catalan missionaries. What is more, they had issued a public decalogue outlining the qualities that African women in Fernando Poo must adopt from their point of view, which were exactly the same roles as those reserved for Spanish women, namely being wives and mothers. The text was given the title "What you must teach your daughters" and made it clear that they had to learn "to cook [...] to wash and iron [...] to make bread [...] while being sensitive and thrifty".[25] The Krio Fernandino women did not share this stereotype, as they had been heirs to an Anglo-American feminism influenced by their initially Protestant religion and culture (Aixelà-Cabré, 2023a).

This general backdrop allows us to understand better the significance of Amelia's marriage to the wealthy and influential William Allen Vivour

(Freetown, 1830–1890). He had been born to a freed Yoruba slave from Lagos, Nigeria, who had settled in Sierra Leone and never forgot his roots. William Allen Vivour was one of the Sierra Leoneans who converted to Christianity upon arrival in Fernando Poo, and he engaged in trade and agriculture. Upon attaining success, he sent some of his brothers to Europe to study. One brother, Jacob Vivour, read law at "Christ Church, Oxford University, obtaining his law degree in 1887", and then medicine, graduating in 1895, when he decided to return to Nigeria to practise medicine (Wellesley Cole, 1987, pp. xv–2).

The Vivour clan had risen to prominence in San Carlos by holding major trading and agricultural interests. For their part, the Barleycorn brothers were known for their "religiousness and stern manner" (Ruiaz, 1928, pp. 83–84), along with their cocoa plantations and companies, which Amelia Barleycorn inherited. By the end of the 1880s, Vivour traded directly with Manchester, as several landowners would do after him, including Manuel Balboa to whom we will return later.

Amelia Barleycorn and William Vivour formed an extremely powerful pair, surrounded by influential persons and numerous collaborators. During his lifetime, William Vivour, and naturally Amelia too, maintained contact with prominent people who visited the island, such as the ethnographer Günter Tessmann, who mentioned them expressly (Tessmann, 2008, p. 124).

William Vivour passed away in 1890. His standing on the island was such that a monument twelve metres tall was shipped over from Liverpool to pay homage to him in San Carlos, the location of his largest plantations. While it cannot be proven from the documentary evidence, there can be little doubt that this act was commissioned by his wife, Amelia, who had always associated with the most prosperous and high-class people of the period and who had also made gifts of various items for the Cathedral of Santa Isabel. The monument cost her 600 dollars at the time (Smith, 1895, p. 165). For the Afro-American traveller Rev. Charles S. Smith (1895, p. 165), commissioning a funerary monument in Liverpool was a clear sign of the Krio Fernandino community in Fernando Poo. Undoubtedly, the intention was to show the Fernandinos' power and authority vis-à-vis the Spanish colonial authorities and the entire population of Fernando Poo, whether white, brown or black.

Amelia Barleycorn and William Allen Vivour had just one child, their daughter Isabel. As is duly stated in Amelia's death certificate in Barcelona, this daughter predeceased her, between the last journey the two made to Barcelona in 1917 and Amelia's passing in 1920. Amelia had sent Isabel to study in England, as we know from the fact that in 1903 Amelia visited her there to check on her academic progress, returning to Santa Isabel via Barcelona. The fact that Amelia and William chose the name Isabel for their daughter over Elizabeth was further proof of the Hispanisation of the island and the profound affection they felt for their city, Santa Isabel, as this name was not of English origin and had no resemblance to others chosen by Amelia's influential brother William Napoleon Barleycorn. Amalia Barleycorn (2021) was incredibly proud of her ancestry, saying, "I am a descendant of Amelia, we are a single branch, from Africa and the English [...] William Napoleon, the bishop, would be the grandfather, but the father William was also a preacher."

As we will see in later chapter, Amelia Barleycorn lived a full life from her widowhood until her death in Barcelona in 1920, although she sold some hectares of her estate, which were bought by other Fernandinos and also by Catalans and Spaniards.

By way of conclusion, it should be noted that the Barleycorn lineage was marked by plantation owners, but also by Methodist bishops, as proof of their English Protestant background that conveyed their educational and religious grounding.

William Allen Vivour, and afterwards Amelia Barleycorn, were not the only major property owners among the Krio Fernandino, but they were the first. In addition, their case allows us to illustrate in great detail how other moneyed Krio Fernandino families, such as the Joneses, Dougans, Kinsons, Collinses and Balboas, operated. As will be seen in the section of the book devoted to the Krio Fernandino in Barcelona, these families would travel to Europe, as did Amelia Barleycorn, some settling until their final days in the city, as in the case of Amelia herself.

In the following sections, we shall take a closer look at some of the influential families, though in less detail than the Barleycorns. I have made significant efforts to use the documentation available to highlight a selection of the most influential women in these families, as once again the invisibility of female Fernandino footprints is repeated.

Mabel Jones

The Jones bloodline gained notoriety thanks to the major role played by its figurehead, Maximiliano C. Jones, who was born in Santa Isabel in 1870 and whose family came from Sierra Leone. He is the product of a later generation than that of Amelia Barleycorn.

Maximiliano C. Jones was a successful entrepreneur from the Krio Fernandino people who set the standard for his ancestry and subsequent generations. His name remains a point of reference when strolling through the city of Malabo in the company of some of his descendants. Sundiata (1996, p. 93) rated him as one of the most promising young men in Fernando Poo in the 1890s, alongside Joseph Dougan, Samuel Kinson and J.W. Knox.

Unquestionably, Maximiliano Jones ended up becoming the most influential African landowner in Spanish Guinea in the first third of the twentieth century. The extent of his lands and properties amazed the mapmaker and explorer Enrique d'Almonte (1908, p. 156). Maximiliano was even appointed by the Spanish colonial authorities as a member of the Royal Order of Comendador on 13 November 1924 owing to his "major plantations in San Carlos". Some of the most important posts he held were as part of the Compañía Trasatlántica in Fernando Poo or as a board member of the Cámara Agrícola de Fernando Poo, although his engagement as a major landowner of plantations was similarly pivotal.

By 1915, Maximiliano Jones was already a figure of undisputed renown. News clippings from the time explain that the "flourishing agricultural endeavours are represented by Firms of great standing, and resounding activity in our trading, such as those of Rius and Torres, referred to as *La Barcelonesa*, Maximiliano C. Jones, [...] Samuel Kinson, Edmundo Collins [...]."[26]

Maximiliano Jones was an entrepreneur. In 1925, he was assigned the installation of the electric lighting network for the capital, Santa Isabel, for a term of years. A further example of the close collaboration that he maintained with the colonial authorities can be seen in his recruiting of a Spaniard to manage this facility. On 18 December 1935, Jones was already the owner of the Electrical Power Station in Santa Isabel and had been awarded a fiscal exemption lasting ten years as he stated that "it did not turn a profit but did give him many sleepless nights" (AGA, box 81/06378). He even had a printing press.

Maximiliano Jones lived a life of comfort and luxury. His person exuded both opulence and a tendency towards profligacy, as was the case with Amelia and other members of the Barleycorn and Vivour families, as well as other well-known Krio Fernandino families such as the Dougans or the Collinses. Numerous news items appeared that underscored his reputation for forward-thinking by importing hitherto unseen products from Europe to the island of Fernando Poo, items that in most of Spain at the time were rarely seen outside of Barcelona and Madrid. Maximiliano Jones' name became synonymous with always being the first to import cars, shore boats and even a cocoa hulling machine for his properties, as can be ascertained from news items from 1912, 1914 and 1921.

The economic, political and social influence exerted by Maximiliano Jones brought power to his entire family. The documentation reviewed reveals offspring, grandchildren and great-grandchildren of both sexes. Worthy of special mention are Moisés Cornelio Jones and Wilbardo Jones Níger. Wilbardo settled in Bilbao in 1923 and his home there became a meeting point for future generations of Joneses, such as Caridad Jones and Miguel Jones Castillo who were his cousins and who in the 1960s attained a certain celebrity status in Spain, the first as an actor and the latter playing for Atlético de Madrid football club. The figure of Wilbardo Jones Níger is highly relevant for understanding how the Jones family fitted in with Bilbao high society and the impact of their life experiences in both Spain and Spanish Guinea. After spending many years in Bilbao, he returned to Equatorial Guinea and was appointed Mayor of Santa Isabel in 1960, under the auspices of the Franco regime, and prior to Spanish decolonisation.

As per the documents consulted from the Alcalá de Henares Archive, on several occasions Maximiliano Jones, and likewise Amelia Barleycorn, acted as mediators to resolve disputes, not only those affecting their families, or the Krio Fernandino community as a whole, but also to help the Bubi people or African workers among the Spanish population, even reaching compensation agreements for different *bracero* labourers.

It is worth highlighting that the peacemaking nature of Jones was both more visible and more sought after than that of Amelia Barleycorn, possibly due to him being a man, who had furthermore converted to Catholicism and maintained close ties with the colonial authorities, as well as the Catalan and Spanish agriculturalists and entrepreneurs. These three aspects would set him aside from Amelia, who embodied quite the opposite. Thus, Jones was a perfect role model of the colonial androcentrism, which was based on rewarding male figures over female ones, as occurred in other nations where women represented influential collectives, for example in Ghana. A key demonstration of this can be found in the text devoted to "Fernandinos ilustres" (Distinguished Fernandino subjects) from 1928, in which not a single woman was given column space, not even Amelia Barleycorn (Ruiaz, 1928, pp. 83–88). These factors bring to the fore the rhetorical and documentary male focus of the period.

As Amelia Barleycorn had displayed her might and wealth on the island by building a new mansion in San Carlos, Maximiliano Jones would soon follow suit. However, Jones' mansion would much more widely discussed in the press in 1916 compared to Amelia's, although hers was chosen as the backdrop for a postcard the state used as "propaganda" for the Spanish Territories in the Gulf of Guinea. This fact would prove that being a wealthy, Protestant black woman was not among the androcentric variables that Spanish colonialism imposed. Spanish colonial authorities sought out masculine figures with whom Hispanisation had succeded.

Among the descriptions of the figure of Maximiliano C. Jones, it is worth considering that all his endeavours in Fernando Poo were widely praised:

> he was an excellent citizen, a model Spaniard, who provided valuable collaboration with the Government's projects [...] While still a child [...] he went to study in Sierra Leone [...] He was always an avid reader, who knew how to combine agricultural tasks with trading concerns simultaneously [...] He undertook during his lifetime significant social endeavours in close collaboration with the general Government.[27]

Similarly, González Echegaray (2013, p. 8) offered words of giddy praise to Maximiliano Jones:

> Maximiliano Jones [was a] Fernandino subject from the Gulf, who was able to amass a great fortune and held the status of the most important African in the colony, respected even by the Governors of this period.

There can be little doubt that the figure of Maximiliano Jones eclipsed all of his descendants. However, one of them in particular, Mabel Jones, is worthy of some consideration, although not much data on her lifetime has been unearthed.

What is known about Mabel Jones comes from some of her regular journeys to Barcelona. Mabel was the daughter appointed by her parents to enter into one of the most prominent Krio Fernandino weddings in the Catalan capital, to Esteban Rhodes, as will be seen in the section in chapter 3 devoted to the lifestyle of Equatorial Guineans in Barcelona. News clippings explained that the couple had chosen to get married in Barcelona, even though he was at the time concluding his studies in London, while Mabel resided in Santa Isabel: "Upon the steamboat named *Cataluña* Miss Mabel Jones boarded in Fernando Poo and docked in Barcelona, who will shortly wed in our city Mr Esteban Rhodes, who lives in London while he finishes his university studies."[28]

Ana María Dougan

The Dougans came to prominence through José Walterio Dougan, a Krio Fernandino whose family originated from Sierra Leone. Given the job of running the major plantation that Amelia Barleycorn had inherited from her husband, William Vivour, Dougan became the proprietor of cocoa estates in Spanish Guinea, as did other many other Krio Fernandino. In 1913, his estates near Santa Isabel were graded in seventeenth place in the ranking of most biggest plantations, behind a majority of Spanish owners

José W. Dougan most stood out for his numerous advertisements, which he frequently placed in magazines such as *La Voz de Fernando Poo* in the first decades of the twentieth century (from 1911 to 1916), and in which he advertised his services as a harvester and an importer of other products, such as manufactured textiles. This was a clear sign that his economic activity was diversified and that he controlled channels of import and export of goods. Indeed, a direct relative of José W. Dougan opened a photographic workshop in 1908, an establishment that advertised being "equipped with the finest instruments available today in the art of photography", premises opened in the central thoroughfare of calle Lepanto in Santa Isabel.[29]

In 1906, the widely known José W. Dougan was one of the few Krio Fernandino appointed as a member of the select group forming the Consejo de Vecinos of Santa Isabel, which mainly consisted at that time of Spanish missionaries, officials and colonists.

Like Amelia Barleycorn and Maximiliano Jones, Dougan made charitable donations to the missionaries in Fernando Poo. For example, he and his family paid, along with other Krio Fernandino, for part of the construction works of the Cathedral of Santa Isabel, which was built in 1916, as well as for some images and altarpieces. In addition, he decided to personally finance the altarpiece and image of San José in the Cathedral.

These charitable actions were in the context of what was a self-interested conversion to Catholicism, since, like Maximiliano Jones, Dougan considered conversion to an effective integration strategy in the Spanish colony after the loss of British influence.

José W. Dougan married Mariana Kinson, who we will discuss in more detail in the next section. Their marriage strengthened the power of both families and increased the scope of their plantations. The missionary magazine *La Guinea Española* explained in 1915 that José Walterio Dougan and Mariana Kinson were very "known and of great significance in the upstanding Krio Fernandino society".[30]

To counteract the general invisibility of Krio Fernandino women, it is worth examining the figure of Lorenza Dougan Kinson. Lorenza was born in Santa Isabel on 8 October 1905. Her trips to Barcelona in the 1950s are well documented. In documents related to them, she declared her profession to be *"sus labores"* (her work), for example in her application for a return visa from Barcelona to Spanish Guinea in 1951, accompanied by her children Lucrecia Jones Dougan and Abilio Balboa Dougan. As we will see, her case is an excellent example of Krio Fernandino endogamy with children from different influential lineages.

Still, among the Dougan women, Ana María Dougan Thomson stands out especially. She studied law in Barcelona and was the first black lawyer in Spain, making her one of the leading Dougan women in the mid-twentieth century. An obituary offered a complete portrait of her, in which it was explained that she had been born in Santa Isabel in 1931 and graduated in law from the University of Barcelona in 1957, following the model of her father Teófilo Dougan Kinson (who graduated in law in Barcelona in 1927) (Radio Macuto, 2017). She promoted the Equatorial Guinea Bar Association of which she was Dean and managed its twinning with the Barcelona Bar Association. She was married to Román Boricó Toichoa, the Minister of Industry in the Autonomous Government of Spanish Guinea and Minister of Labour in the first government after independence, who was assassinated in the 1970s.

Mariana Kinson

The Kinson bloodline was originally from Sierra Leone and gained widespread notoriety in early twentieth century Spanish Guinea. Among the family were two male figures, Daniel Kinson and Samuel Kinson.

Daniel Kinson was a prominent member of the Consejo de Vecinos of Santa Isabel from at least 1905, and at least until the late 1920s. At meetings of the Consejo de Vecinos, all manner of information was reviewed, both strategic and concerning other minor matters. For example, it is striking that in 1924 Daniel Kinson (and Eduardo Oribi) were denied the construction of country-style houses with a zinc roof. Plus, of course, Daniel Kinson's popularity among the authorities of the colony was also due to the fact that he was one of those who provided more financial aid to the missions on a regular basis, as can be seen in the Suscripción Popular en Santa Isabel (Popular Subscription in Santa Isabel) of 1904, where his name appears next to those of Eva and Francisco Knox as one of the trustees who contributed the most.

Another important Kinson figure was Samuel Kinson. Certainly, in 1915, *La Guinea Española* reported that he belonged to one of the houses that represented "the flourishing agriculture" of the colony. Amongst the document consulted, deeds and documents were found that were submitted to the Notary of the Colony between 1923 and 1925 about the granting of a loan with a mortgage guarantee to Samuel N. Kinson in December 1924. Moreover, in 1919, the Kinsons and Collinses were the first Fernandinos to own a motor car in Spanish Guinea, even before any of the Spanish colonists. In fact, the first vehicle had been brought over for the Banapá Mission in 1913. The flood of cars to Fernando Poo would not arrive until 1928, when 145 vehicles were counted.

In 1911, Samuel Kinson married Julia Vivour Barleycorn, a relative of Amelia Barleycorn. The wedding was announced in *La Voz de Fernando Poo*, which explained that lavish preparations had been undertaken.[31] It explained that lavish preparations had been undertaken and that it would be a major event. This kinship relationship between the Kinsons and Vivours brought the personal relationships between Amelia Barleycorn and Samuel Kinson closer, as will be seen. They occasionally travelled together to Barcelona.

Regarding the women of the family, Mariana Kinson is particularly notable. As mentioned above, she married José Walterio Dougan and they were one of the most well-known couples at the beginning of the twentieth century. Mariana Kinson appeared in numerous news stories alongside her husband, especially when baptisms, deaths or marriages were celebrated. For example, when the couple baptised their son José Walterio, according to a news clipping, "the church could not hold the crowd because the cream of the indigenous population was in attendance [...] The godparents were Luís Lolín Camblé and the girl Juliana Dougan y Kinson."[32] Similarly, the note on the death of a daughter, Anita Sara Dougan Kinson, at ten months old proves the high infant mortality rate at those times in Spanish Guinea that similarly ravaged the Fernandino people.

Mariana Kinson was linked to different charitable activities along with other Fernandino women, or as a wedding bride or mother or godmother of baptism. Mariana Kinson de Dougan served on the choir committee of the Archdiocese of Santa Isabel and founded various associations with other Krio Fernandino in the mid-1910s (see chapter 4). Mariana's dynamism in the 1910s underscored her female leadership in the Kinson family.

Sara Collins

The Collins family was one of the Krio Fernandino families with large estates, as noted in the 1915 list of the major agricultural powerhouses published by *La Guinea Española*. Ramos Izquierdo and Navarro y Beltrán (1912, p. 29) referred to the plantations of Vivour, Maximiliano Jones and Collins, among others, in San Carlos as the most important farms in that locality at that time. According to Aranzadi (2016, p. 254), the Collinses came from Sierra Leone, like the Macfoys, Kinsons, Joneses and Dougans.

One of the figures who stands out in this family is Edmundo Collins. Edmundo Collins is credited with creating the Club Fernandino. The 1914 most influential fellows included Samuel Kinson, Claudio Cole Vivour and Collins himself. As García Gimeno (2013) notes, entry to the Club was forbidden for whites unless they were influential in the colony. In addition, the Collinses, like the Kinsons, were the first to own a car in Spanish Guinea in 1919.

In the Alcalá de Henares Archive there are numerous deeds and other documents presented and accepted by the Notary of the Colony between 1923 and 1925. To give two examples, there is a deed of sale from April 1923 in the name of Edmundo Collins, which includes as a witness Emilio Barleycorn, and from July 1925 a judicial sale by Edmundo Collins.

Figure 3. Aerial image of the Club Fernandino, Santa Isabel, 5 October 1963. General Archive of the Administration, 3 (82) F/ 01311, envelope 45.

Although it is difficult to appraise the labour conditions of the Krio Fernandino's farm labourers – which is why it is suggested that they did not differ much from those of the Europeans – it should be noted that the odd specific complaint was lodged, in this case regarding Edmundo Collins' plantation. In the Communication of 8 August 1919 of the corporal of Rebola, it was stated that four of the six *braceros* hired by Edmundo Collins for one of his plantations did not receive enough rations but did not dare to complain, and that when they were asked for the reasons behind their grievances they said that they did not understand why the corporal of Rebola had said that, because was not true since their employer had always provided them with abundant rations.

The high profile of the Collins family at the beginning of the twentieth century in the press came from the hand of Edmundo's widow and his son, also called Edmundo, as adverts placed by the Widow Collins and her son appeared in *La Voz de Fernando Poo*.[33]

As with other families, the Collinses joined forces with the Joneses. For example, the daughter of Edmundo Collins and Juana Jones was Juana Elena Collins Jones, who was born on 22 June 1925 in Santa Isabel. When she was older she visited her uncle Eduardo Jones in Santa Isabel from her residence in Barcelona.

Also of note is Edmundo Collins Jones, a descendant of Edmundo Collins from whom he received his name, who he played an important role in the 1960s. He married Lucrecia Jones Dougan at Santa Isabel Cathedral in 1956. The continuity of that lineage in Barcelona was seen with his death in Barcelona in 2011, as reported in an extensive note in a sports newspaper, summing up the exile of this Fernandino family to Barcelona after the establishment of the Macías dictatorship. Other descendant who gained notoriety was José Luís Collins, known as Pepe Collins, who was born in Santa Isabel in 1962 (Chiquillo, 2017). There was also an interview in *El Periódico* (Merino, 2011) with Eddy Collins Jones, born in Santa Isabel in 1956, who worked serving glasses and making cocktails for "the heady nightlife of Barcelona culture" and who explained: "I am a descendant of African slaves."

Regarding the entire bloodline, Sara Collins was one of the most visible women in the family, travelling abroad, including to Barcelona, whenever her responsibilities permitted. Even without being able to corroborate this completely, there are indications that Sara was one of the Collins women who led the first demonstration against colonial power in 1915, a demonstration of Krio Fernandino women that received a certain amount of attention in the press published in Spanish Guinea at that time (see chapter 4). This leadership on the part of the Collins women shows their influence on the Fernandino society of Santa Isabel.

Consuelo Balboa

The Balboa family had Manuel Balboa as its figurehead on Spanish Guinea. The Balboas are Fernandino descendants of the emancipated Cubans sent to Fernando Poo during the 1860s. To say that it would have been a few decades since the arrival in Santa Isabel of those first poor Cubans that were identified in the lists by a first name and marks on the skin whose majority responded to signs of slavery and letters.

The major difference between the Fernandinos of Cuban origin and those of African origin is that they followed the Catholic faith, rather than Protestantism. Aranzadi explains (2016, p. 259) that other "Cuban surnames still remain such as Moreno, Castillo, Riquito, Mata, Rivas, Balboa, Valcárcel, etc." The documentation reflects their Catholic marital links with Krio Fernandino of other origins, such as the marriage of José Salinas to Paulina Peter in 1909, showing that the merging of Cubans with Africans was a reality at the beginning of the twentieth century.

Manuel Balboa owned farmsteads in the bay of La Concepción (D'Almonte, 1908, p. 145). His agricultural and export activity began in 1890, attaining international recognition at the beginning of the twentieth century. He received medals at the Paris and London Exhibitions: a Grand Diploma and gold medals at the 1905 Paris Exhibition of Foodstuff Products and the 1906 London Colonial and Indian Exhibition.

Manuel Balboa was said to have intervened in various unofficial commissions, supporting government initiatives, and was, together with Daniel Kinson, one of those who collaborated in the implementation of indigenous work by 1907. Like the rest of the Fernandinos under study, Manuel Balboa carried out charitable activities with the missionaries established in the colony. For example, records show his gift of two recliners to the Mission in 1904.

Manuel Balboa was also remembered for bringing the first cine-camera to Santa Isabel in 1904. This was reported on in a news item published in *La Guinea Española*, where it was explained that on his return from Barcelona, he had brought it to "amuse and comfort the spirit [...] at the same time as reporting some profit to the owner."[34] The device had cost 1,000 pesetas and made it possible to reproduce objects and scenes in motion. The one that was going to be installed in Santa Isabel was comparable with those existing in two only theatres in Barcelona. The movie theatre Cine Santa Isabel worked for decades screening films of interest, such as *Sin novedad en el frente* or *Caballero de noche* in 1933. Yet beyond bringing Fernando Poo such an innovative device, which was still lacking in many European cities, the film screenings became a means of bolstering the Spanish colonial mission. As proof of the foregoing, as would happen on the peninsula, the Governor General demanded to be informed prior to the monthly cinema screenings to ensure the supposed morality of the colony.

However, it should also be noted that not all Krio Fernandino subjects blindly followed Spanish colonial regulations. For example, the sale of wine to the *braceros* in the employ of the Collinses and Balboas is known even though it was prohibited, which is why they were issued a fine for ignoring the prohibition on 27 August 1919. In reality, in an authorisation that Balboa received to open a new factory on the Basakato estate on 20 January 1920, he was forbidden from selling wine and alcoholic beverages, nor was he permitted to pay labourers with articles so that they would not be forced to consume if they did not want to. This shows that these abusive practices must have been widespread amongst the owners of Fernandino plantations, and likewise the Spaniards and Catalans.

One of Balboa's most renowned descendants was Manuel Balboa During. *La Guinea Española* dedicated a tribute to him, as well as to other renowned Fernandinos, descendants of their ancestors who had amassed prestige and power in the city. In this, it was said that their activities represented the civic and economic life of Santa Isabel. He was described as a man "of an enterprising spirit, a workaholic and tireless."[35]

Other known descendants were Abilio Balboa Arkins, who in turn called his son Abilio, and who as a landowner had interests with the Catalan J. Pérez Portabella, the manager of the trading company Comercial Frapejo SA. Abilio was the son of Lorenza Dougan Kinson.

Still, the Balboas were not the only Cubans on the island. Another example of a marriage between Cuban and Fernandino citizens was that of Luís Lolín Camblé to Constancia F. Coker in 1908. It was said that "the religious act covered all the solemnity possible: the altar was spectacularly lit, a solemn psalm was sung". It was added that they were married by the popular Father Juanola, who gave his address in Spanish and then in English, given the ethnic and linguistic diversity of the spouses who, according to the note, "produced a lively sensation in the crowd".[36]

Among the Balboa women, Consuelo stands out. Consuelo Balboa was the sister of Abilio Balboa Arkins and stood out for studying singing in Barcelona, gaining a modicum of fame as a soprano in the Catalan music scene of the 1930s and 1940s. She married Catalan bourgeois businessman Fausto Ruíz Espuñas (Gargallo & Sant, 2021, p. 89) in what was a mixed marriage. *La Vanguardia* reported on a review of one of her performances in the Casa del Médico in which it was said that it "caused a deep impression in the select audience";[37] however, perhaps due to her status as a black African or for her limited quality, she was not known to have performed in the Liceu or the Palau de la Música.

2.3. Everyday life in Santa Isabel

The historical reconstruction of life in Santa Isabel provides data to help us understand the reality of the colony, because understanding the urban social dynamics better clarifies the referential framework within which Equatorial Guineans, Fernandinos, and other Krios and Africans moved, as well as Catalans, Spaniards and other Europeans in general.

To show the city's characteristics and transformation, population factors, the cost of living and public services of Santa Isabel have been taken into account, since only in this way can the social dynamics of Santa Isabel and Barcelona be successfully compared.

The ultimate aim is to understand, on the one hand, what the socio-occupational and economic framework was in which Krio Fernandino women and the Equatorial Guinean community as a whole had to operate, and, on the other, what experiences could be projected to their stays in Barcelona, as the unofficial capital of the mainland during the first third of the twentieth century.

Population of the colony

The majority of the population of Santa Isabel was African, regardless of whether they were considered Spanish subjects or foreigners. Their origins and provenances were very diverse, which gave the city a highly Afropolitan and scarcely European character. European cultural influence in the city was limited until the first third of the twentieth century.

The available population data for Santa Isabel are very detailed and demonstrate the diversity of the city. Unzueta (1947, p. 277) provided details from an extract of the Population Census of Santa Isabel de Fernando Poo, produced on 31 March 1856 (see Table 3), in which it was noted that almost half of the African population that lived there either worked as artisans or as servants (419 people, 42.6% of the total population).

The groups most influenced first by British culture and then by the Spanish were initially the Krio community in general, and the Fernandino in particular, but this fact did not cause them to lose awareness of their African identity, since their identity affirmation was mostly based on Africanity, not Europeanness, which probably also limited the scope of their mixing with the Cuban minority.

If we consider the classification by religion issued in 1862 (see Table 4), it can be seen that Protestantism was the majority religion (42.3%) and that it necessarily was followed by a substantial part of the African population, since the white population made up only 14.7% of followers, among which only four were women. The next category after Protestantism was "without known religion" (39.7%), which would mostly refer to the cult of ancestors. The Catholic faith amounted to a paltry 18%, which shows that the missions were spreading the word at a snail's pace.

Ramos Izquierdo and Navarro y Beltran (1912, p. 26) also provided data on the inhabitants of Santa Isabel as of 1912. At that time, they considered

Table 3. Population breakdown for Santa Isabel, 1856

	Origin	Men	Women	Total
English residents	England	6	1	105 (10.6%)
	Sierra Leone	47	21	
	Accra English	20	1	
	Cabo Costa	6	3	
Freedmen by English warships believing that they were English subjects	Lagos	12	28	238 (24%)
	Aboh	36	29	
	Calabar Viejo	22	24	
	Cameroonians	14	15	
	Kabenda	6	13	
	Congo	16	18	
	Fopoh	1	1	
	Azu	2	1	
Orphans of former colonisers, arrived with Captain Owen	Santa Isabel	22	21	43 (4.4%)
	Fernando Poo	89	91	180 (18.4%)
Residents who are neither English slaves nor freedmen and work as artisans and servants	Bonny	14	6	419 (42.6%)
	Portuguese (Principe/S. Tome)	33	8	
	Dutch Accra	7	1	
	Bimbia	55	13	
	Calabar Viejo	4	21	
	Cameroonians	44	13	
	Aborigine	29	9	
	Benin	1	1	
	The Americas	-	1	
	Jamaica	1	-	
	Krumanes	158	-	
	Total	645	340	985

Source: Unzueta (1947, p. 277).

Table 4. Population of Santa Isabel. Census of 1862

Inhabitants	Men	Women	Total	Percentage
Residents of Santa Isabel	350	296	646	62.3%
Garrison servicemen	115	-	115	11.1%
Kruman civil servants	69	1	70	6.7%
Kruman private individuals	206	-	206	19.9%
Total	740	297	1,037	100%
Classification by race	Men	Women	Total	Percentage
White	148	4	152	14.7%
Mulattos	10	11	21	2%
Morenos	582	282	864	83.3%
Total	740	297	1,037	100%
Classification by religions	Men	Women	Total	Percentage
Catholicism	176	10	186	18%
Protestants of various branches	214	225	439	42.3%
No known religion	350	62	412	39.7%
Total	740	297	1,037	100%

Source: Compiled by the author. Documentary Collection of the Instituto Nacional de Estadística. *Anuario 1860–1861*.

Fernandinos to be, after seventy years of living in the city, "the natives of the capital of Santa Isabel", who were grouped as *morenos* among the natives of Santa Isabel and other parts of the island. They added that "they amount to 1,300 and 200 are natives of foreign colonies, to which are added 170 Spaniards, 4 English, 5 Germans and 11 Portuguese" (Ramos Izquierdo & Navarro y Beltrán, 1912, p. 26). These data also show that at the beginning of the twentieth century the English presence was almost non-existent after decades of the slow process of Hispanisation.

Comparing the censuses of the late nineteenth and early twentieth centuries allows us to see the gradual distinction being made between the white minority and the African majority population, as well as the slow arrival of Spaniards, whether as part of colonial, military or settler cadres, in particular the Catalan community (Gargallo & Sant, 2021). Until the 1930s, and coinciding with the advent of the dictatorship of Francisco Franco in Spain, population statistics did not always systematically distinguish the population by their skin colour, even though it was the most common proof of colonial racialisation.

Everyday life in Santa Isabel among groups from such diverse backgrounds – Africans, Europeans and to a lesser extent Latin Americans – was not straightforward. As can be seen in Tables 5 and 6, the population was very segmented: being European or Spanish, male and white guaranteed successful integration, except on rare occasions.

Likewise, the needs of agricultural plantations led to the massive hiring of *braceros* through bilateral agreements with various African countries such as Liberia, and these treaties stipulated how long they could remain in the country and their working conditions (Martino, 2012).

The arrival of unregulated immigration was evident in the 1930s when the need to establish regulations was noticeable. On 1 August 1934, a Regulation was proposed, but its basis was the "convenience of adopting a procedure to acquire Spanish nationality for people for many years in Guinea" (AGA, box 81/07189). As stated in the documentation consulted, there was a reiterated interest in "becoming Spanish subjects" on the part of

> numerous individuals born in other parts of the African Continent, for having resided for a long time in our Possessions, speaking our language, being owners of agricultural or industrial holdings, for affection for the country of residence or for having contracted unions with indigenous women and having had of these descendants.[38]

In the proposal for a Regulation, it was recalled that there were only two means of acquiring Spanish nationality: by obtaining a naturalisation charter or by recognition of their neighbourhood in any town of the Kingdom. This second option would be very difficult to prove due to the scarcity of civil and consular records in the colony and specifically in Fernando Poo after the effective colonisation of the territory.

During the 1930s, statistical data on the colony began to be collected in a systematic manner, which allows us to estimate the composition of the native and foreign population, segregating the population by the racialised categories of "people of colour", "black" or "white". The data of Table 5 show the population increase and greater mixing and interethnic coexistence, with a percentage of women always lower than that of men.

Table 5. *White population* in Fernando Poo, 1942 and 1950

1942		1950	
3,319		3,937	
2,880 men	439 women	2,721 men	1,216 women
2,693 Spanish	375 Spanish	2,493 Spanish	1,102 Spanish
114 Portuguese	39 Portuguese	139 Portuguese	64 Portuguese
20 Germans	5 Germans	45 Lebanese	30 Lebanese
17 Syrians	4 Syrians	23 Germans	10 Germans
11 Italians	1 Italian	8 Indians	1 Indian
2 French	2 French	5 Italians	3 Italians
3 English	1 English	4 British	1 British
20 others	12 others	4 others	5 others

Source: Compiled by the author. Resúmenes Estadísticos del Gobierno General de los Territorios Españoles del Golfo de Guinea (1945, pp. 30–32). Resúmenes Estadísticos del Gobierno General de los Territorios Españoles del Golfo de Guinea (1953, pp. 26–27).

Certain statistics provided data that categorised the African population by the European empire from which they came (see Table 6). This particularity made it possible to demonstrate that the majority of Africans who were settled in Santa Isabel came from English colonies (49%), with a large gap to the next categories, which were French (12%) and Portuguese (0.8%). Of the total population of Santa Isabel, which was 9,280, Spanish Africans in the city numbered only 2,267 and Europeans 1,785. The rest, 5,228 people, were Africans from other European colonies (56.3%).

It should be noted that, at the urban level, the houses of the Krio Fernandino in Santa Isabel stood out compared to those of the Europeans at the beginning of the twentieth century. Saavedra (1910, p. 114) recalled "the residences of the wealthy Fernandino families, what might be called 'island aristocracy', the Joneses, Kinsons, Barleycorns, Balboas, Lolíns, Noxes, Princes, etc., all of them cheerful and well cared for, complete and beautify the perspective of the capital."

Decades later, the urban development expanded the centre of the capital with military barracks and housing for officials, intermingled with the existing wooden houses typical of the island. Lighting and sewerage works were carried out that improved the flow of the floodwaters that

Table 6. *Coloured race* population of Santa Isabel, 1942, by nationality

Nationality	Consejo de Vecinos of Santa Isabel			Eastern Demarcation			Total on the islands		
	Men	Women	Total	Men	Women	Total	Men	Women	Total
Spanish Territories	1,239	1,028	2,267	2,554	3,155	5,709	5,938	5,692	11,630 (38%)
Republic of Liberia	34	7	41	21	0	21	105	7	112 (0.3%)
French colonies	1,244	750	1,994	1,202	43	1,245	2,802	884	3,686 (12%)
English colonies	2,294	766	3,060	7,697	99	7,796	14,085	930	15,015 (49%)
Portuguese colonies	74	59	133	42	7	49	143	75	218 (0.7%)
Total	4,885	2,610	7,495	11,516	3,304	14,820	23,073	7,588	30,661 (100%)

Source: Compiled by the author. Resúmenes Estadísticos del Gobierno General de los Territorios Españoles del Golfo de Guinea (1945, pp. 34–35).

are so abundant in the rainy season in a tropical country. Some of this infrastructure was not subsequently maintained in the independence period, with it being a recurring theme that the exasperated citizenry would rhetorically wonder why the infrastructure had been "of a higher standard" during the colonial period than since independence, especially considering that independent Equatorial Guinea was in the early 2000s one of the largest oil extractors on the African continent.

Products, prices and the cost of living

Santa Isabel was the capital of the colony and although it was well provisioned it was an expensive city if one compares the prices of products there with a European city like Barcelona, in part because most products were imported. Travellers such as Muñoz y Gaviria (1871a, p. 15) were surprised by the cost of living in the last third of the nineteenth century and provided a detailed account of the cost of different products (see Table 7).

Table 7. Prices of staples in Santa Isabel, 1871

Type	Reales*
Basket of potatoes	40
Chicken	10
Dozen eggs	12
Lard (pound)	8
Oil (pound)	4
Wine (barrel)	100
Pig (whole)	180
Sheep (whole)	170
Beef (pound)	5

Source: Compiled by the author. Muñoz y Gaviria (1871a, p. 15).
* The real was exchanged at 0.25 pesetas.

Some of the documentation consulted reflects the problems of supply and the cost of products, as well as facts of the social life of the city. In the minutes of a session of the Consejo de Vecinos of Santa Isabel held on 6 June 1906, attended by Daniel Kinson, Rolando Barleycorn and José Dougan, it was explained that the high cost of flour would have a bearing on the prices at the bread oven. The state and problems of the slaughterhouse and the reserve of meats in the city were also discussed, as was the postponement of a bullfight. In other minutes of meetings of the Consejo de Vecinos, in this case from 1905, a greater supply of gunpowder was requested to guarantee hunting, since "the amount of meat available to the population was insufficient".[39]

At the beginning of the twentieth century, Ramos Izquierdo and Navarro y Beltrán (1912, p. 26) explained that it was already possible to buy all kinds of footwear, clothes and umbrellas, and also all kinds of luxury and superfluous items in Santa Isabel. The same occurred with food and drink, with there being numerous reports that the best whiskey and champagne could be found in Santa Isabel. These products were not available to everyone; only the most affluent families could afford them, especially the Fernandino Krio community. The Cooperativa Annobonesa's price chart of 4 June 1920 indicates that the products were sold in stores as well as through various cooperatives. Its factory's price list dates from May 1920 and shows prices of 78 pesetas for a silk scarf, 4 for socks, 4 for swimsuits, 62 for English cretonne, 308 for a navy blue suit, and 50 for one of the umbrellas so highly prized by Fernandino women.

Santa Isabel's booming trade could also be seen in the fact that, at the end of the 1920s, some Fernandinos and Catalans announced that they were importing materials for construction in a city that, from the twentieth century, had begun to grow in terms of number of inhabitants and not only with wooden houses.

Thus, the cost of living in Santa Isabel was high by the mid-twentieth century, as can be seen from Table 8 on to prices and Table 9 on basic services. In the 1940s, prices continued to rise, influenced by the post-Civil War shortages.

Many products arrived by sea, meaning that European tensions and conflicts had an impact on the availability of products and their prices. Anyone who travelled could always be easily detained somewhere if there was a war underway, just like their goods. These limitations were observed with the American tensions regarding Cuba, but also with the First and Second World Wars. For example, in *La Voz de Fernando Poo* it was said that:

> The commercial stoppage due to the war is complete here, but in a total way in the continent where all the branches are being closed because they do not do even the least amount of business [...] The price of rice that is the main element of life [...] is through the roof. At 50 pesetas for 50 kilos!!! Unheard of![40]

The cost of living hindered the survival of Africans, Krio and the few non-Fernandino Equatorial Guineans who lived in Santa Isabel and, of course, of the African *braceros* who lived far away on the farms, because their monthly salaries would, hopefully, hover around the 200 pesetas they spent in the plantations' commissaries (see Table 9).

The salaries of the African *braceros* were almost ten times higher than that of the Equatorial Guineans (Sepa, 2011, p. 247), and the salaries of Spaniards thirty times higher (see Table 10).

For example, in the *Boletín Oficial de los Territorios Españoles en el Golfo de Guinea* of 30 August 1907 it was stipulated that the salary of a Bubi man would be 1 peseta per day (including rations), and that of Bubi women and those under fifteen years of age would be 3 *reales* (0.75 pesetas at exchange) (Miranda Junco, 1945, pp. 320–231).

Table 8. Prices of main European staples in Santa Isabel, 1946–1947

Items	Unit	1946		1947	
		Max.	Min.	Max.	Min.
Bread	Kilo	4	4	4.16	4.16
Rice	"	3.20	3	3.20	3.20
Potatoes (from Moka)	"	2.50	2.25	2.50	2.50
Onions	"	3	1.65	3.50	2.50
Beans	"	4.42	4.42	6	6
Fresh tomatoes (from Moka)	"	2.50	2.50	2.50	2.50
Fresh tomatoes (from Canary Islands)	"	5	4	5.65	4.40
Garlic	"	13	7.50	13.50	13.50
Beef	"	13	8	13	8
Pork	"	13	13	20	20
Chicken	Single	35	25	40	25
Chorizo	Kilo	60	35	85	70
Salami	"	100	55	115	90
Fresh fish	"	8	5	8	5
Turtle meat	"	5	5	5	5
Condensed milk	Tin	4.15	3.80	8.50	4.50
Eggs	Dozen	24	12	24	7.20
Sugar	Kilo	11.05	5	6.55	6.55
Cheese	"	50	35	60	40
Soap	"	4.15	4.15	7	5.24
Electricity	kWh	3	3	3	2

Source: Compiled by the author. Resúmenes Estadísticos del Gobierno General de los Territorios Españoles del Golfo de Guinea (1943, p. 178).

Table 9. Prices of basic services in Santa Isabel, fourth quarter 1941 (in pesetas)

Items	Unit	October		November		December	
		Max.	Min.	Max.	Max.	Min.	Max.
Middle-class rent	Month	200	125	200	125	200	125
Working-class rent	Month	150	60	150	60	150	60
Electricity	kWh	1.50	1.50	1.50	1.50	1.50	1.50

Source: Compiled by the author. Resúmenes Estadísticos del Gobierno General de los Territorios Españoles del Golfo de Guinea (1943, pp. 32–33).

Table 10. Indigenous Equatorial Guinean and Spanish monthly salaries on a 1959 coffee plantation (in pesetas)

Worker	Salary
Indigenous Equatorial Guinean *bracero*	216
Spanish estate manager	6,297
Spanish estate director	8,000

Source: Compiled by the author. Balance sheet, Hacienda Virgen de Montserrat 1959. Fondo Giménez Ferrer (IMF-CSIC).

These aspects are key to understanding the wealth of the Krio Fernandino community and the fact that the richest consumed expensive products that were imported from Europe, such as Victor Clicquot champagne.

The high price of Santa Isabel's standard of living was also reflected in the complaint about the salaries received by the Spanish military. Thus, the salary of a sergeant or a corporal in the Colonial Guard was 250 pesetas per month in 1914, an amount that did not allow them to take their families with them. In fact, the complaint was that salaries were low for the high standard of living of Santa Isabel and should be increased, or products provided to soldiers, because "the life of the European should not conform to that of the indigenous [...] With the rare exception of some indigenous products, the others are imported from Europe."[41]

Those concerns continued for decades, as monthly wages were low compared with the costs of rent and basic necessities. These facts also led those who rented houses, including owners who were Krio Fernandino women, having to face defaults and initiate eviction claims. One example identified in the documentation is the civil case filed by Susana Barleycorn. She had her residence in calle del General Franco and sued Pascual Sepa de Batete on 13 June 1941 for a debt 187.50 pesetas corresponding to five months of unpaid room rent at the rate of 37.50 pesetas per month. The judge resolved the case in favour of Susana Barleycorn, giving the tenant eight days to pay the debt (AGA, box 81/08538).

It is worthwhile knowing how payments were made and what kind of mechanisms were used for sending and receiving money, given the significant profits of the owners of the plantations, as well as understanding whether the Krio Fernandino carried cash or used other means to finance their trips to the Iberian Peninsula or other countries.

Ramos Izquierdo and Navarro y Beltrán (1912, p. 26) explained that at the beginning of the twentieth century in Santa Isabel, bank transfers of bank branches located in Spain, England and Germany worked normally. In the case of the Barleycorns, they had a close relationship with Liverpool, thanks to the companies with which they traded and, of course, with the bank that the English operated. For example, the Bank of British West Africa Limited was one of the banks of reference. In 1903, this bank announced that it had a capital of 10,000,000 pesetas, offering a collection of bills, advances, drafts, deposits and checking accounts, and agents in Fernando Poo.

Thus, in Santa Isabel at that time, the use of banks was widespread, especially among Europeans and Krio Fernandino. For example, in *La Guinea Española* there was news of the visit of A.C. Reeve, the manager of the Bank of British West Africa, who said he had received "great evidence of sympathy and consideration from the Fernandino colony".[42] And as we shall see, there was no shortage of initiatives by the Krio Fernandino to strengthen their bank from the 1920s onwards, which certainly greatly worried the colonial authorities, who did not wish Fernandino empowerment.

But Fernandino people also like to have gold at home. As we will see in section 4.2., after the death of Amelia Barleycorn in 1920, the policemen who went to testify to the theft that occurred in her mansion in San Carlos explained that she kept money in trunks in different European currencies and that she had abundant gold.

In any event, although cash in different currencies, or even metals and gemstones, were always an available resource, money orders had become a very popular form of economic exchange.

In short, daily life in Santa Isabel was in some aspects very similar to that in other African cities, but it also reflected issues found in large European cities such as Barcelona, despite the profound differences between Europe and Africa. For example, the high cost of many essential products in Santa Isabel compared to wages and the cost of houses, rentals and other services, such as lighting, showed the scarce purchasing power of the majority (see Tables 8 to 11). It is also striking that the price of some products was so high in Santa Isabel with respect to Barcelona, as can be observed by comparing some tables on the cost of products that, despite being from different decades, do allow for certain indications to be extracted (see Tables 7, 8 and 25).

Colony services

The development of infrastructure and services in the city of Santa Isabel took place after the effective colonisation of the Kingdom of Spain. From the beginning of the twentieth century, improvements would be accelerated to ensure better exploitation of the colony, with expansion works in the port of Santa Isabel, in that of San Carlos and the extension of the Santa Isabel to San Carlos railway in 1916. Construction of homes and shops had been continuous since the late nineteenth century, and the city's lighting had been deployed by 1921.

The budgets of the city allow us to know the expenses and income of Santa Isabel, which was the largest city in Spanish Guinea. They show the high tax rates that had been imposed to reduce spending in the general state budget: Spain invested mainly in infrastructure, health and safety, and the income it collected allowed it to balance its accounts to a certain extent in different periods of the twentieth century. Despite the Spanish civilisational rhetoric, the colonial state's investment in education was laughable.

The economic power of the Fernandinos rebounded on its socio-political influence, though not on the administrative sphere: the presence of Fernandinos in certain decision-making or problem-solving bodies was constant in commercial or associative entities, but very limited in colonial bodies. Therefore, members of the Krio Fernandino collective were an established presence in minor colonial bodies, like in the Consejo de

Vecinos of Santa Isabel, but the relevant colonial administrative bodies were exclusively reserved to Spaniards from the peninsula, not to African Spaniards.

The Spanish unwillingness to incorporate Fernandinos into the colonial administration was maintained until the late 1920s, at which point certain Fernandinos began to occupy administrative positions. In that sense, the Fernandino Teófilo Jorge Dougan Kinson is worth mentioning, since he was the first Equatorial Guinean to practise law in Santa Isabel after graduating in Barcelona in 1927. From the 1930s onwards, Equatorial Guineans of other ethnicities – Bubis, Fangs, Ndowes, Bissios and Annoboneses – would also begin to occupy certain positions in the colonial administration, although in their case always limited to junior and low-skilled positions, such as manual labourers, watchmen or assistant teachers.

For this reason, for decades the Krio Fernandino were the only Equatorial Guineans who occupied the most important positions, even in the courts, thanks to their first-rate academic training in Barcelona and in some other Spanish cities.

The order and security of the colony remained in the hands of the Colonial Guard and the Civil Guard. Eventually, the Equatorial Guineans who had joined the Colonial Guard and the police were part of the colonial administration because, without them, the Spanish state would not have been able to take control of the territory. This situation was overturned, ultimately, in 1959 when Spanish Guinea became a Spanish overseas province, and in 1963 with its subsequent conversion to a Spanish equatorial region. These periods marked a certain widening of the rights and opportunities of Equatorial Guineans, who saw an improvement in the treatment they received, subtly alleviating the lack of opportunities and racial segregation that had prevailed in the colony for decades and that was still in force.

The schooling carried out by the Spanish Catholic missionaries, most of them Catalan Claretians, would gradually spread throughout the territory. Catalan missionary schooling in the early 1940s was also already well established for European pupils (see Table 11).

The system of scholarships for the training of Equatorial Guineans would be gradually established, yet would be limited to study in Spanish Guinea. In the twentieth century, a few scholarships were granted to study on the peninsula, especially to train Equatorial Guinean teachers, who

Table 11. Santa Isabel Mixed School (European pupils), 1942

Initial intake		New recruits		Cessations		End intake		Total
Men	Women	Men	Women	Men	Women	Men	Women	
12	8	13	13	11	6	14	15	29

Source: Compiled by the author. Resúmenes Estadísticos del Gobierno General de los Territorios Españoles del Golfo de Guinea (1945, p. 48).

Table 12. Monthly teaching salaries in Spanish Guinea, 1930 and 1933

Spanish primary school teacher (1930)	3,500 plus bonuses worth 7,000 = 10,500 pesetas (Accommodation costs of 250 pesetas per month were received in the form of a gratuity)
Indigenous primary school teacher (1933)	500 pesetas

Source: Compiled by the author. Alumni data statistics, Teaching Inspectorate. Spanish Territories of the Gulf of Guinea, March 1930 (AGA, box 81/08123). Documentation on Teaching Staff in Rural Schools in Fernando Poo and Annobon, March 1933 (AGA, box 81/08123).

were called "indigenous teachers" and who, for example, in 1933 were only allowed to earn what was called a "gratification" of 500 pesetas, 4.7% of what a Spanish teacher earned (see Table 12). The indigenous teachers had a subordinate and very precarious position with respect to Spanish teachers, who maintained very high salaries and considerable status in Spanish Guinea.

The first scholars to study on the peninsula were named in the period between 1916 and 1925, one of the most well known cases being that of Pilar Momo in 1925, a Bubi woman from Baney who was honoured by the entire Equatorial Guinean community in the postcolonial period. From the 1930s onwards, there would be other cases. Therefore, it can be said that a notable increase in the system of scholarships granted to Equatorial Guineans, both to study in the colony and to study in Spain, took place between the period of the Civil War and the beginning of the Franco dictatorship, later accelerated by the Falange Española. This scholarship system of the metropolis had the purpose that, after their studies, those who travelled to mainland Spain, many to Madrid, would return to the colony. However, this was very different from what actually happened with the Krio Fernandino collective, which had been self-financing the studies of their descendants, preferably in Barcelona. Some of the Krio Fernandino who studied there ultimately chose to settle in the city.

The Hospital de Santa Isabel was also built, as the issue of health had been identified as being especially important for guaranteeing the development of the colony and safeguarding the health of the Spaniards. One issue was the repeated epidemics – no longer only leprosy, malaria or fevers,[43] but also Spanish flu. This ravaged the population in 1918 and led to the promulgation of an edict to guarantee the disinfection of steamers, facilities, shops and homes in Santa Isabel.

The Spaniards, like the Krio Fernandino, when they had a disease that was difficult to treat in the colony, moved to the peninsula to be treated in hospitals and better-stocked medical centres. For example, Barcelona of the early twentieth century offered different clinics and hospitals providing healthcare (Hochadel & Nieto-Galán, 2016).

In the early 1940s, various diseases were very prominent, and the lack of medical resources led to numerous deaths throughout the colony, including in Santa Isabel (see Table 13).

In relation to leisure, the first recreational space in Santa Isabel was the exclusive Club Fernandino, created by the Fernandino community in 1914. The board featured names such as Samuel Kinson, Claudio Cole Vivour and Edmundo Collins. The entrance to the Club was limited to Fernandinos, which was like acknowledging that whites were not allowed, although there was flexibility on this for the more influential Europeans in the colony. In the magazine *La Guinea Española* it was reported that it was a place of amusement for the "indigenous". The chronicle did not mention that it was the first dance and music venue that the city had, although the founders Luís Lolín y Camblé, Samuel Kinson, Claudio Cole Vivour and Edmundo Collins were noted.

Alongside the Club Fernandino, restaurants such as Manuel Fita's Gran Restaurant Peninsular and other venues attended by both Fernandinos and Europeans had been opened, proof that intersectionality by social class superseded the parameters that were used to racialise cultural differences and justify the disparities in rights and duties that existed between the colonisers and the colonised of the colony. This is not to overlook the fact that the island of Fernando Poo, and specifically Santa

Table 13. Causes of death in the Spanish Territories in the Gulf of Guinea, 1942

Cause of death	White race	Indigenous
Pertussis	0	1
Tuberculosis	0	24
Malaria	2	6
Syphilis	0	2
Rheumatism and gout	4	118
Avitaminosis and chronic poisonings	2	0
Meningitis	0	21
Heart conditions	1	118
Bronchitis	0	5
Pneumonia	4	138
Genital diseases	1	6
Suicide	1	11
Others	9	302
Total	24	752

Source: Compiled by the author. Resúmenes Estadísticos del Gobierno General de los Territorios Españoles del Golfo de Guinea (1945, p. 39, p. 46).

Isabelian society, was strongly segregated by skin colour through a colonial Regulation. It was thus on the basis of racial differences, beyond the attributions and rights of the Krio Fernandino, that Equatorial Guineans were prohibited from attending certain events or sharing a list of spaces with the white population, no matter how much like Spanish subjects the Africans appeared – although this did gradually become more flexible.

The existence of recreation and relaxation spots is an important issue since the intersectionality and desacralisation of the Krio Fernandino community was evident, while the racial segregation of the rest of the Equatorial Guinean and African population of other origins remained visible.

The Cathedral of Santa Isabel, just built in 1916 (Memba & Villaverde, 2018), was a meeting place for Spanish colonisers, Fernandinos and other Equatorial Guineans who had converted to or accepted Catholicism. Sunday Mass was a meeting point for the authorities and people of

Figure 4. Aristocratic wedding, Fernando Poo. Undated (likely 1910s). General Archive of the Administration, 3 (84) F/ 00797, envelope 30.

influence in the colony, in addition to many women visiting the church that day. Sunday was also a day of meeting up for Methodists too.

Thus, in general, the most illustrious Krio Fernandinos held social events in Santa Isabel and San Carlos with Catalans and Spaniards, as illustrated by different news items, this one that was published in 1916: "On the occasion of the birthday of Alfonso XIII luxurious festivities have been celebrated in San Carlos [...] [like] regattas [...] The Cup was awarded to [...] Mr Jones."[44]

Over the years, restaurants such as La Rosaleda and recreational venues such as the Casino were opened, the latter said to have excellent facilities, while the Club Fernandino continued to operate successfully. It should be noted that the venues for leisure that were advertised were scant and highly select, often Spanish in terms of the cuisine served, and there was no lack of French champagne during the meetings and celebrations.

And of course, numerous banquets were held to honour diplomats, or for christenings and any other celebrations. This was reported in the magazines of the time. But above all what was most celebrated were weddings, the Fernandinos' being the most opulent and crowded.

At the end of the 1940s, in addition to the Club Fernandino, the Casino, the restaurants, the cinema and the theatre, Santa Isabel also boasted a tennis court.

Still not everything was harmonious, as we will see in the next sections dedicated to conflicts in Santa Isabel and Fernando Poo, and it was the courts that ended up solving all kinds of issues, including minor accidents. One example is the case that the Krio Fernandino Juliana Barleycorn filed against Hilario Enguras, a native of Punta Mbonda, relating to a bicycle collision, which the judge resolved in her favour with the imposition of compensation of 25 pesetas (AGA, box 81/08553, file 96). The documentation also records abuses and usury of Catalan and Spanish companies against the population, as seen in some of the complaints that reached the courts.

But social life in Spanish Guinea was complex. Regarding the colony's racial segregation, numerous oral testimonies have been found, as well as documentation. For example, one new article worth highlighting explains that in 1916 the Dependents Association decided to allow attendance at its theatrical performance of what it called *"morenos"*. The term *"moreno"* was intended to hide – unsuccessfully – that Spanish racism was alive and well (Aixelà-Cabré, 2021). The article explained that this measure had caused part of the "natural population of Santa Isabel",[45] the Krio Fernandino community, to refuse to attend to express their disagreement.

As we will see in the next section dedicated to colonial repression, the decline of Fernandino power became widely noted from the 1950s onwards, as part of the community began to occupy subordinate positions in the colonial administration or jobs that afforded scant recognition, for example electricians. The socio-economic decline of the Krio Fernandino was well underway by that time, although it was evident that certain families maintained a modicum of political influence, as observed in the important role that some of them had in Spanish Guinea during the provincialisation of 1959 and the autonomous period of 1963, forming a powerful core power that promoted political parties and that was invited to participate in the meetings that would ultimately lead to the independence referendum in 1968, already as Equatorial Guinea. However, it should be said that the Krio Fernandino's economic decline did not lessen its prestige as a group, which was always recognised by the rest of the population and upheld until modern times, as Amalia (2021), the descendant of Amelia Barleycorn, explained.

2.4. Tensions and conflicts: surviving under colonial repression

The official documents and press articles tallied in their efforts to undervalue, infantilise and reject Africans from the supposed Spanish moral superiority. Within the Spanish colonial framework, it was understood that police and military control duties were vital. The repressive Spanish system revealed itself in numerous ways. Living together in such a diverse city was complex. Tensions that were witnessed appeared in the press at the time and in the lawsuits filed in Santa Isabel, which are available at the Alcalá de Henares Archive.

While the British and Spanish revelled in the perks of their status as colonists, the power exerted by the colonial structure and military or police corps, with the Krio Fernandino receiving the protection resulting from their assets and plantations, meant that Equatorial Guineans had to endure vastly inferior living conditions, much worse than the labourers brought in to work on the coffee, cocoa and timber plantations.

In the forthcoming sections, I will list some of the tensions that came to light due to the whites' impunity, the abuse of African women and girls, skirmishes between the Krio Fernandino and the Spanish Colonial Guard and between Spaniards and the indigenous Colonial Guard, the regulation of migrations within the colony, and the backtracking on full emancipation. All of these factors reveal the tensions and conflicts that arose during coexistence, the limits of Krio Fernandino empowerment, and the pitiful injustice to which the large majority of Equatorial Guineans in Santa Isabel and on the island of Fernando Poo were subjected to between 1900 and 1968.

Spaniards above the law

Colonial regulations had as their aim encouraging the development of the colony and granting privileges to the colonial population, as was described down to the last details by Mudimbe (1988). The result of this discriminatory policy was that whenever an accident or mistreatment occurred, it went largely unpunished, as arrests or imprisonment were generally the exception rather than the norm, as can clearly be seen in Table 14. The table clearly points to the types of crimes that were committed, with the columns for non-indigenous or Europeans solely naming three white people detained out of a total of 1,210.

Table 14. Arrests made in Santa Isabel, 1946

	Population					
Crime	Europeans			Indigenous		
	Men	Women	Total	Men	Women	Total
Public order offences	0	0	0	0	0	0
Forgery	0	0	0	9	1	10
Gambling and raffles	0	0	0	53	0	53
Injuries	0	0	0	11	4	15
Deceit	0	0	0	4	7	11
Robbery	3	0	3	46	2	48
Theft	0	0	0	168	16	184
Other crimes	0	0	0	590	302	892
Total	3	0	3	881	329	1,210

Source: Compiled by the author. Resúmenes Estadísticos del Gobierno General de los Territorios Españoles del Golfo de Guinea (1949, p. 148).

To offer a paradigmatic example of Spanish impunity, when a Spaniard ran over an African with his vehicle, this went unpunished as, in a somewhat dubious account, the white man stated that the African had lain down in the middle of the road for a nap. This case is listed in the record of 7 July 1937, in which it is noted that the Nigerian labourer Peter Akpan had been struck by the vehicle of the Director General of the San Carlos Territorial Administration, José Munuera, who affirmed that he did "run over and kill the Nigerian, but it was because the latter had taken a nap in the middle of the road, and despite swerving he could not avoid hitting and killing him" (AGA, box 81/08024). The case was filed because the Lieutenant Commander who signed the report had witnessed the accident. In general, the documentation leaves little doubt that Spaniards were always free to do as they wished and always covered each other's backs. What is more, as can be seen from Table 15 on crimes in Santa Isabel, the whites' standing above the law was almost unlimited: almost no Spaniards or Europeans were detained. The whites were almost always declared innocent.

Table 15. Crimes in Santa Isabel, second semester 1941

Crimes	By place				By number of detainees			
					Non-indigenous		Indigenous	
	Public highway	Waste-ground	Private houses	Public establishments	Men	Women	Men	Women
Public indecency	-	1	-	-	-	-	1	-
Forgery	-	-	2	4	-	-	5	-
Gambling and raffles	-	-	32	-	-	-	35	-
Murder	-	-	-	-	-	-	-	-
Injuries	10	12	5	6	-	-	10	-
Deceit	1	2	2	-	-	-	3	-
Robbery	2	3	14	3	-	-	22	-
Theft	7	20	50	24	-	-	126	5
Embezzlement	-	5	14	5	-	-	23	3
Other trickery	-	2	3	2	-	-	2	-
Indecency	191	10	30	16	-	-	165	86
Public disorder and drunkenness	6	-	5	-	-	-	4	2
Others	31	4	16	6	-	-	23	11
Total	248	59	173	66	0	0	419	107

Source: Compiled by the author. Resúmenes Estadísticos del Gobierno General de los Territorios Españoles del Golfo de Guinea (1943, p. 12).

Corrective measures against those who dared to challenge the colonial racial pyramid were harsh. An example of the foregoing is the communiqué dated 17 March 1920 on the ill-treatment meted out to a labourer by a European, in which it was stated that the labourers could not take justice into their own hands, however severe their treatment was. The document said that, following the relevant inquiries

> and in the presence of all labourers on the estate, duly formed, Mbiti was then ordered to receive twenty-five strikes of the pole, warning the other labourers that when they wish to file a complaint, this must be done at the command post (AGA, box 81/07190).

It is also worth stating that, with the Krio Fernandino on the crest of an economic and commercial wave in Santa Isabel between 1880 and 1930, tensions towards them must have been well known. In 1905, an incident that was referred to as the "Accidente desagradable" (Unpleasant Accident) took place, and while there were not many details provided in the press, the information was of interest as the incident had occurred between a white assistant at the exclusive establishment Casa Casajuana and a *"moreno* Fernandino". The news item stated: "we will not pause to comment as this subordinate to some extent spoiled the local festivities that were due to commence in Santo del Rey that afternoon."[46] Certainly, in accordance with the intersectionality approach, and despite racialisation justified on the grounds of skin colour, the African Krio Fernandino wielded more power than the dependent white Spanish counterpart, a fact which was widely known by the Santa Isabel citizenry and redounded in a matter of class status, rather than skin colour.

At the end of the 1960s, the Krio Fernandino's decline was already underway, as well as the access of other Equatorial Guinean groups to the status of limited emancipation. The sense that there was a loss of acknowledgement was duly corroborated in a meeting in which certain Fernandino claimed greater respect and more rights. The Fernandino meeting was in 1933. It would transpire that while the Fernandino wielded power, they enjoyed full emancipation, and that this began to dissipate, firstly with the passing of the Royal Decree of 17 July 1928 and, most notably, with the Law of 30 December 1944 that would distinguish between classes of emancipation: full, limited and unemancipated (Miranda Junco, 1945, pp. 1384–1385). This was to be the means by which there would be in the city a negligent path to attaining limited emancipation status for Equatorial Guinean staff who worked for the colony in lowly positions.

The abuse of black women and girls

Abuse meted out against Equatorial Guinean women and girls in the colony occurred in diverse forms. It was not limited to abuses of authority, as these women and girls formed the base of the Equatorial Guinean pyramid, but also took the form of sexual abuse. This is because the African female was hypersexualised in the Spanish mindset, which resulted in persistent sexual abuse aimed at women and the need to control the supposed unchecked virility of men.

As I have already stated in a previous work, and along the same lines as Nerin's study (1999), the sexual abuse of Equatorial Guinean women, who were named *"miningas"* ("woman" in the Fang language), was widely undertaken by colonists, military servicemen and even also missionaries (Aixelà-Cabré, 2021).

The possible harassment of Equatorial Guinean women would emerge as a further colonial perk. It is important to state, however, that this abuse of Equatorial Guinean women was limited in the case of Krio Fernandino women, who, due to their belonging to the emancipated African elite, were better protected in terms of status and breeding. Indeed, Fernandino women reported abuses committed by Spaniards against Equatorial Guinean women, with the Fernandino women themselves acting as accusers. For example, this happened in the case reported by Lorenza Dougan of the sexual abuse suffered by a Bubi girl in Santa Isabel on 12 February 1932. Mrs Dougan accused the Spanish citizen Luís Gabriel Peñalosa of raping a five-year-old girl, Eugenia Meaca Bubi. The case is noteworthy as there are very few written documents on the abuse of minors taking place in colonial times, as the aim was probably to leave no record. However, evidence of the abuse is provided by oral testimonies.

Irrefutable proof of the sexual abuse of Equatorial Guinean women being so widespread and deemed a "perk" for Spanish men during the colonisation period is provided by the engaging text written by the Colonies' Managing Director dated 27 June 1941. The missive was accompanied by the *Anteproyecto* and *Proyecto regulando la inmigración de estos territorios* (Pre-project and Project regulating immigration from these territories) and informed the Governor General that Article 5 of the Pre-project, which stated that "cohabitation with women of coloured race is strictly forbidden", had been rejected, and explained that Article 6, whose wording said any civil servant who cohabited with women of coloured race would be expelled had to be deleted (AGA, box 81/08156, file 3). In the definitive Project published on 27 June 1941, it was specified in Article 1.f that one had to "display cultural levels superior to the average of the indigenous people to prevent a dependent indigenous employee reasonably believing themselves superior to a European" (AGA, box 81/08156, file 3). Article 2 says it is not permitted "for European women to enter unless they were civil servants or were going to live with relatives" (AGA, box 81/08156, file 3). Article 9 graded as serious offences

> Sexual relations with indigenous women that are made public, or bearing children with indigenous women, or illegitimate offspring, or also promoting the prostitution of indigenous women taking advantage of their cultural shortcomings, or sexual relations with indigenous women under the age of 18 years (AGA, box 81/08156, file 3).

These issues relating to sexual relations being permitted or prohibited with Equatorial Guinean women laid the groundwork for a genuine colonial declaration of the manifest absence of rights to which African women were entitled. Furthermore, it was little more than hypocritical posturing, as it basically demanded that if there were relations with Equatorial Guinean women, then this should be kept "behind closed doors".

Despite the above, the colonial authorities were fully aware of the fact that sexual abuse was widespread. With that in mind, the fact that there was noticeable concern in Madrid by the mid-1940s regarding sexual abuse of Equatorial Guinean women is further proof of the difficulties tackling what was seen as a generalised practice from the beginning of the colonisation period.

The Spaniards exercised a series of rights that trampled on the African people, including women's rights. In this regard, it is particularly revealing to consider the bloodthirsty aggression that an Equatorial Guinean woman, Mercedes Mbolo, and a Krio Fernandino citizen, Domingo Davies, were subjected to by ten white and indigenous Colonial Guards. In a document dated 17 August 1933, Mercedes Mbolo made a complaint about police mistreatment of her person, and of the Krio Fernandino citizen who defended her. Following the witness statements, it was established that while the police did beat them, this did not constitute abuse because it was claimed that she was his lover and because he confronted them aggressively. From the document, it is patently obvious how hard it must have been to trust the justice system, as one of the police officers had told the Fernandinos' lawyer that he would do as he liked because the judge would never believe the lawyer's version. Against this backdrop of repression and hierarchy, the strident efforts that this Equatorial Guinean woman had to make to report the abuse on the part of the Colonial Guard are clear, knowing full well that her testimony would be worth less than theirs, and that to escape justice they could denigrate her.

In the file of this report, we also have the ruling issued by the judge against the complainant, Mercedes Mbolo. In the proceedings, testimonies of four Equatorial Guineans, employees and guards had been taken, alongside that of the European who managed the establishment where the assault took place. It is also added that, "in accordance with the legislation, all drinks that are served to indigenous persons in bars must be consumed in the very same establishment" (AGA, box 81/08156, file 5). In the background facts contained in the proceedings against Domingo Davies, it stated that "he had been arrested for being drunk and disorderly, using an abusive tone or driving under the influence, though nothing serious" (AGA, box 81/08156, file 5).

In the ruling, the violence unleashed by the Colonial Guards against the woman and the Krio Fernandino was never called into question. Moreover, it was justified through the fact that indigenous people could not consume wine outside a bar, a clear warning that this privilege was only applicable to white women, and not black ones, whether emancipated or not. This left no doubt that race was treated above class, as the same rule was applied to an emancipated Fernandino.

The highlighted cases and the legislation reviewed show that there was a general framework in which abuse was widespread, with Krio Fernandino women often the ones who reported these disgraceful situations, or who would finally organise actions to protect certain privileges of a social nature, which was proof of their power and influence. However, these actions were unable to prevent some Krio Fernandino men from also abusing young African women and having illegitimate children Bubi women.

In any event, an awareness of the abuse carried out against Equatorial Guinean women is necessary in order to understand the vast difference in way of life that their migration to Barcelona during colonial times entailed, as inequalities and lack of rights were much more pronounced in the colony than in mainland Spain. The case of the Krio Fernandino differed as their settling in the city did not give rise to major differences with regard to the freedom they enjoyed in Santa Isabel.

The Krio Fernandino against the Spanish and Indigenous Colonial Guards

The complexity of relations between the Spanish population and the Krio Fernandino and other Equatorial Guineans can be clearly identified from the documentation consulted, as numerous conflicts can be revealed in which the Spanish population were always cast in a favourable light, either because no sentences or fines were ever imposed or because they barely had to face the consequences of their actions. This casuistry is observed in two cases that are worth looking at more closely.

One is the case discussed above involving Mercedes Mbolo and Domingo Davies, in which the violence inflicted on the two of them was justified by claiming that they were hostile persons. The other case involved a servant of the Fernandino Edmundo Collins. The complaint lodged by Collins on 10 May 1917 expanded on the reality that relations between the Colonial Guard, labourers and the Krio Fernandino population were far from smooth, patently proving the Indigenous Colonial Guard's status as being above the law and its clashes with Fernandino subjects as boasting both power and influence (AGA, box 81/07956). The dispute had to be resolved by Maximiliano Jones, as the most influential Krio Fernandino in 1917, who finally appealed to Spanish benevolence as a means of not calling into question on colonial power, thus demonstrating the complex web of favours that clearly show the "you scratch my back" ethos in place between the Krio Fernandino, who mediated on many occasions for other Equatorial Guineans.

As far as the relations between the Indigenous Colonial Guard and the European colonisers are concerned (see Table 16), it is worth noting that these were similarly tense and often a source of controversy and dismissal on the part of the Spanish, as the latter were white.

Below I have selected some examples of conflicts that allow us to see the effects of racialisation during the complex coexistence in colonial times.

To exemplify the dismissal on the part of the Spanish population of the Indigenous Colonial Guard's jurisdiction, it is worth mentioning the complete statement reporting the aggression that four white men inflicted

Table 16. Colonial Guard workforce in the Spanish Territories in the Gulf of Guinea 1946

Personnel		Number
Europeans	Chiefs, officers and similar	21
	Assimilated	47
	Total	68 (8.9%)
Indigenous	Sergeants	13
	Corporals	44
	Guards, musicians and sailors	631
	Total	688 (91%)
	Total personnel, European and indigenous	756

Source: Compiled by the author. Resúmenes Estadísticos del Gobierno General de los Territorios Españoles del Golfo de Guinea (1949, p. 140).

on two indigenous Colonial Guards in 1920. In the documentation, it was explained that the two black guards had gone into a venue to quash a disagreement and restore order in their roles as security officers, yet this had been impossible for them as the four white men refused to acknowledge their authority because they "were blacks". The fact of the matter is that the four white men had behaved improperly and had been admonished for their conduct, given that the colonial regulations vis-à-vis matters of security and the duties of the Colonial Guard were very clear, remaining above the everyday discourse on race and the racist practices commonplace among the colonists with regard to the African population. This was such that in the upper section of the statement mentioned, there was an annotation in the margin that highlighted this was a file that authorities "had tried to make disappear" (AGA, box 81/08024).

This example of the whites against the black Colonial Guards shows that the exchange of roles and power bestowed upon black men through their status as Colonial Guards did not save them from tensions and conflicts, as disagreements contravened the grounding of the monopoly of the colonial force built around skin colour. The fact that someone tried to cover up the aforementioned statement and the fact that there were very few arrests or imprisonments of white people, are clear markers that the (white) majority of the Spanish authorities preferred for matters to go unnoticed, either *motu proprio* or through the engagement of an influential family in the colony.

It must be borne in mind that this practical limitation that the Indigenous Colonial Guard had to overcome to exercise their authority over the white population did not exist with regard to the African population, as Equatorial Guinean Colonial Guards attained a measure of power within their own community. Plus, joining the Colonial Guard afforded benefits that set them apart from other Africans, Equatorial Guineans and *braceros* of other nationalities; however, this was not the case for the Krio Fernandino and all those who had already obtained fully emancipated status.

This is not to overlook the fact the indigenous Colonial Guards were also victims of mistreatment on the part of their white superiors, or even abuse during the performance of their duties, in comparison to their white Colonial Guard counterparts.

These examples of coexistence and conflict allow us to shed light on a hierarchical structure that led to serious tensions in which intersectionality plays a key role by calling into doubt the status inherent in skin colour, situations that in Barcelona did not occur so violently or openly.

Expulsion of Spanish Africans from the colony

The regulation of migration to the colony from the 1930s was closely linked to the widespread practice of expelling Africans, which had been commonplace in the colonial structures of the Spanish Gulf Territories for decades. This deterrent measure was applied to all those who did not respect colonial authorities since the effective colonisation of the island, starting in 1860. Although these expulsions in Spanish Guinea were not constant, they showed the pressure that the metropolis exerted on the African population, including Equatorial Guineans: all the inhabitants had to submit to the Spanish colonial power and the imposed norms. The impunity of the colonial authorities in relation to these practices fanned the flames for a major social mobilisation in the city of Santa Isabel in 1920 with the aim of demanding the cessation of the expulsions of Africans, something that, skipping forward through time and space, would also occur in Barcelona in the early 1990s.

Next, I shall review the impunity with which the government of the colony exercised its powers in the expulsions of Peter John Stone in 1879 and of the Krio Fernandino citizen Carlos G. Vivour in 1907. The two men were of very different status, since the former was an unknown, whereas the latter was a Fernandino related to the influential Amelia Barleycorn de Vivour. Stone's case is interesting since it shows the inflexibility of the authorities in not allowing his return, largely due to the fact that he did not an influential figure in his corner who could obtain a report to reverse his expulsion. In the case of Vivour, I have already outlined how the Fernandinos were the ones who enjoyed the most room to manoeuvre, although they had to resort to lawyers to seek legal counsel to dismiss cases like that of Carlos G. Vivour, which also required the intercession of Amelia Barleycorn. These case studies are key to understanding the coercive measures that the Spanish state wielded against the citizens of Santa Isabel and the rest of Spanish Guinea, because if they did not wish to be expelled from the colony, they had to submit to colonial power, avoiding as far as possible clashes with the colonial authorities or with influential people.

Peter John Stone, according to his handwritten signature on one of the documents uncovered, was expelled from Santa Isabel in 1879. Spanish authorities would refer to him as the African Pedro Juan Stone, thus Hispanising his name in the same way as they did with a good part of the Equatorial Guinean population in an attempt to erase English colonial traces. His expulsion from Santa Isabel is recorded, along with his application for pardon in October 1881, which he made from his residence in London, and the refusal of readmission pronounced in March 1882. The file indicated that he had been expelled because he had no means of subsistence or the intention or ability to obtain them, which was summarised in the request for return as him having been expelled from the colony "for being an incorrigible cad and recidivist" (AGA, box 81/06939, file 5).

The second file reviewed was the one opened in relation to Carlos G. Vivour on the occasion of insults directed towards Lieutenant Joaquín Carlos Roca in 1907, which actually covered up an attempted rape of Carlos' wife Sarah Vivour (AGA, box 81/06340). The file reproduced the statements of all the parties and witnesses, and the trial and sentencing of Vivour to be expelled from the island for a term of five months. It is worth bearing in mind that, when he was expelled, his wife was pregnant. In the documentation, it was explained, according to Roca's complaint, that when he sent his clothes to be washed by the wife of the defendant, Sarah Vivour, the wife of Carlos Vivour, she refused to wash anything else and claimed that he owed money to her.

In the statement given before the judge, Sarah Vivour said that she knew Lieutenant Roca as she was the washerwoman of his clothes, of which he is resentful owing to the continuous indications her husband is not up to the job for which she was necessary to let him know. She claimed that on the day she was to return Lieutenant Roca's clean washing to him, he made advances to her, wanting to indulge in "his carnal appetites", to which she replied, "Sir, I am both married and I am pregnant I have no need of another man; I am more than well-served by my husband" (AGA, box 81/06340).

The file included a document signed by Mr Allendesalazar dated 8 July 1907 and addressed to the Acting Governor General of the Spanish Territories of the Gulf of Guinea (AGA, box 81/06340), attesting to the fact that, after the mediation of Vivour's lawyer and the more than probable diplomatic contacts of Vivour's own widow Amelia Barleycorn, it was clear that the Equatorial Guinean population would not be sympathetic to colonisation if the abuse they suffered remained unpunished.

The two cases bring to light the mechanisms used by the colonial authorities to rid itself of undesirable settlers, showing the functioning of the expulsion orders and the variability of their effectiveness depending on who was affected and if he had relatives or influential friends to reverse the situation.

It is worth noting that the expulsion orders would ultimately attract the population's wrath. The African community of Santa Isabel rebelled against the expulsion of Africans, whether Equatorial Guinean or not, organising two large-scale mobilisations, described by the reporters as "widely attended",[47] on 23 September and 5 October 1920.[48] These demonstrations had been preceded by the first known demonstration in Santa Isabel, which was led by Krio Fernandino women in 1915.

The expulsion of Africans had been the subject of unclear regulation for decades. It was only after the African mobilisations of 1920 that the foundations were laid for putting in place different measures that would control the arrival of immigrants to the colony from 1930 onwards. However, these legal measures, such as the 1934 Regulation, constituted the practices of expulsion of citizens, who were forever at the mercy of the authorities.

Regulation of immigration to Fernando Poo: the gradual transit between Spain and Spanish Guinea

The social rejection of expulsions of Africans, reviewed in the previous section, prompted the government of the colony to approve an Immigration Regulation in the 1930s, the aim of which was to govern the movements of people – both Africans and Spaniards from the mainland. A file from the Government Police offers a description of immigration in Fernando Poo from the perspective of the colonial authorities.

In the dossier, the Chief Inspector explained that most foreigners acquired authorisation for unpaid work which allowed them to circumvent the action of the authorities, while the vast majority of the detainees were foreigners, in addition to the fact that they thieved and the loot was sent directly to their home country, thus being recidivists since they was no space for them in prisons, they had to be released, which he lamented because "the fear of punishment that awaits them in these Territories is almost non-existent" (AGA, box 81/08156, file 3).

The description of the types of African immigrants arriving and of the consequences of half of those arriving remaining on the island without apparently having a trade laid the groundwork for a somewhat restrictive Regulation on the immigration of Spaniards to the Spanish Territories in the Gulf of Guinea passed on 1 August 1934. Article 14 of that regulation sets forth that "Spaniards convicted of committing any crime, as well as those whose presence is considered dangerous or undesirable, may be expelled from the Colony" (AGA, box 81/06467). In practice, the "Spaniards" being referred to were those of African origin. Furthermore, Article 14 added that "those expelled from the Colony will not be allowed to re-enter [...] until the expulsion ruling has been revoked by the Governor General" (AGA, box 81/06467). Both specifications constituted blackmail that in practice meant a clear loss of rights of Spanish Africans because, on the peninsula, no Spaniard could be expelled if they held Spanish nationality, a topic that I will address in the coming section. Indeed, in the documentation, the deportation of only one Spaniard from the peninsula from Fernando Poo was found.

Only a year later, a decree was approved and published in the *Boletín Oficial* of 1 January 1935. The legal changes meant that foreigners were made equal with Spaniards in the colony in terms of the requirements for their arrival.

There would be still further reforms to regulate migration in the following decades. In particular, we can highlight the reform of June 1946, in which an ordinance was approved making it mandatory to deposit 25,000 pesetas for all those wishing to travel to Spanish Guinea and who did not have a contract of employment or could not prove sufficient financial standing to settle with their own means or to carry out other activities making it mandatory to deposit 25,000 pesetas. This meant that the needs of Spanish settlers had been covered by the mid-1940s and that they preferred to reduce the number of arrivals of Spaniards from the mainland. Likewise, in that decade the gradual arrival of Equatorial Guineans to mainland Spain commenced, many decades after the arrival of the first Krio Fernandino to Barcelona. The gradual to-and-fro transit between Spain and Spanish Guinea was becoming well established (see chapter 3).

In conclusion, we should reflect on the way in which negative stereotypes of African immigrants have been devised since the first third of the twentieth century from Africa. The colonial reports on irregular immigration contained some highly pejorative value judgments involving, for example, the spread of diseases (understood to mean venereal) through African women who prostituted themselves not of their own will; the supposed relationship between foreigners and criminals in terms of the flight of foreign currency when thieves sent the proceeds of their crime to their countries of origin; and immigrants' supposed "slovenliness", with the result that they were treated as vagrants who should be repatriated because "here they engage in unlawful acts with impunity" (AGA, box 81/08156, file 3). This never-ending array of myths hindered the immigrants' integration and permanence, and recalls the narratives put into circulation in Europe at the end of the twentieth century to reject the arrival of Africans on the European continent.

It is similarly surprising that, despite having organised two large demonstrations in Santa Isabel, with hitherto unseen diverse and widespread citizen support, to request an end to the expulsions and better treatment of the African population by the Spanish authorities, the various regulations that were approved not only did not bear these requests in mind, but rather continued to forestall immigration to the colony based on gross and denigrating arguments against the African populations who wished to settle in Santa Isabel.

A rescindable emancipation: Krio Fernandino under the spotlight

Spanish measures to ensure adherence to colonial norms were especially severe for the Equatorial Guinean population. Full emancipation was the legal formula that was used to make the rights of some African Spaniards equal to those of the Spaniards of mainland Spain the metropolis. In principle, a letter of full emancipation was reserved for the Krio Fernandino community, although with the passage of time, other Spanish Africans – namely the Bubis, Fangs, Annoboneses, Ndowes and Bissios – benefited thanks to the services they provided to the colonial administration. Some of them achieved the highest status possible with limited emancipation. It should be noted that the withdrawal of a letter of emancipation granted to someone of Krio Fernandino origin was a situation that surely caused great concern in the community.

Below, I shall describe two case studies that underscore the diminished economic and socio-political influence of the family of Amelia Barleycorn de Vivour, as well as indicating the legal pressure that the Krio Fernandino had begun to face. The first deals with the withdrawal of the letter of emancipation of Daniel Omonie Barleycorn between 1942 and 1945 for breaching regulations on alcoholic beverages; the second refers to the consequences of the denial of visas that could have been the subject of inquiries by the colonial authorities, as happened in the case of George Armando Barleycorn.

The Alcalá de Henares Archive contains a report on the fact that the President of the Patronato de Indígenas returned the letter of emancipation to Daniel Omonie Barleycorn on 16 August 1945, which had previously been withdrawn. The emancipation file of Daniel Omonie Barleycorn stating the different procedures that the applicant had undergone to obtain the status of emancipation on 15 January 1936, ratified on 3 December 1937. In the document, it was said that the "indigenous" Daniel Omonie Barleycorn,

> having regard to the present file [...] which regulates the benefits of emancipation of the indigenous [...] and in accordance with the agreement adopted unanimously [...] on 4 November 1936, approval was granted [...] for the definitive validity [...] of emancipation of the indigenous Daniel Omonie Barleycorn (AGA, box 81/09058).

Years later, the file was modified to include a new document from the Governor of Bata, which stated that he had "provisionally withdrawn the Letter of Emancipation from the indigenous Daniel Omonie Barleycorn for breach of the Alcoholic Beverages Regulations" of 30 July 1942 (AGA, box 81/09058). From the documentation, it is clarified that Daniel Omonie Barleycorn appeared in Bata on 3 April 1945, noting that his emancipation was provisionally withdrawn on 21 July 1942 and that he requested that it be returned. Finally, in another file dated 14 July 1945, he was allowed to recover the letter of emancipation in Bata, three years after his sentence, meaning that his request for the sanction to be lifted was accepted.

The second case study shows that the Colonial Police, at the request of superiors, made reports on Krio Fernandino during the times of the Falange Española. This was an indication of the legal and criminal consequences they could have against them if the colonial authorities pointed them out. One of these files concerned the application they had received for George Armando Barleycorn Boricó to study in Nigeria, which had finally been approved on 12 March 1962. However, the documentation contained a highly detailed confidential report against him, relating to the opposition to colonisation that his father, Juan Walterio Barleycorn Jones, had exhibited against Spain, adding that his father was similarly "favourable to Protestantism" (AGA, box 81/09058).

Below, the report is reproduced partially. It is particularly ening to read the reasons why the visa was finally denied, as it is a torrent of mistrust, anger and value judgments:

> [T]his [Government Police] Service estimates that [...] The only thing Mr Juan Walterio Barleycorn Jones intends, in the typical Fernandino vein, [...] is to maintain the flame of heartlessness and lack of affection for the Homeland in which he was born, so that his son can be brought up in an environment of ideologies completely opposed to the Catholic ethos and society that the Spanish regime provides [...] Juan Walterio Barleycorn Jones was enrolled in the proceedings instructed in November-December 1959 for anti-Spanish activities and had contact with the Protestant Pastor Gustavo Mbela during his stay in Santa Isabel in November 1959. Therefore, the Chief of Police considers that it is not appropriate to approve the request (AGA, box 81/07611).

The report was signed on 1 March 1962. At that time the provincialisation of Spanish Guinea had been approved and the consideration of granting it the status of an autonomous region was underway, legal changes that had supposedly meant a recognition of the rights acquired by Spanish Africans. And yet, the text shows unequivocally that, one hundred years after colonisation, the Krio Fernandino collective continued to symbolise the tensions over the legacy they represented of the British and Protestant imprint on the island. An upsurge in anti-Spanish sentiment had been kindled throughout the colony which was beginning put the gears in motion to demand independence from colonial rule.

2.5. The connection between Malabo and Barcelona since 1968: Equatorial Guinean exile

The celebrations for the achievement of independence from colonial rule on 12 October 1968 were short-lived. The advent of the dictatorship of Macías Nguema in March 1969 prompted the exile of Krio Fernandino and Equatorial Guinean on a journey of no return to African and European countries, especially to Spain. Although the promises of the second dictatorship of Obiang Nguema in 1979 initially seemed to favour the possibility of return, this was rapidly curtailed given the fact that the national reconciliation of the presidency of Obiang was a resounding failure.

Colonial independence meant the end of the privileges of the small Spanish population that still remained there, which had to flee with the advent of the dictatorship of Macías. The socio-political development of independent Equatorial Guinea was cut short in only a few months and many Equatorial Guineans decided to emigrate before the establishment of the terror regime established by the Macías dictatorship. What is more, fear of Macías led the Spanish airlines Iberia to transport not only Spaniards from the peninsula, but also the former African Spaniards who had lost their status of Spanishness, alongside numerous foreigners who had no other means of escape.

In the documentation in the Alcalá de Henares Archive, certificates of residence from after October 1968 can be consulted, such as that of José Manuel Bdyogo Owono, a resident of Santa Isabel, from 30 December 1968, a document that he had to request in order to leave the country legally for Spain. The documentation also includes permits granted for the purchase of tickets for flights on Iberia aircraft, dating from 15 January 1969 and from 30 December 1968. Such ticket permits were also granted for citizens of Equatorial Guinean origin, such as the aforementioned José Manuel Bdyogo Owono. That flight from Santa Isabel to Madrid cost Anselmo Boleko Brown 7,925 pesetas, and he made the trip with many Spaniards, as happened on other flights, as recorded in Iberia's invoices that can similarly be consulted. Lists of British and American passengers who left Spanish Guinea on charter flights in August 1968 for Spain also indicate the concerns at the time about the unravelling of independent Guinea.

Colonial independence resulted in elections agreed to by Spain after the Constitutional Conference. In 1967, the Fernandino Democratic Union (UDF) party was created, "which was divided into two, the Democratic Union (UD) and Fernandino Union (UF). In the first government [...] the community of Creoles had ministers, deputies and other representations appointed" (Iyanga Pendi, 2021, p. 42). Yet, merely a few months later, the dictatorship of Macías Nguema was established. Many Krio Fernandino were property expropriated, while others fled. Even so, a minority stayed during the first dictatorship, including Amelia, as her descendent Amalia (2021) explained. However, there were some initial exceptions, such as John Barleycorn, who owned a relatively large plantation in Santa Isabel and who became manager of La Vigatana from 1969, after the expulsion of the Spaniards by Macías. Aranzadi (2016, p. 253) recalls that many Fernandino families "still remain in Bioko, such as the King, Jones, Dougan, Arkins and Collins families", although these same families, like others reviewed, established their formal residence in Barcelona, Madrid and Valencia, and so their bloodlines persist today on two continents, Africa and Europe.

During the hundred years of effective colonial occupation in Bioko and the sixty years on the continent, thousands of Equatorial Guineans died, a fact that was repeated during the subsequent dictatorships (Ndongo, 1977; Iliescu, 2017). That of Macías (1969–1979) was so violent that it was responsible for the death of more than 10,000 people. This has since been used by his nephew, Obiang Nguema, to guarantee the paralysis of Equatorial Guinean society by stirring up the country's collective memory of specific episodes of terror or of the constant and arbitrary arrests, torture and selective murders.

Only some of the population was able to emigrate to other countries in the 1950s, but the flow of migration would become extensive especially in the late 1960s, and in the early 1970s sought international shelter with the advent of the first dictatorship (Aixelà-Cabré, 2011). Thus emerged a transnational migration of Equatorial Guineans that would extend well into the 1990s.

No less than a quarter of the population emigrated, bearing in mind that Spanish Guinea had 245,989 inhabitants in the 1960 census.[49] Until the early 1970s, Equatorial Guineans mainly went to African countries, such as Cameroon, Gabon and Nigeria, or to Spain, and then from there a few went on to other European countries or the United States. At that time, the typical profile of an exile was usually a man who emigrated alone or with his closest relatives. The first migrants were opponents of the colonial regime, then students of both sexes, and finally exiles, although the movement of people had been one of the characteristics that had been repeated on the borders of the continental territory with Cameroon and Gabon.

Students who migrated in the mid-1960s, like others before them, did not have the support of relatives in the new destination because the family network would only appear later, with the next generation of Equatorial Guineans residing abroad, a fact that explains why the Equatorial Guinean network began to be available in the mid-1970s, and was solid and strong from the mid-1980s onwards. The documentation consulted also showed who was able to leave the country by sea, by obtaining a visa in extremis after independence, like Trinidad Collins Jones on 17 October 1968. However, the most delicate moment was when the Krio Fernandino had to leave Guinea at the start of the Macías dictatorship. For Bolekia (2003), this was a disappointment for them, since many Fernandinos had believed that, as the most academically advanced section of the population, they would be granted a decisive role in the construction of the country's future. Instead, they encountered the expropriations Macías embarked upon, as he wished to expel the most educated people from the newly independent country.

Spain ended up being the epicentre of the Equatorial Guinean exile for decades, as well as the platform of arrival or departure for other migratory destinations in Europe, the Americas and Asia. Of course, some African destinations, such as Cameroon and Gabon, and also Nigeria, remained viable options, as had happened long before. International political efforts would make it possible to establish pacts with different governments such as that of Gabon, Nigeria, Sierra Leone or Egypt, so that refugees were not sent to Equatorial Guinea, although the situation of Equatorial Guineans in the different countries would be characterised by a precariousness that would force them to perform painful and low-paying jobs. Finally, some of them decided to move to Spain. In the case of those who were in Cuba, Venezuela and East Germany, Ndongo (1977, p. 277) recalled that

Table 17. Equatorial Guineans in Spain, 1961–1996

Country	Before 1961	1961–1970	1971–1980	1981–1990	1991–1995	1996
Equatorial Guinea	227	220	495	966	1,780	338

Source: Census of Population, Instituto Nacional de Estadística (2001); Aixelà-Cabré (2011, p. 91).

Table 18. African tourists in Spain, 1970–1973

Foreigners with passports	1970	1971	1972	1973
Africa	1,003,496	1,203,510	1,456,974	1,031,320

Source: Statistical Yearbook (1974); Aixelà-Cabré (2011, p. 92).

they decided to stay in Spain instead of continuing the summer holiday trip to Equatorial Guinea.

It is important to note that from 1970 there was a flood of Equatorial Guineans migrating to Spain, which with a quick regularisation process and rapid granting of Spanish nationality, would obtain Spanish citizenship without being able to distinguish them from the total. It is almost impossible to locate them in the population statistics as Equatorial Guineans, since the figures are still very low with regard to the expected population that left Equatorial Guinea in a hurry, some of whom went to Spain.

This general invisibility can be seen in the following historical table of the Equatorial Guinean presence in Spain, from 1961 to 1996 (see Table 17).

In the Statistical Yearbooks of Spain, finally, unexpected figures were uncovered in the data on African tourism: the number of foreign tourists from Africa was unusually high compared to other European countries for which Spain was a burgeoning tourist destination (see Table 18). This is what leads us to deduce that many of the Equatorial Guineans who arrived in Spain were probably subsumed in that African group and did so in the guise of "tourists", changing their status shortly after arriving, through some of the options offered by the Spanish state to regularise their situation in the country. Other Equatorial Guineans entered Spain with their national identity cards or with the Spanish passports that some of them had been able to procure towards the end of the colonial period.

The issue of migrants not being categorised by geographical origin was identified in the 1990s, decade that started their classification by nationalities, so that by the end of that decade and during the 2000s it began to be possible to categorise people by origin.

The available data thus lead us to affirm that since the independence of Spanish Guinea, transnational Equatorial Guinean migrants residing in Spain have settled in the mainland and have ended up holding dual nationality – Spanish and Equatorial Guinean. The exceptions are those who have claimed political asylum and who therefore only hold Spanish nationality, and those descendants who were born in Spain and hence automatically obtained Spanish nationality by full right.

Another issue was the effect that the Equatorial Guinean collective residing in Spain had on interest in acknowledging Spanish colonial memory, along with xenophobia and racist aggressions, factors that would make themselves felt with regard to the shortfall in employment and socio-political opportunities, a situation that several Equatorial Guinean women tried to overcome via literature and essay writing (Aixelà-Cabré, 2020a).

For their part, much of the Krio Fernandino also emigrated to the peninsula, many to Barcelona, taking advantage of the family networks that had historically been established in the city, but also to Madrid, the Canary Islands and Valencia. Their past was obscured and the footprints of those who came before their forefathers were erased from a collective memory, which ruled out the recovery of black Spain imprints and their settlement in the Iberian Peninsula and Catalonia (Aixelà-Cabré & Rizo, 2023), something that this book will help to reverse.

2.6. Conclusions

Amelia Barleycorn became the wealthiest person in Spanish Guinea upon inheriting property from her husband William Allen Vivour in 1890. From a highly influential Protestant family, she did not cease to practise that faith, showing her generosity through various gifts to her own church as well as its Catholic counterpart. She had a daughter whom she outlived, meaning her legacy passed to her closest Barleycorn relatives and perhaps some Vivours, which is why the properties she had not sold before her death were split between the descendants. As a woman, she saw herself as being in the position of overcoming European androcentrism that was ill at ease with women as interlocutors, as well as defeating European racialisation through her lofty social class that managed to neutralise a large part of the perverse effects of racial segregation. The support and aid she provided to various members of the Barleycorn and Vivour families also showed a more sympathetic human side faced with the delusions to abuse and oppress the Equatorial Guinean population.

Regarding the comparison of her or other Krio Fernandino, as "black colonisers", with the "white colonisers" in terms of abuse inflicted on the population, it must be said that, in the documentation consulted, only a handful of acts against *braceros* on Krio Fernandino farmsteads could identified that could allow us to compare white impunity with Fernandino impunity. Much more common were episodes in which whites should have felt uncomfortable with their presence, even somewhat "inferior". In that regard, it is worth mentioning that the Krio Fernandino acted like other bourgeoisie and economically powerful groups in a capitalist system: seeking profit at the lowest cost. This did not mean that they legislated or imposed unjust regulations in the same way the Spanish authorities or the government of the mainland itself did, yet it is clear they took full advantage of their position of power to further their own interests as far as possible, sometimes trying to maintain a certain justice in relations between whites and the rest of the unemancipated Equatorial Guineans, since they were fully aware that unemancipated status constituted an abuse and an injustice in any country.

The analysis of the social reality of Krio Fernandino and other Equatorial Guinean women in the city of Santa Isabel required a historical reconstruction of the European and Spanish colonial context in the city and in Fernando Poo. The shift from English to Spanish influence in the mid-nineteenth century left traces on religious issues, with the loss of visibility of Protestantism to the benefit of Catholicism; in the language, with the Hispanisation of a colony that could not prevent the pichi from continuing to speak their language; and economically, because the push the British gave to an African elite such as the Krio Fernandino was questioned after the Catalan and Spanish appropriation of trade and agricultural production. On a legal level, African Spaniards, who were recognised as subjects of Spain, were deprived of rights in comparison to the Spaniards of the peninsula, except for those who received letters of emancipation, which gave them equal rights to the Spaniards, as was the case in general of the Krio Fernandino diaspora.

The formation of the Krio Fernandino group has also been studied in this chapter, with an emphasis on the Barleycorn family and especially on Amelia Barleycorn de Vivour, as well as other influential families such as the Joneses, the Dougans, the Kinsons, the Collinses and the Balboas. This has allowed their wealth way of life, activities and customs to be portrayed. These aspects were fundamental, as these descriptions allowed us to understand that they were a very wealthy and Afropolitan community, which maintained multilocal, transcontinental, transnational links, as could be seen from their constant travels and their ability to insert themselves in very different contexts, whether African or European.

Likewise, a sketch was made of everyday life in Santa Isabel in terms of population, cost of living and services in the colony has been provided, since these were key to understanding the standard of living and social dynamics of this African city. These data also help to provide a consistent comparison with the city of Barcelona.

However, Santa Isabel was beset with tensions caused by the rights and visibility of the Krio Fernandino with regard to Spaniards, Catalans and other Europeans. Therefore, it was essential to review the conflicts that emerged in their coexistence since the colonial repression was constant, making colonial impunity evident. I explained the existence of the abuse of women and girls, the conflicts that arose between Spaniards and indigenous Colonial Guards, as well as the repressive measures of the Spanish authorities, such as the expulsion of the Spanish Africans or the rescission of a full emancipation that was thought permanent.

It should be said that the data analysed allow us to observe that, despite the fact that all the writings described the Krio Fernandino collective as a select and educated community, their exceptionality came from the close commercial and political relations they maintained with the European colonial authorities, first the British and then the Catalan and Spanish. Therefore, it should be borne in mind that it was their collaboration with these that endowed them with a special status.

Precisely it is this position they held as a hinge between Europeans and Africans that afforded them major advantages.

In that regard, it should be borne in mind that their courteous treatment did not prevent them from exercising their power ironically. An example of this is the fact they exerted pressure on the *braceros* by reducing their food rations (Barleycorn estate in 1919), including abuse and mistreatment of the foremen (Dougan estate in 1917 and 1920).

Finally, a review of the connection between Barcelona and Malabo since independence in 1968 and the beginning of Equatorial Guinean exile has made it possible to understand the destinations chosen during the massive flight caused by the advent of the dictatorship of Macías and the reasons why the Krio Fernandino community today continues to be a group anchored between Africa and Europe.

CHAPTER 3

The Fernandino in Barcelona during colonisation and post-independence

The necessary comparison of the social, employment and economic context of the Krio Fernandino and Equatorial Guinean population between Santa Isabel and Barcelona entailed a reconstruction of life in Barcelona in terms of population, cost of living and services, aspects that were relevant to understand why it was worthwhile for the Fernandino to embark upon such an expensive investment in trips and stays given their already high standard of living. Ultimately, Barcelona afforded many advantages and fewer disadvantages than residence in Santa Isabel.

As has been noted, the cost of living in the capital of the colony was just as high as in Barcelona, alongside the fact that the educational and health systems were notably superior in the Catalan capital, affording greater opportunities for educational progress and medical treatment. What is more, their daily dealings in the city were not affected by race issues since racial segregationism was not subject to regulations, as was the case in Santa Isabel.

These aspects, together with others that will be reviewed, led certain Krio Fernandino to choose to settle in the Catalan capital. In fact, delving into the Fernandino dynamics in their commercial, recreational and even social life in Barcelona, was of significance, since they explained the plurality of reasons that brought them to Barcelona and the heady lifestyle they enjoyed there.

The Krio Fernandino mobility between Africa and Europe demonstrates its multi-sited, transnational and transcontinental residence, variables contained within an Afropolitanism context that should increase the interest in revealing African footprints in Barcelona and on the Iberian Peninsula (Aixelà-Cabré, 2023b), promoting the study of black Spain.

3.1. Barcelona and Santa Isabel

Barcelona in the final third of the nineteenth and early twentieth centuries was a diverse and cosmopolitan city. The colonial ties between Santa Isabel and Fernando Poo developed around commercial interests, while the rhetoric about the benefits of Spanish colonisation in Africa was at a high point, through, among others, the Catalan Catholic missions that from the outset sought to Christianise Fernando Poo. As we shall see, the arguments that racialised Africans could also be seen in performances such as human zoos and universal exhibitions. However, the outcry about these "exotic shows" was limited, as they took place in a city historically accustomed to coexistence between people from different continents (Fauria & Aixelà-Cabré, 2002).

Thus, while African populations were undervalued and undermined, Catalan society had the opportunity to mingle with the elite Krio Fernandino community, a group that was able to refute any type of stereotype that linked Africans with the primitivism and savagery that different political groups of the Spanish state claimed they had in order to justify the exploitation of Africa.

As will be shown, the colonial ties between Barcelona and Santa Isabel were close. It was probably the cosmopolitanism of Barcelona that most facilitated the welcome of the Fernandinos during the large part of the twentieth century.

Cosmopolitan Barcelona

The cosmopolitan nature of Barcelona has been attained gradually over time. Its status as a Mediterranean port city built upon cultural diversity has given it a marked multicultural stance that has confirmed its international outlook since the Middle Ages onwards. Already then there was a strong European presence and various merchant families owned slaves of various origins, including Africans (Tatjer, 2002, p. 134). Furthermore, in the sixteenth and seventeenth centuries the city played host to immigrants from different backgrounds, although the true expansion of Barcelona would take place in the eighteenth century (Tatjer, 2002, p. 135). It was in the nineteenth century that "the cosmopolitanism of Barcelona would be accentuated in a swifter manner, both numerically and qualitatively" (Tatjer, 2002, p. 135). The expansion of the textile companies of the Catalan bourgeoisie, along with the industrialisation of Catalonia, made it equal to England in its development,[50] and required a large workforce and marked commercial expansion.

By the early twentieth century, and especially in the 1920s, there was "a significant expansion of the migratory field, both peninsular and international" (Tatjer, 2002, p. 139). In 1917, Barcelona was the most populous city in Spain, with a population of 1,197,601, followed by Madrid with 953,300 and Valencia with 926,486 inhabitants.[51]

By looking at the population statistics of Barcelona, we can see that the cultural diversity of the city was relative at a statistical level, although in qualitative terms it was relevant. It is worth remembering certain other conditions that enable us to identify diversity. On the one hand, there is the fact that cosmopolitanism had been evident in the cultural and artistic circles of Barcelona of the early twentieth century, with painters such as Picasso, Dalí, Miró and Fortuny. In addition, it was from the modernism of Gaudí and Puig i Cadafalch that so many architectural jewels arrived in the city. Conversely, and in another context, there is the fact that Barcelona is one of the cities in the world that, despite not being a capital, has become home to a sizable number of foreign consulates, a clear after-effect of the wide range of nationalities represented in the city.

This cosmopolitan Barcelona of the mid-nineteenth and early twentieth centuries shared a space with a curiosity about otherness that often tended to exoticise those who were different. An emblematic case is human zoos, which mixed the exhibition of people, showbusiness and supposed scientific dissemination (Sánchez Gómez, 2006; Pardo-Tomás et al., 2019, p. 6). As García Bravo recalls (2019, p. 162), in the exhibitions of humans that took place in the late nineteenth and first third of the twentieth centuries in various Spanish cities, there were cases in which some countries did not send "any couple of living indigenous people", but rather mortal remains, skulls, etc.[52]

It was within this framework of exotic diversity that the exhibition of Senegalese in Tibidabo Park took place in 1913. The news item explained that there had been a large number of attendees on the first day of the exhibition

> of the black Senegalese [...] They have arranged their dwellings in such a way that they serve as an evocation of their cabins and although the landscape does not help the fiction through [...] the panoramic view [...] revealing a great

modern city [...] meaning that the blacks continue with their very special kind of life.[53]

The article went on to explain the cold the blacks experienced because the temperatures in the month of March in Barcelona were like winter for them. It continued with statements full of stereotypes about Africans, as, for example, when talking about their dances, which were described as being "barbaric, primitive and even wild".[54] Yet the Senegalese were not the only ones to be exhibited as objects or animals. Only a few years later, in 1925, the exhibition in the Tibidabo of a large tribe of black *Fulahs* from tropical Africa was announced.[55]

At that time, the enthusiasm of the Barcelona elites for internationalising the city gained widespread backing. With that spirit in mind, the Feria de Barcelona (Barcelona Fair) of 1919 was devised as "a public limited company that [...] proposed the organisation of fairs, exhibitions, contests."[56] The initiative, which was spearheaded by the Catalan bourgeoisie, was complemented by the Universal Exhibition of Barcelona was held in 1929, where again human beings, in this case Moroccans, were exhibited in the Moroccan pavilion (Martín Corrales, 2002, pp. 198–199).

The press was a fertile medium to record the presence of people of other geographical and cultural origins in the city. Surveying a hundred years of the Barcelona newspaper *La Vanguardia*, covering the period 1900–1999, showed the reasons why they were given so much publicity. During the first half of the twentieth century, most news articles linked them to robberies, cons and thefts; this began to combine in an increasingly intense way with reports of their religious practices and beliefs, with their recreational or cultural activities, with the world of work and employment, with their begging and charitable activities, with commercial exchanges, with diplomatic visits, with international politics, with tourism, with their studies, and with the racism and xenophobia to which they were often subjected, that is, from the 1990s.

Colonial ties between Barcelona and Fernando Poo

The effective colonisation of Spanish Guinea had begun in the mid-nineteenth century, its pace intensifying between 1880 and 1900. This was when the first Krio Fernandino arrived in Barcelona, at the same time as the Spanish state, like other European countries, was encouraging the "necessary civilisation" of Africa. Therefore, the arrival of Spanish Africans on the mainland must not be detached from any colonial political context.

When Amelia Barleycorn de Vivour arrived in the informal capital of the mainland, which was then Barcelona, Spanish slogans about what was expected of colonisation in Africa imposed a socio-cultural superiority that denigrated African populations. A grammar of alterity had been sold as the norm which, in an orientalist house of mirrors (Baumann, 2002, 2004), projected an image of European superiority that simultaneously relegated the African to an inferior status. As the Catalan Eduard Giménez Ferrer (2016) recalled, whose coffee production in Spanish Guinea was always marketed from Barcelona, "what they explained to us was that the blacks [...] lack culture."

Given the Spanish colonising rhetoric defended by figures such as Ramos Izquierdo and Navarro y Beltrán (1912, p. 348) at the beginning of the twentieth century, and taking into account that the former had been Governor of the Spanish Territories in the Gulf of Guinea and the latter an engineer at his command in the colony, the cultural and racial clash in the cultural dis-encounter[57] that Barcelona was headed for would seem inevitable, since they proclaimed that Spain should "govern primitive peoples [...] [and promote] rational assimilation" (Ramos Izquierdo & Navarro y Beltrán, 1912, p. 348). Only after undertaking their civilising mission did Ramos Izquierdo and Navarro y Beltrán (1912, p. 348) hope "to grant [the] autonomous regime under the supervision of the mainland when [the colony] has the legal standing to administer its own matters."

Ramos Izquierdo and Navarro y Beltrán (1912, pp. 351–352) were highly explicit regarding how each race should be treated and the need to preserve whiteness:[58] "there is the white race that is the superior, and the rest that can be mixed together." In fact, the term that the colonial authorities applied to the colonised Africans and that flooded all the official documentation was "indigenous". However, since the term did not specify skin colour, ultimately the terms that were also extended to establish the differences between Spanish Africans and Spaniards of the peninsula were *"moreno"* and "black", as, in Ramos Izquierdo and Navarro y Beltrán view, these did allow for the local population to be racialised through their skin colour. Indeed, according to Ramos Izquierdo and Navarro y Beltrán (1912, p. 352), mixing should be avoided because it turned a person into "quarantine, half-caste, *mulatto*", which "are the names of when the races intermingle".

It must have been similarly difficult to detach oneself in Barcelona from the descriptions that the Catalan missionaries bandied about regarding the Krio Fernandino, despite the fact that some, namely Amelia Barleycorn, always helped them financially, even if they were Protestants. For example, the Claretian Ruiaz (1928, pp. 87–88), after devoting lavish praise to different Fernandino figures of major importance, such as Balboa, Jones and Kinson, criticised their way of life in Santa Isabel. This speech against the Krio Fernandino was promoted in parallel to the Fernandinos' claims regarding the treatment they received in the colony.

In a document from the files of the Alcalá de Henares Archive dated 25 May 1933 and compiled by Enrique Martino, the community's discomfort was explained in a meeting organised in Santa Isabel by prominent Fernandino figures. The document, which was drafted by the colonial Government Police and was the result of their espionage, stated that the Krio Fernandino had always wanted to assert their rights through legal channels:

> The meeting was convened by Manuel Balboa During, Samuel Kinson, Alfredo Jones, José Edgerley, Gustavo Mentz, Claudio Ricardo, Benito Macfoy, Edmundo Collins and Roberto Barleycorn. The purpose was to protest against the contributions and similarly the lack of freedom that indigenous people were granted in this Territory despite it being their country, not receiving proper treatment anywhere and their rights not being recognised, even those indigenous people who had been granted emancipation.[59]

Moreover, the concern of the colonial authorities regarding the Krio Fernandino along with Catalan involvement during colonisation was notable. Rodríguez Vera (1900, p. 87), who was a frigate captain, expressed the opinion of many in concluding that "if the flourishing trade with Catalonia were curtailed, the island would cease to be Spanish in a short time."

Thus, the intercultural encounter between Catalans and Krio Fernandino was determined by colonial logics and shifted through different phases when another Equatorial Guinean population settled in Catalonia and Spain. Decades later would Bubi, Fang, Ndowe, Bissio, or Annobonese people begin to arrive, with whom the ties were hierarchical for those who knew them in the Spanish colonies. Only with time, Barcelona, as the main destination, was replaced by other places like the Canary Islands, the Valencia Region, the Basque Country, or the

Community of Madrid, to which students and the population in general would move.

As happened in other European cities to which rich and elegantly dressed African polyglots flocked in the last third of the nineteenth century, it is likely that the greatest culture shock affected the existing Catalan population in general with respect to Krio Fernandino, and not vice versa, despite the cosmopolitan character of Barcelona. This was because, as has been shown, the Fernandino diaspora was accustomed to dealings with the British, Portuguese, Germans, Italians and French, frequently making trips to different cities of the European empires, in addition to the fact that the Krio Fernandino, like other Africans, were accustomed to coexisting with the European population in the colonies, not always the other way round. Now, the disencounter in Barcelona should not have been so disruptive, given that the high social class and European education of the Fernandinos should have softened the rejection that could have been targeted to a black and African minority, despite Barcelona's multicultural stance.

This hypothesis that between the population of Barcelona and Santa Isabel colonial ties were established that were not overly marked by predictable inequality can be confirmed with the reconstruction of Fernandino life in Barcelona until the first half of the twentieth century. As an example, which I will take up in the coming section, there is the photograph of a wedding between the Jones and Dougan families, taken by the well-known Catalan photographer, Josep Maria Segarra i Plana. The photograph was published in *La Vanguardia* in 1932 and shows the Krio Fernandino couple surrounded by members of the Catalan bourgeoisies who had not wished to miss either the event or the photograph.

However, it is important not to overlook the fact that race discourses during Francoism were markedly racialised, despite the supposed benefits of the rhetoric of the Hispanic race, with this finding greater resonance in Madrid, as the nation's capital, than in the rest of the peninsula. This blunt racialisation of the African would eventually hamper cultural encounters, especially when members of other Equatorial Guinean groups began to arrive from the colonies who had not been afforded access to the same education or enjoyed the same lifestyles as the Krio Fernandino community, an issue that, as we will see, would worsen in the postcolonial period, particularly from the late 1980s onwards with the rise of transnational African migrations and other origins.

The arrival of the Krio Fernandino diaspora in Barcelona coincided with the occasional arrival of other Africans from the mid-nineteenth century, especially in Madrid. These cases appear in some chronicles. One of them was the African who brought the Viscount of San Javier, Muñoz y Gaviria (1871b), between 1860 and 1870. Muñoz y Gaviria (1871b, pp. 142–143) explained that he acquired from a black king "an eight-year-old black child" in Benin for two bottles of brandy. He said that he saved him from certain death, as he was to be sacrificed in honour of a snake, and that he took him to Madrid where he became his cook. However, he added that the boy rubbed the whites up the wrong way and had acquired bad habits in Madrid and Malaga, so he decided to send him back to Fernando Poo. He called this young man Tiberius (Muñoz y Gaviria, 1871b, p. 185), ironically expressing what his fate could be in the case of good behaviour, since the treatment that was offered to the young man, according to the news story, highlighted the objectification faced by many Africans: Muñoz y Gaviria took him to his home in Madrid as a souvenir, but this young man, without an African name, was ultimately returned to Fernando Poo, which was not even his country, when "his master" got tired of having him with him. His narration minorise and widespread disregard for African people:

> By acquiring the little black kid I had saved his life [...] This little *"negro"* stayed with me after all my time in Africa, and I turned him into an excellent cook. The bad habits he acquired [...] forced me to send him to Fernando Póo again, where [...] today he lives peacefully in the midst of a savage tribe (Muñoz y Gaviria, 1871b, pp. 142–143).

In another vein, the economic and trading relationship Santa Isabel enjoyed with Barcelona must be appraised due to its close nature. The commercial exchange was highly intense between the colony and the city, while some of the imported products were distributed from Barcelona, with its port serving as the departure point for a large part of the materials exported. Some of the most important Catalan entrepreneurs who based their interests in the colony were Salvador Trinitat Rius i Torres, Francesc i Joan Buxeres i Joan Font, La Vigatana by Miquel Trias i Trias, Jaume Riera i Caralt and Josep Vilarassa i Arenas, Antonio Pérez López, Joaquim Rodríguez Barrera (with the Montseny and Montserrat plantations), Joan Domènech, Bonaventura Roig Serra, Salvador Sendrós, and Francesc Potau (Sant, 2015).

Table 19. Selection of products exported from Barcelona to Santa Isabel, October 1915

Construction materials	Cotton, iron, zinc, cement, bricks, plaster, refractory earth, vegetable oil, iron, glass, trellis
Parts, machinery and hardware	spark plugs, pulleys, hardware, turpentine, colours, hardware, paint, electrical material, oars
Clothing and fabrics	fabrics, clothing
Food	cod, vegetables, butter, corn, flour, beans, potatoes, onions, sweet fruits, rice, chickpeas, sterilised milk, olives, hams, bacon, paper bag, legumes, cheeses, salt, cereals, biscuits, sugar, butter, garlic, sardines, pasta for soup, cocoa, sauce, olive oil, sausages
Alcoholic drinks and beverages	table wine, vermouth, spirits, mineral water, beer, cognac, brandy, anise, gin, whisky
Hygiene and pharmaceutical products	syrups, soap
Household items and personal use	trunks, lamps, footwear, furniture, mattress beds, perfumery, hats, books, bellows, scales, brooms, suitcases, writing paper

Source: Compiled by the author. *Ébano*, 13, 12-11-1939.

The exchange of trade between Santa Isabel and Barcelona at the beginning of the twentieth century was notably high. Some data are offered by Ramos Izquierdo and Navarro y Beltrán (1912, pp. 306–307). As an example, the documentation consulted includes an itemised breakdown of a shipment that arrived in Santa Isabel from Barcelona in October 1915 containing all kinds of products in terms of food, hygiene, home, clothing, construction materials, pharmaceuticals, hardware, and alcohol and drinks, products that both Catalans and the Krio Fernandino could import (see Table 19).

Consulting the *Itinerary of the line of Fernando Poo* of the Compañía Trasatlántica from the year 1911, it was stated that the services left Barcelona every 2nd of the month at 4 pm. They arrived in Sierra Leone every 19th of the month, reaching Monrovia on the 20th of each month and finally Santa Isabel on the 26th of each month at 7 am. The same

Table 20. Movement of passengers by sea through ports of origin and destination Santa Isabel, 1942

Ports of origin or destination	Inbound			Outbound		
	Men	Women	Total	Men	Women	Total
Barcelona	133	71	204	164	62	226
Bilbao	35	21	56	40	25	65
Cádiz	274	119	393	267	81	348
Las Palmas	403	26	429	189	61	250
Santa Cruz de Tenerife	10	17	27	30	9	39
Valencia	34	22	56	54	21	75
Vigo	1	-	1	7	5	12
Total Spanish ports	925	293	1,218	831	304	1,135
Calabar, Nigeria	220	280	500	1,366	136	1,502
Douala, Cameroon	40	-	40	27	14	41
Other foreign ports	145	12	157	167	17	184
Total foreign ports	405	292	697	1,560	167	1,727
Overall total	1,330	585	1,915	2,391	471	2,862

Source: Compiled by the author. Resúmenes Estadísticos del Gobierno General de los Territorios Españoles del Golfo de Guinea (1945, p. 110).

steamer stopped for a few days in Santa Isabel, from the 26th to the 2nd of the following month, when it would set sail again at 3 pm, arriving in Barcelona on the 25th day of the month at 4 am. Therefore, a boat from Santa Isabel and Barcelona always left at about the same time. This schedule was maintained over the decades.

However, the transnational travel of Africans and Europeans altered markedly over time, being highly conditioned by their social class. If among the Krio Fernandino community, men and women travelled to the peninsula in first class with a certain regularity, this was not the case for other Africans. Equatorial Guineans who wished to embark on the steamer needed to have certain permits and authorisations, which were difficult to obtain, in addition which, at first, most would be funded by the colony that would only cover third-class tickets, as was the case of some Equatorial Guinean students who were granted scholarships in 1935.

In the case of the Spaniards from the peninsula, the type of passage they were able to take reflected the different roles they had in the colony. Thus, apart from highly ranked officials, landowners or important merchants, who always travelled in first class, sometimes with their families, the rest of the passengers did so in second class if they were middle class, or in third class if they were common soldiers or people recruited to perform subordinate tasks. Indeed, the Compañía Trasatlántica applied a 30% discount on tickets for the trips officials made to the colony, as per the official discount. It was clear that the steamer made money through the transportation of goods, but also of people, with the passage of soldiers and officials.

Regarding the costs of travel, it should be noted that a first-class ticket from Las Palmas to Fernando Poo on the steamer *Ciudad de Cádiz* cost 410 pesetas in 1911. In Barcelona, it cost three times as much. In 1924, passengers from Santa Isabel to the port of Barcelona paid 1,250 pesetas for first class, 900 pesetas for second class and 350 pesetas for third class, half if they were only travelling to Las Palmas.

Likewise, the movement of passengers by sea allow us to identify the busiest ports of the maritime route, chief among them Barcelona, and how many women travelled, either alone or accompanied, whether African or Spanish (see Table 20).

3.2. Amelia Barleycorn heading to Europe

If anything characterised the Krio Fernandino community, it was their multilocality, and their transnational and transcontinental mobility, especially between Africa and Europe. Their mixed and Europeanised status facilitated their socio-cultural fit against the backdrops in which they settled. As will be seen, they made trips to various different countries. Below, I reproduce some of the places they visited in Africa and Europe, stopping especially in Barcelona.

The reconstruction of the mobility of Amelia Barleycorn and other Krio Fernandino and Equatorial Guineans has been made possible by a thorough review of the passengers who embarked on some of the steamers that connected Barcelona and Santa Isabel between 1903 and 1921, using the lists published in the magazine *La Guinea Española*. A more general

Table 21. Residence and travel permits in Santa Isabel in 1941, 1942 and 1943

Year	Documentation	Total
1941	Passports for indigenous people	2,635
	Passports for Europeans	194
	Residence permits for indigenous people	7,116
1942	Passports for indigenous people	3,627
	Passports for non-indigenous people (European)	334
	Residence permits for indigenous people	4,433
1943	Passports for indigenous people	3,338
	Passports for non-indigenous people (European)	-
	Residence permits for indigenous people	-

Source: Compiled by the author. Resúmenes Estadísticos del Gobierno General de los Territorios Españoles del Golfo de Guinea (1943, p. 13). Resúmenes Estadísticos del Gobierno General de los Territorios Españoles del Golfo de Guinea (1945, p. 125).

research was undertaken from that date until the 1940s, after which I replaced the consultation of tickets on the steamers from the magazine with the granting of visas to travel to Spain until 1968, which are available in the Alcalá de Henares Archive (see Table 21).

The work's findings make it clear that transcontinental mobility was not exclusive to Spaniards and Catalans from the mainland towards the African colony, but rather that there was also widespread movement of African Spaniards towards the mainland. The data show that the first to travel to Europe were the Krio Fernandino, mostly to Barcelona, from 1870 until the end of the 1930s. After that, other Equatorial Guineans joined in from the 1940s, not solely travelling to Barcelona but also to other cities such as Madrid, Valencia or the Canary Islands, a new flow that would occur in unison with the Fernandinos' journeys to the Catalan capital that remained uninterrupted, albeit diversified to other cities.

As will be shown in the forthcoming sections, this mobility would persist until colonial independence in 1968, and would accelerate in the period of the provincialisation and self-government of Spanish Guinea (1959–1963), making it clear that the possibility of travelling to the mainland had ceased to be the exclusive birthright of the wealthy and powerful Krio Fernandino families.

Barcelona as the main destination for Amelia and other Krio Fernandino and Equatorial Guineans

In the 1860s, Santa Isabel was still poorly linked with the Iberian Peninsula, as the sea route connected the island of Fernando Poo with England, especially with Pilmont, London and Liverpool, which, in turn, connected with Santa Cruz de Tenerife. This explains why the first trips by Spanish Africans to Europe from the port of Santa Isabel involved a British final destination since, after all, this nation had actually initiated the effective colonisation of what would become Spanish Guinea. Muñoz y Gaviria (1871a, pp. 15–16) discussed this:

> Fernando Poo's communications with Spain are few and far between. Occasionally, a Catalan ship docks to load palm oil. Every two months the government sends a steamer to carry food and money from the salaries of the employees and the garrison of the colony.

However, only a few decades later, this situation had been reversed, since 148 steamers had been counted in 1908.

The Barleycorn family's first trips to Europe began in the mid-nineteenth century. Their destination was England. They had major agricultural landholdings with the British as their exports were sent to the United Kingdom. These ties favoured constant transcontinental trips of the Barleycorn family, thanks to the connectivity that existed via the sea route and that also incorporated the central and western African coasts. The Barleycorn family then travelled to the cities of Liverpool, Manchester and London. Their journeys are recorded as being for study, medical, commercial, ecclesiastical and leisure purposes, while they maintained their businesses in the plantations of Fernando Poo, as was the case of the family of Amelia Barleycorn and her husband William Allen Vivour.

It should be noted that the first to make trips to Europe was the patriarch Napoleon Barleycorn, who, after his visits, decided to send his children to study at Bourne College in Quinton, near Birmingham. Among them was Amelia's brother, William Napoleon Barleycorn. He married Dorcas Fanny de Barleycorn, who died in London in April 1889 while undergoing a five-month medical treatment which commenced in 1888,[60] during which time she was accompanied by Amelia Barleycorn. The death of Dorcas Fanny de Barleycorn coincided with William Napoleon studying in Barcelona in 1889. It is also worth noting that the burial of Dorcas Fanny in London was attended by numerous dignitaries from the faith, proof of the influence that William Napoleon held in the Presbyterian community.

William Napoleon Barleycorn left London in May 1889 upon the death of his wife. Although it is unknown whether his visits were made from Barcelona or from Fernando Poo, he still visited England in 1892 and 1893, though despite having accepted his request for a visit in the following years, he never returned. William Napoleon Barleycorn's in Barcelona for his studied in 1889 had been preceded by another, in 1884, to obtain a certificate of Spanish education. It is likely that by then Amelia Barleycorn was already travelling to Barcelona with some regularity, although it has not been possible to verify whether she was sent to study at Bourne College in Quinton with some of her brothers or rather to Barcelona.

In this family context of such boundless transcontinental mobility, it is possible to imagine that for Amelia it was not difficult to travel to Europe. Furthermore, as I pointed out, there was a seemingly endless stream of ships that connected Fernando Poo directly with England. We cannot date her trips to Barcelona with certainty using the passenger lists published in *La Guinea Española*, nor can we to ascertain whether she made journeys from Spain to England, or had stopovers in the Canary Islands. However, what is known for certain is that during the first decades of the mid-nineteenth century one could travel to London directly, but not to Barcelona.

In that regard, the beautiful house that Amelia Barleycorn rented in London in 1881 is known, thanks to the fact that a photograph was linked to her name that was inscribed in the census of the city.[61] The house was located at Castle, 81 Holloway Road, Islington, and beyond that no other addresses in the city are known. It is proof that when travelling she sought to have a very comfortable home befitting her social class and status. This rental was earlier than others that she later had Barcelona, because, at a minimum, it is known that she passed away in a house located in Sant Gervasi street, in the exclusive Barcelona neighbourhood of Sarrià-Sant Gervasi. At that time, this area was comprised of single-family residential houses, one or two storeys high – very similar, therefore, to the house she had leased in London.

Why Amelia Barleycorn chose Barcelona and not another European city as her main European destination since the 1890s was explained at the beginning of this chapter, where it was argued that trade with Santa Isabel passed from British to Catalan hands. The fact that Amelia's brother studied in Barcelona might also have convinced her, though without being a decisive factor.

This mobility of the Krio Fernandino and other Equatorial Guineans to Africa and Europe, and especially to Barcelona, was significant from the end of the nineteenth century and especially from the beginning of the twentieth century onwards. Logically, the regularity with which the steamer *Fernando Poo* under the flag of the Compañía Trasatlántica connected the island of Fernando Poo with the peninsula since 1892 it was one of the factors that influenced why the Krio Fernandino and other Equatorial Guineans travelled to Barcelona, thanks to the fact that the powerful slave trader, Marqués de Comillas, made Spanish Guinea its destination.[62]

Added to this, undoubtedly one of the most relevant issues that arises from all these data was that the transcontinental mobility of Amelia Barleycorn de Vivour made her one of the first African women of the last third of the nineteenth century to visit Europe of her own volition, because she was self-reliant and independent, travelling many times alone, or accompanied by family, friends or with her service staff. The profile of the Krio Fernandino Amelia Barleycorn was similar to that of certain European women, rich and educated, visiting Africa at that time, as was the case of the English writer Mary Kingsley (1862–1900) in 1897 (who, as we will see, dedicated a few words to the Fernandino minority), however Amelia Barleycorn did not claim to travel to Europe as an explorer of foreign lands as they advocated in the opposite sense, in addition to her Nigerian roots together with her knowledge of European cultures, stimulated her Afropolitanism.

Yet, before we continue with the visits of Amelia Barleycorn and other Krio Fernandino to Barcelona since the end of the nineteenth century, we can briefly mention that the Fernandino maintained close contact with their families and their interests and properties in other African countries, from which many came, in particular Liberia, Sierra Leone and Nigeria.

Among the rationales behind the trips between Santa Isabel and some African countries were business and studies, although also escape from the rainy weather, and seeking out better temperatures and climatic conditions. In the 1920s, to mention only some of these trips to other African countries that have been recorded in the documentary sources, we can consider those that were destined for Liberia. For example, there are the trips made by Gertrudis and Mabel Barleycorn (relatives of Amelia

Barleycorn, probably daughters or granddaughters of her brother, William Napoleon) to Monrovia in 1920, in this case also accompanied by José Dougan and Manuel Balboa, among others, that same year. There is also the journey of José Walterio Dougan from Santa Isabel to Monrovia, likewise in 1920. In all truth, the travel to and from Liberia was so significant – largely due to the need for *braceros* in the plantations of Fernando Poo – that a request was made to create a Legation House of Spain in Monrovia on 10 July 1923. However, there were also abundant trips to Sierra Leone, such as Sara W. Dougan returning from Sierra Leone in June 1909 or Walter Dougan sailing there in November of the same year from Sierra Leone to Santa Isabel.

Returning to the route to mainand Spain, it should be said that, although Amelia Barleycorn constitutes a precedent, she was not the only Krio Fernandino who journeyed to Barcelona. However, she undoubtedly became a real magnet for her family at the beginning of the twentieth century. Thus, we know that in 1903 Amelia Barleycorn visited her daughter in England and that she did so from Barcelona, just as, in 1904, the arrival of the popular steamer *San Francisco* made the news, and among the passengers who disembarked were Mariana and Roberto Barleycorn, in addition to Claudio L. Cole and, above all, Manuel Balboa, who that same year had returned to Santa Isabel with the first cine-camera of Spanish Guinea. As a matter of fact, Balboa would be one of the most frequent travellers on steam passages during the first quarter of the twentieth century and he talked openly about his Barcelona home. But going back to 1904, there is no doubt that the Barleycorn family enjoyed the city, as in another news story it stated that the same boat that had arrived with Mariana and Roberto Barleycorn set sail on 26 September towards Santa Isabel with two other relatives of Amelia, Emilio and Jeremías Barleycorn. A year later, Jeremías Barleycorn and Maximiliano Jones made the return journey to Barcelona. In 1909, Domingo and Emilio Barleycorn also travelled, whom the reporter described as *morenos*, a word that, as I have already mentioned, racialised the African population more than the traditional term "indigenous".

In the 1910s, the Krio Fernandino's visits to Barcelona increased, as other Barleycorns, as well as Amelia Barleycorn, and the Vivours travelled frequently to Barcelona, joining the descendants of Balboa, Jones, Dougan, Kinson, Macfoy and Wilson, to name but a few. The Collinses also travelled to Las Palmas, such as the trip made by Sara, Edmundo, Reina and Manuela in March 1913. That year, 1913, also saw the return of

Balboa to Barcelona in April, although only a few days later he went back to Santa Isabel.

Undoubtedly, seafaring voyages during that time had their difficulties and drawbacks owing to the First World War. Francisco Wilson faced many hurdles in returning to Santa Isabel from his stay in Europe since the First World War had broken out in 1914. He had to go via six or seven boats, having made the trip on both German and English ships, with war merchants, and in the end he was able to reach Concepción by boat.

Other Krio Fernandino women who travell like Amelia did were Sara W. Dougan, Sara Collins and Raquel Jones. For example, we know of a trip to Barcelona in June 1916 by Sara Collins and Raquel Jones, who were labelled by *La Voz de Fernando Poo* as housewives. The magazine reported on the visit in Barcelona, with an article that said: "we have had the pleasure of greeting the important Fernandino owners Miss Raquel Jones and Miss Sara Collins who on a leisure trip have recently arrived aboard the steamer *Ciudad de Cádiz*. We wish you a pleasant stay among us."[63] The news clipping is interesting as it shows that there was contact between Catalans and Krio Fernandino beyond Fernando Poo, with Barcelona being a meeting point, in addition to the fact that since the magazine represented commercial interests of the Catalan bourgeoisie, Miss Raquel Jones and Miss Sara Collins must probably have been received by the editor himself or someone in a position of prominence.

In 1917, we know of a voyage of Amelia Barleycorn, Isabel Vivour de Kinson and Isabel Níger to Barcelona on the steamer *Cataluña*, together with Samuel Kinson and accompanied by a servant (on the subject of service, see section 4.3.). These long trips in the company of other members of the Krio Fernandino diaspora presumably mean that they maintained a formal relationship between themselves, at least exchanging pleasantries, since the constant endogamy of the community bolstered the Fernandino group. It was already mentioned in the section dedicated to the Kinsons that they had married one of their daughters to the Jones family. In October 1917, Alfredo J. Jones and Bernardo J. Jones also arrived in Barcelona. On the same steamer another Krio Fernandino was aboard, Adelaide Macfoy.

The year 1918 was also dotted with visits. In March, the three Jones sisters – Mabel, Juana and Raquel – travelled to Barcelona. In addition, their trip was for professional reasons, as it was stated that trade was engaged. Eduardo C. Barleycorn also returned to Barcelona, and was classified as a farmer. That year Samuel Kinson travelled to Barcelona in July and his return was in August, enjoying a two-month stay in summer. It is likely that on the way he was accompanied by María L. Kinson de Dougan or Susana Dougan Kinson and that they were not appear on the passenger lists reported in the press, because these sometimes had to be selective and could be incomplete. On the return trip to Santa Isabel in August, José W. Dougan was also listed, who perhaps accompanied the Kinsons as they were all travelling together. In the list, the name Collins was followed by Carlos, Beatriz, Margarita, Williams and Fanny Collins, so it was understood that a good part of the Collins family had travelled.

Between 1919 and 1930, voyages by the Krio Fernandino took place even more regularly. As examples, the visit to Barcelona of women of the Dougan, Kinson and Collins families in 1919, some of whom would stay for July and August, is worthy of special mention. Indeed, in summer there were many families travelling on the steamers: "María L. Kinson de Dougan, I. Susana Dougan Kinson, José Walterio Dougan [...] Carlos L. Collins, Beatriz Collins, Margarita Collins, Fanny Collins."[64] It is also worth noting that in April 1920 Mildred Jones travelled to the Canary Islands, coinciding with the trip of Encarnación, Francisca and Susana Castillo, Fernandinos of Cuban origin, also to Las Palmas. Or even the trip of Samuel Kinson to Barcelona in May 1929; aboard the same steamer was Manuel Balboa, as recorded in the passenger list.

The data gathered suggest that Amelia Barleycorn de Vivour was probably the first Krio Fernandino woman to decide to live to between Santa Isabel and Barcelona, just as Manuel Balboa would be the first Fernandino.

The 1930s brought with them certain peculiarities. In 1928, the regulation on emancipated and non-emancipated status had been approved in Equatorial Guinea, which shortly afterwards would allow certain non-Fernandino Equatorial Guineans to access emancipation status. Even then, the Catalan bourgeoisie began to loosen its stronghold in the colony, with other regions and especially Madrid becoming the main draw. By the end of the 1930s, Barcelona had ceased to act as the main destination for the Krio Fernandino diaspora. Finally, some Equatorial Guineans would embark bound for the peninsula but travelling via other Spanish cities, not only Barcelona.

All these factors combined indicated the beginning of the decline of Fernandino power in Santa Isabel and the expected emancipation of other Equatorial Guinean groups.

Diversification of Equatorial Guinean migrations

From the 1940s onwards, and until colonial independence, the Krio Fernandino's constant trips to Barcelona and other cities in Spain would continue, although from 1952 many would travel by plane to the peninsula, specifically to Madrid. This was a sign of their purchasing power, since this service was faster and more comfortable than the crossing by ship. Furthermore, the fact the bureaucracy for granting safe passage and sixty-day visas was centralised in Madrid, as the national capital, had an influence on this shift.

The decade of the 1950s also saw an increase in travel by other Equatorial Guineans from the Fang, Bubi, Ndowe and Annobonese ethnicities to Spain. In most cases, these were trips for study, using missionary channels or scholarships provided by the colonial authorities, but they were also for dealings in trading, visiting family or simply leisure trips. The Equatorial Guineans who travelled to Spain via missionary channels, for example, from the mission of Banapá, were students selected directly by the missionaries, having shown a "convinced" conversion to Catholicism. In the case of Spanish scholarships, Equatorial Guineans could obtain aid from the colonial authorities to study on the peninsula or places on some training courses, including military or technical studies.

This change in the profile of Equatorial Guinean passengers and the chosen destinations, since most journeyed to Madrid, and to a lesser extent, Salamanca, Cádiz or towns in the Basque Country, as well as the uninterrupted movement of Krio Fernandino, made Madrid as a destination undergo an expansion with regard to the type of travellers arriving and departing. Many of those who moved to the city would settle in university residences and the private homes of Madrid families.

A selection of cases is provided below so that the aforementioned changes can be perceived, with respect to the ethnic groups requesting travel to Spain, the reasons given for the journeys and the final destination cities of these groups. The documentation available enables the comparison of requests made by the Krio Fernandino community with those of other Equatorial Guineans from the Fang, Bubi or Ndowe ethnic groups that will be reviewed subsequently.

Regarding the Fernandinos' travels in the 1950s and 1960s, it is worth highlighting some of the trips made by the Barleycorn, Balboa, Jones, Vivour and Collins families. They mostly travelled to Barcelona, they showed a wealthy position, and the rationale behind the trips was for trading, employment, study, leisure or health reasons. It must be stressed that, as in the documentation issued of visas to travel to other groups Equatorial Guineans no Krio Fernandino, all applicants held Spanish nationality, something that in the colony never gave them equal rights to Spaniards living on the mainland, except for those who were full emancipated.

Below is a selection of the visas and safe-conducts consulted from this period (see Table 22). Some cases are presented in detail to show the content of the petitions and the relationships that the plaintiffs maintained with the cities they visited, which, as we will see, in this case was mostly Barcelona. Sometimes it was stated that the usual residence was Barcelona, not Santa Isabel or other cities on the Iberian Peninsula.

In the sources, there were documents of Susana Barleycorn Norman, born on 15 March 1879, of Spanish nationality, widow, a housewife by profession, who applied for a visa in 1956 to move to her home in Barcelona where she resided. It was recorded that she would make her trip with Isabel Barleycorn Macfoy, born on 6 May 1907, of Spanish nationality, unmarried, a housewife by profession, who applied to move to Santa Isabel after her residence in Barcelona.

Another Barleycorn example is that of Veracruz Barleycorn Boricó. There were three exit cards from the country issued by the Government Police of Santa Isabel. The first, from 1954, stated that she was born on 11 May 1927 in Santa Isabel, was a commercial teacher, unmarried, and that she left for Barcelona by boat bound for carrer Consell de Cent 393. In her occupations, trade was stipulated. The second exit card was from 1957 and stated that she worked at the Patronato de Indígenas, which was engaged in trading, and that she left by plane to Madrid. The third exit card was from 1958 and requested permission to travel to Spain, France, Portugal and Italy.

There was the further case of Eugenia Barleycorn Inta, born on 29 December 1951, unmarried, the daughter of Jeremías Barleycorn and Gertrude Ita, residing in Santa Isabel, who had a 1956 departure card to travel to Barcelona for leisure purposes.

A different case is the 1963 file of Juan Walterio Barleycorn Jones, born in San Carlos on 23 October 1922, married, an industrialist and son of Eduardo and Carolina, domiciled in Santa Isabel. He applied for a passport and permit for his daughter Celestina Barleycorn Bioco, aged

19, to move to Monrovia (Liberia) to study, although ultimately they had decided that she would study in Barcelona, visiting her aunt, bearing the costs of travel and stay.

To outline also the documentation of Eduardo Barleycorn Atti from 1944–1956. On the 1956 departure card, it stated that he was born on 24 February 1890 in Santa Isabel, married, a farmer, the son of Jeremías Barleycorn and Sally Atti, and lived in Barcelona on Ronda de San Pedro.

Just as the Barleycorns travelled, so did the Collinses. For example, Eduardo Collins Edgerley, on 8 September 1927 in Santa Isabel, married, the son of Alberto and Isabel, a welder, had a 1961 departure card to leave for Madrid to study for his accelerated vocational training. His case also reflects a loss of influence of the Collins family in the 1960s, as they got him a scholarship, but as a welder, which put him on a par with the rest of Equatorial Guinean groups.

Of course, the Balboas also travelled, as was the case of Abilio Balboa Arkins, born on 6 January 1906 in Barcelona, of Spanish nationality, married, an agriculturalist, with permanent residence in Barcelona, in the smart Avda. Calvo Sotelo 5, who requested in 1957 to move to Santa Isabel with his son Abilio to return to his home in Spanish Guinea. They left via Madrid by plane.

There was also a safe-conduct granted on 26 January 1961 to Susana Vivour Lolín, born on 13 January 1950 in Santa Isabel, of Spanish nationality, unmarried, a student, so that she could move to Santa Isabel to meet her father Esteban Vivour.

The Joneses appearing in the documentation gathered are represented by Wilbardo Jones Castillo, born on 8 April 1932 in Santa Isabel, of Spanish nationality, unmarried, a veterinarian, who requested a visa in 1966 to be able to move from his permanent address in Bilbao to Santa Isabel with his brothers Pablo and Fernando Jones Castillo in order to rejoin his family.

Regarding the trips of other Equatorial Guineans groups, outside the Fernandino, a selection has been made (see Table 23) to show some general trends that allow for data to be compared alongside the information collected on the Krio Fernandino diaspora (see Table 22). Most of these Equatorial Guineans departed from Madrid, with there being a minority who journeyed to Barcelona, since there was a remarkable geographical spread in the destinations. In general, these requests reveal their economic dependence on state aid, as well as missionary channels, for study,

Table 22. Selection of Krio Fernandino members who travelled between 1950 and 1960

Passenger name	Dates travelling	Occupation	Reason	Origin/ Destination
Guillermo Barleycorn Beckeley	27 November 1944	-	-	Santa Isabel/ Barcelona – Madrid
Veracruz Barleycorn Boricó	7 January 1954	Trade	Patronato de Indígenas	Santa Isabel/ Barcelona
Elena Collins Jones	18 February 1955	Housewife	Returning home	Madrid/Santa Isabel
Isabel Barleycorn Macfoy	2 March 1956	Single	Returning home	Santa Isabel/ Barcelona
Eduardo Barleycorn Attlee	2 August 1956	Agriculturalist	Returning home	Santa Isabel/ Barcelona
Susana Barleycorn Norman	2 August 1956	Housewife	Returning home/ Leisure	Santa Isabel/ Barcelona
Eduardo Barleycorn Atti	16 September 1956	Agriculturalist	Returning home	Santa Isabel/ Barcelona
Abilio Balboa Arkins	12 December 1957		Trade/Family visit	Barcelona/ Santa Isabel
Susana Vivour Lolín	26 January 1961		Student/ Family visit	Madrid/Santa Isabel
Eduardo Collins Edgerley	21 January 1961	Welder	Studies	Santa Isabel/ Madrid
Eugenia Barleycorn Ita	30 January 1962	Housewife	Returning home/ Leisure	Santa Isabel/ Barcelona

Passenger name	Dates travelling	Occupation	Reason	Origin/Destination
Nicolasa Barleycorn Edgerley	3 December 1962		British chaplaincy teacher/ Daughter visit	Santa Isabel/ Nigeria
Eugenia Barleycorn Inta	20 June 1963		Student/ Family visit	Madrid/Santa Isabel
Juan Walterio Barleycorn Jones for Celestina Barleycorn Bioco	26 August 1963	Student	Studies	Santa Isabel/ Barcelona
Wilbardo Jones Castillo	29 March 1966		Veterinarian/ Family visit	Bilbao/Santa Isabel

Source: Compiled by the author. AGA, box 81/08465; AGA, box 81/08349; AGA, box 81/07579; AGA, box 81/07615; AGA, box 81/08376; AGA, box 81/07605; AGA, box 81/07502; AGA, box 81/07605; AGA, box 81/08349; AGA, box 81/08437; AGA, box 81/07614; AGA, box 81/8497.

professional training or business trips; it was only a minority who had an obviously comfortable economic status, as in the case of the Krio Fernandino, which allowed them to activate their family networks so that they could be received at their destination by their own families. These circumstances are logical since the Krio Fernandino elite enjoyed major economic power that allowed them to be self-reliant, in addition to the fact that they had been building family support networks in Barcelona for over fifty years.

Thus, it is observed that in the case of the rest of Equatorial Guineans, those who stayed in Madrid were there because they had to attend schools and entities located in that city. It should be noted that it was precisely this arrival of Equatorial Guineans to Madrid that would constitute the solid basis for the Equatorial Guinean migrations to the Community of Madrid that were so numerically significant the post-independence period.

Table 23. Selection of Equatorial Guineans who travelled between 1950 and 1960

Passenger name	Dates travelling	Occupation	Reason	Origin/ Destination
Beatriz Maho Chuaham	7 March 1952	Sister of the Cloth	Studies	Madrid/ Santa Isabel
Adelaida Buaki Botuy	2 October 1952	Sister of the Cloth	Studies	Madrid/ Santa Isabel
Pius Akpan	10 May 1960	Cook	Cook	Santa Isabel/ Las Palmas
Expedito Pedro Boleko Browne	8 September 1960	Student	Studies	Santa Isabel/ Barcelona
Jesús Ndongo Buendi	5 October 1960	Banapá seminarian	Studies	Santa Isabel/ La Coruña
Reginaldo Makendengue Bodabo	5 October 1960	Banapá seminarian	Studies	Santa Isabel/San Sebastián
Leoncio Joaquín Edjang Avoro	5 October 1960	Banapá seminarian	Studies	Santa Isabel/ Palencia
Leoncio Paciencia Bilelo Lopez	5 October 1960	Banapá seminarian	Studies	Santa Isabel/ Palencia
Crescencio Rufino Copoboru Bonahi	15 October 1960	Student	Studies	Santa Isabel/ Madrid
Gerardo Boneque Borilo	22 November 1960	Student	Studies	Santa Isabel/ Madrid
Donato Oyono Mbo	21 January 1961	Navy	Work instruction barracks	Santa Isabel/ Cádiz
Pedro Biatiche Chuyo	21 January 1961	Electrician	Studies	Santa Isabel/ Madrid
Reginaldo Chicampo Solebapa	21 January 1961	Government police officer	Studies	Santa Isabel/ Madrid

Source: Compiled by the author. AGA, box 81/8497; AGA, box 81/07605; AGA, box 81/08376; AGA, box 81/07605.

Below is a discussion of some of the visas granted to Equatorial Guineans who travelled between Spanish Guinea and the Iberian Peninsula.

The documentation contains the departure card of Jesús Ndongo Buendi, issued in Santa Isabel in 1960. He was born on 1 January 1937, he was a bachelor and a seminarian from Banapá, who left for La Coruña to continue his studies. His trip coincides with those of other seminarians from Banapá around the same dates, such as Reginaldo Makendengue Bodabo and Leoncio Joaquín Edjang Avoro, who disembarked at other destinations on the mainland. All three are a standout example of the missionary networks that were activated from Spanish Guinea so that they could go to Spain to receive ecclesiastical training.

Two cases of nuns are those of Beatriz Maho Chuaham and Adelaida Buaki Botuy. Beatriz Maho Chuaham was born in Rebola on 13 January 1940, was single and a member of a convent, and resided in Madrid at calle Ferraz 85. Her departure card from Spain was from 1952 and included safe-conduct to visit the mission in Fernando Poo. Adelaida Buaki Botuy's situation was very similar. They are thus examples of Equatorial Guinean nuns who returned after the completion of their education in Madrid. However, from the documentation, it is very revealing that these two young Equatorial Guineans travelled with three Spanish nuns on the same date, one of them Catalan from Mataró, and these three white nuns had requested to travel in first class rather than in third as the Equatorial Guineans did, which was granted to them, since it should be remembered that they were considered official passage and travelled on account of the colony. The fact that the Spanish nuns travelled in first class and the Equatorial Guineans in third symbolises the hierarchy through skin colour that was commonplace between black and white Spanish Africans on the mainland.

There was also documentation pertaining to Donato Oyono Mbo, born on 8 August 1943 in Rio Benito, unmarried, from the Navy Training Barracks, who left for Cádiz to return to his work on 21 January 1961. Another example that of two young Equatorial Guineans, also enrolled in the Spanish navy, who went to sit their tests in Cádiz but who were forced to return to Spanish Guinea because they had failed them and who claimed that "they were too poor to pay for a degree as a doctor or lawyer and could only return with the ticket paid for by Spain" (AGA, box 81/07605).

A further example is the case of a chef born in Calabar, Nigeria, Pius Akpan Akpan, who had a departure card from Spanish Guinea in 1960, in which he stated that he was a cook in Santa Isabel, unmarried, and departed for Las Palmas to continue working for his employer. Another a young man with a 1960 departure card was Leoncio Paciencia Bilelo Lopez, born on 9 January 1948 in San Carlos, Fernando Poo, unmarried, who left for Madrid. Another is Expedito Pedro Boleko Browne, born on 19 April 1942, in Basapu, unmarried, a student, who left for the Residence School of Passeig de la Bonanova in Barcelona to continue his studies, giving his address as carrer d'Aragó 271 and had a departure card issued in Santa Isabel in 1960. The case of Expedito Pedro was similar to that of Milagrosa Bernardeta Epam Kopa, who attended the same well-known school in Barcelona.

Among the women who went on family visits, there were only two – Bernadeta Buapache Donson and María Mochoma Soka – who did so to Barcelona, the only city in which the lengthy experience of Krio Fernandino settlement and an Equatorial Guinean minority had allowed for family networks to be weaved over the decades. Of all the women for whom I have departure cards, only two made their trips for health reasons – Laureana Botala Ripelo and Bernabe Sorizo Becelebó.

Alongside the foregoing were, one would expect, Equatorial Guineans who applied to enlist in the Spanish army, for example Luciano Mba Mba.

In all the dossiers reviewed, there was no indication that supplementary reports of "good behaviour" had been issued, or if it was preferred that visa applicants be apolitical in relation to Spaniards' interests. However, in the days of Franco's dictatorship, supplementary reports were very frequently issued.

Below, I shall briefly offer a selection of examples to ascertain the type of problems that gave grounds for personal reports to be issued, as they reflect the concerns of the Spanish authorities regarding the pro-independence movements that began to come to the fore in the mid-1950s (Aixelà-Cabré, 2011). The files selected are those of Luís Nanga, Inocencio Lawson Mecheba, José María Loeri Comba and Cirilo Mba, as the four were pointed out as dangerous to the Spanish state due their ideas clashing with the colonial regime. Other cases that I will not delve into were those of Tomás Boriko Baupe, Idelfonso Mecha Bikechi, Francisco Edu Ela, Antonio Nsue Nkuku and Santiago Nsogo Mico.

Luís Nanga's file stated that he was born in Rio Muni and that in 1963 he applied for a six-month scholarship to reside in Spain to learn how to mend typewriters, which in principle was completed without any issues.

However, another classified document of 1963 provided contrary reports, saying that:

> the applicant displays very poor political behaviour as he is labelled as decidedly anti-Spanish in almost all the files of the province [...] He is considered one of the main activists of this continental region, he has attended several meetings, all of them of a political nature, acting as liaison for the activists [...] [C]urrently, he continues with the same political ideas and in the files, he is widely suspected of engaging in anti-Spanish activities [...] For all the above reasons [...] the applicant should not be granted whatever he requests (AGA, box 81/07615).

Regarding the secret file of Inocencio Lawson Mecheba, favourable political and social reports were issued indicating that he worked as a teacher's assistant in the Christopher Columbus school group in Evinayong and that he was married to a teacher who worked in the same school group. However, it was revealed that he had made statements in favour of Nigerians when he travelled to Madrid in January 1963, which were published his statements in the journal *Municipalia* during his residency at the National Institute of Local Administration in Madrid. The report added as a demerit that, in 1960, he received a visit from his brother Mauricio, who had fled to Douala in 1949 for political reasons.

In the case of José María Loeri Comba, there is a private communication from the General Government of the Equatorial Region for the different Delegates of the Government in Rio Muni and Santa Isabel on 30 April 1963 notifying that this Bubi citizen claimed to be the secretary of the pro-independence Luís Maho and that they were planning to stay there permanently to avoid colonial opposition. The report stated that José María Loeri Comba was one of the five Bubis exiled to Cameroon and, repeating statements from the National Congress of Free Trade Unions, said that they claimed that "we live like slaves" (AGA, box 81/07615).

For his part, Cyril Mba appeared in a file issued by the Government Delegation of the District of Santa Isabel of 27 June 1963 that censored him due to the fact he had penned an article that he sent to the *Ébano* magazine entitled "Nosotros, los africanos protestamos" (We Africans protest), a text that was highly critical of the colonial regime (AGA, box 81/07615).

These four examples of socio-political repression to prevent the colonial independence of Spanish Guinea show Spain's interest in drafting reports that would mark people out who had questioned colonisation or who had criticised the Spanish dictatorial regime. It is of the utmost significance that these reports were drafted at the same time as Spain was in international organisations, such as the UN, promoting the significant changes that had facilitated the provincialisation of the colony of 1959 and the consideration of Autonomous Region status in 1963, preserving Equatorial Guinean rights. Furthermore, apart from the empty rhetoric of the Spanish state, the anti-colonial political movements of Equatorial Guineans continued to be repressed, meaning this Spanish Africans faced obstacles if they made a request to travel to mainland Spain. In that regard, it should be noted that the anti-colonial mobilisation that was emerging at the end of the 1950s pushed some Equatorial Guinean leaders to go into exile in the neighbouring countries of Gabon and Cameroon. It is worth stressing then that the anti-colonial struggle led to the dissidents being expelled from the Spanish territories while the Spanish state sought to repress all those who made statements criticising the colonial regime (Pélissier, 1963).

3.3. Life in Barcelona

The settlement of African women in Barcelona in the nineteenth and twentieth centuries coincided with the overwhelming demand of Catalan women to create spaces for them and occupy others that until then had been reserved solely for men, an attitude found not only among wealthy, upper-class Catalan women, but also among those from other social strata. It should be remembered that, in Spain, women could not freely access universities until 1910 (Segura, 2011, p. 55) and that they were not entitled to vote until 1932 (Rotger, 2017, p. 93), once the Spanish Republic was proclaimed in 1931.

Historically, European androcentrism in general had advocated that men, rather than women, were the ones who had the capacity to articulate a community outlook for the benefit of all society, and also that they were the ones who gave the family lineage its identity via patrilineality, those who led the political spheres and those who managed economic resources. These factors were supported by a deeply androcentric view of monotheistic religions (Aixelà-Cabré, 2005). In Spain, all these parameters encouraged a male centrality of the spheres of power and authority in which men monopolised the limelight in public or private acts of socio-political relevance.

Now, it must be said that these ideas were also intrinsically linked to class as well as geographical and cultural origin, and ended up providing greater visibility to white, bourgeois and aristocratic men. However, contexts of high cultural diversity are rife with disruptive elements masterfully described by the concept of intersectionality. The term evidences that upper-class women have more influence than men belonging to the middle or lower classes, thus breaking the presupposition that men, in all circumstances, are able to hoard greater power and authority than women. This finding should not overlook the fact, however, that a woman with greater power, if she is black or mixed race, could experience racism or xenophobia.

These issues are at the fulcrum of understanding the general framework of the settlement of Krio Fernandino women in Barcelona since the end of the nineteenth century, as, although they seemed to be Europeanised, black, rich and powerful women, belonging to the upper or upper middle classes, they maintained a strong African identity that went against the grain of the white society's androcentric and imperial logic that, at that time, justified the exploitation and abuse of Africans under the supposed European civilising endeavours.

Even knowing that at the beginning of the twentieth century there were already certain influential Fernandino men and women residing between Barcelona and Santa Isabel, it is nevertheless not surprising that, in the photographic testimonies of banquets and meetings of groups of Catalan businessmen with interests in the Spanish Territories of the Gulf of Guinea, only white men were seen, and exceptionally the odd African man invited as a sign of tokenism that with the passage of the decades would become more flexible. Such was the case, for example, of Dougan's official visit to the Barcelona Chamber of Commerce in 1930. Regarding the absence of African guests whose images did not appear in the photographs that were published of the banquets and meetings that took place in Barcelona at the beginning of the twentieth century, some of which were published in *La Voz de Fernando Poo*. The conspicuous absence in practice of African men, much less African women, even if they were Spaniards, from these photographic testimonies is because they were never invited, because they turned down the invitation or because the photographer ruled out immortalising the encounters. The foregoing was a clear symptom of the segregation that still existed in commercial events when they took place in European contexts. The same happened in other social events that were held in the Catalan capital, in which the African women who participated where nowhere specifically in the photographic evidence. However, and fortuitously, this was not the case when the Krio Fernandino diaspora were the host, since they invited different Catalan bourgeois families to certain social events.

Below, further population factors, the cost of living and public services in Barcelona are discussed as they offer a general framework of what everyday like was like there, while allowing us to gain a better understanding of the advantages that the city offered to the Fernandino community compared to life in Santa Isabel. The latter will allow us to compare the context and social dynamics of the Fernandinos vis-à-vis Santa Isabel, as well as to understand the precedent that meant that African women such as Amelia Barleycorn de Vivour forged themselves a place in Catalan society.

Population of Barcelona

As was seen at the beginning of this chapter, the cultural diversity of the city of Barcelona was remarkable in qualitative terms. Studying extracts from statistics allows us to reconstruct the cultural diversity of Barcelona and the location of migrants by district.

In this regard, it should be noted that, in 1902, Barcelona already had 533,000 registered inhabitants. Of these, 20%, or 113,340, were from other Spanish provinces and 1.5%, or 7,624, were from abroad. Among the foreigners were more than 4,000 French people who lived in Eixample, Ciutat Vella, Sant Martí, Sants-Montjuïc and Sarrià-San Gervasi; more than 1,500 Italians who occupied the area of Ciutat Vella and Sants-Montjuïc; more than 500 English people who lived in Gràcia and Sant Martí; more than 500 Germans who lived in Eixample and Gràcia; almost 200 Argentines who resided in Eixample; almost 100 Mexicans who lived in Sant Martí and Eixample; about 30 Peruvians who lived in the area of Eixample and the Military Hospital; 30 Chileans who lived in Eixample and Gràcia; and 15 Moroccans who resided in Sant Martí and Eixample.[65]

The Krio Fernandino diaspora were not reflected in the figures because being African Spaniards was not classified as foreign.

The cultural diversity observed at the beginning of the twentieth century had increased by the middle of the century: in 1949, Barcelona reached 1,205,509 registered inhabitants. Of these, 33%, or 409,547, were from other Spanish provinces and 2%, or 24,091, were from abroad. Among the foreigners were more than 8,000 French people living in Sant Martí, Sants-Montjuïc and Sant Andreu; more than 2,000 Germans residing in Eixample and Gràcia; more than 2,000 Argentines living in Eixample; more than 1,100 Italians living in Sant Martí and Eixample; more than 400 Mexicans residing in the Ciutat Vella and Eixample area; more than 400 Algerians living in Sant Martí and Sants-Montjuïc; more than 300 English people living in the Ciutat Vella and Eixample; more than 300 Chileans living in Eixample and Sarria-Sant Gervasi; more than 300 Moroccans living in Sant Andreu and Eixample; more than 100 Peruvians residing in the Eixample and Sant Martí area; and 38 Ecuadorians living in the Sarrià-Sant Gervasi. Again, the Krio Fernandino community still did not appear in the statistics because of their status as African Spaniards, and not foreigners.

Likewise, by the end of the twentieth century, specifically in 1996, Barcelona had 1,508,805 registered inhabitants. Of these, 30%, or 431,855, were from other Spanish provinces and 4%, or 58,385, were from abroad. Among the foreigners were more than 3,100 Moroccans who lived in Ciutat Vella and Sants; more than 2,700 Peruvians who lived in Eixample, Sants-Montjuïc and Sant Martí; more than 1,700 French who lived in Eixample and San Gervasi; almost 1,700 Italians who lived in Eixample and San Gervasi area; more than 1,500 Germans who resided in Eixample, Gràcia and Sarrià-San Gervasi; about 1,100 Argentines who lived in Eixample and Ciutat Vella; almost 1,000 English who resided in Eixample, Sarrià-San Gervasi, Gràcia and Ciutat Vella; more than 600 Chileans who lived in Eixample and Ciutat Vella; more than 600 Pakistanis who resided in the Ciutat Vella area; more than 500 Chinese who lived in Eixample, Sants-Montjuïc and Sant Martí area; more than 400 Hindus who lived in Eixample and Ciutat Vella; more than 200 Equatorial Guineans who lived in the Nou Barris and Sant Martí area; and about 200 Algerians who mainly lived in the Old Town and Eixample. In this case, when the statistics began to gather immigrants' nationalities, it was possible to count the members of the Equatorial Guinean community, although, as we saw in section 2.5., it was not possible to quantify all those who obtained Spanish nationality.

As had been discussed in previous sections, the arrival of the Krio Fernandino and Equatorial Guineans to the city was constant, although gradual. Barcelona was enriched by Fernandino Afropolitanism with music, tastes, gastronomy, art[66] and sports, as well as by the desire to attain new horizons on the part of the various populations that also settled from other origins.[67]

A brief report that *La Vanguardia* published in 1962 on African students revealed the situation of the Equatorial Guineans in the early 1960s in Barcelona. The author of the article had asked the municipal offices "how many blacks would there be in Barcelona?", to which the reply was that "it is impossible to know. Skin colour is not recorded in the register."[68] This detail is not to be dismissed, as in the colony all the statistics separated populations by skin colour. Thus, the author, faced with the difficulty of obtaining absolute or relative figures, focused on offering an approximation of the true picture of Africans in Barcelona through those who had arrived for studies, thereby ascertaining that, of the 681 students from 29 countries enrolled in the School of Modern Languages of the University of Barcelona, "there is only one student of colour, a Moroccan".[69] Francisco Pérez Portabella, a former settler of Santa Isabel who then served as host for this group, told the author of the article that there were 37 African students in total who lived in Barcelona and its surroundings, and introduced him to Samuel Ebuco Besebo and a male of probably Fernandino of Cuban roots, Manuel Castillo. Both explained that they frequented the Ateneu Barcelonès. From the responses that the journalist received from them, it became clear to him that in everyday life they spoke "*pichinglish*" (Pichi) and that they did not like to be referred to as "black". Besides, they were used to living in capitals; as they themselves told him, they liked living in Barcelona, though "it was nothing new to them. Many of us have lived in Paris, London or Madrid beforehand."[70]

The interviewees explained that other students residing in Barcelona included the Krio Fernandinos Jorge and Mariana Dougan, who were siblings of the first Equatorial Guinean lawyer in the colony, and Piedad Granje Kake. In that year, there were only three African enrollees in the Faculty of Political, Economic and Commercial Sciences of the University of Barcelona: Samuel Ebuco Besebo and Piedad Granje Kake, who were Equatorial Guineans, and Allou Kouame from the Ivory Coast. They told the journalist that some of the things the young Equatorial Guineans like to do were to walk through the Gothic Quarter or go to the Museu Marés, the Museu Etnològic or the Museu Nacional d'Art de Catalunya (Museum of Romanesque Art) – which they referred to as "Barcelona with character". They added "in [Equatorial] Guinea you breathe Catalan air",[71] referring to the numerous Catalans who had commercial, trading and agricultural business dealings there.

The journalist concealed his surprise at the swift settling of the Equatorial Guineans in Barcelona and to his question about whether it had been difficult for them to make friends, they had answered with some anger: "Why would we not be able to make friends? We see no obstacle [...] between us and the boys and girls of Barcelona. Conversely, most of us live in family-type pensions, which puts us in immediate contact with Barcelona family circles."[72] The news item ended by concluding that the Equatorial Guineans "felt a bit *Barcelonés*" (Barcelonaish), and offered a more accurate reflection of how the arrival of Equatorial Guineans students had changed:

> Several years ago, the children of the powerful families of Santa Isabel and the continent came to study in Spain. Today, coloured students already come from middle-class families [...] eager for their children to acquire a culture that was denied to them.[73]

Products, prices and cost of living

Life in Barcelona, as in other European cities of the early twentieth century, was expensive. Among vastly different social classes – from the industrial bourgeoisie to the liberal professionals, the service professions, and civil servants of all scales – wages varied widely. The most common wage scales in 1914 ranged from 3 to 5 pesetas a day. Others who were more fortunate could earn, depending on their profession and salary scale, between 8 and 27 pesetas a day gross (calculations made from the data in Table 24).

Low wages were combined with commodities whose cost was not compatible with a high-protein diet. A kilo of beef or veal cost 5 pesetas per kilo, lean meat 2.50 pesetas, cheaper fish, especially sea bream, 0.75 pesetas, potatoes 0.50 pesetas, and dried chickpeas 1 peseta (see Table 25). Furthermore, wages were low. The cost of renting or buying somewhere to live was expensive. To provide context, it should be noted that prices were high in the city in the first third of the twentieth century, something

Table 24. Annual public salaries by profession in Barcelona, 1914

Profession	Category	Annual salary (in pesetas)
Chief engineer		10,000
Bookkeeper		6,000
Commander municipal guard		6,000
City police force		4,500
Inspector or director general		4,500
Butler		4,500
Inspector		2,125
Musical band soloist		2,000
Auditor		3,000
Chaplain		1,900
Concierge		1,825
Clerk		1,825
Municipal guard		1,825
Stonecutter		1,643
Bricklayer		1,505
Security guard		1,460
Gardener		1,460
Cleaner		1,460
Locksmith		1,400
Labourer		1,017
Watchmaker		1,000
Midwife		600

Source: Compiled by the author. *Gaceta Municipal de Barcelona* 3, 20-1-1914, pp. I–XVI.

Table 25. Main prices of consumer items in the markets of Barcelona, 1914

Products	Pesetas per kilo
Meat dishes	
Leg of lamb	2.50
Sirloin steak	5
Beef tenderloin steak	5
Live hen	6
Quarter chicken	1.50
Live chicken	3
Eggs (dozen)	1.30
Lean meat	2.50
Fish dishes	
Hake	2
Red seabream	0.75
Monkfish	1
Vegetables, fruits, legumes and others	
Lettuces	0.05
Peppers	0.40
Potatoes	0.15
Tomatoes	0.15
Onions	0.10
Rice	0.50
Pears	0.40
Olives	1
Sugar	0.90
Soap	0.75

Source: Compiled by the author. *Gaceta Municipal de Barcelona*, 1, 4-11-1914, pp. 4–5.

that, over the decades, became consolidated. In *La Voz de Fernando Poo* of 1921, houses and villas were advertised in Barcelona as well as in the advertising section of *La Vanguardia*. Added to this, it is highly likely that some of the Krio Fernandino who settled in the city made their initial contact with a view to a purchase, rental or real estate investment through the pages of *La Voz de Fernando Poo*.

As an example of the type of ads that the wealthy Krio Fernandino who wanted to travel to or settle in the city would have consulted, we can highlight the "House Rental" section in *La Voz de Fernando Poo* in 1921. Preceding the section "Offers", it had ads for the sale of villas and country houses in places like Mataró with vineyard included for 75,000 pesetas; in Sant Gervasi, a "beautiful house in high point of Sarrià, tram at the foot, with all modern conveniences, surface 86,000 palms and price 150,000 pesetas"; in Santa Coloma de Gramanet, "a large house with garden, price 30,000 pesetas"; in Premià de Mar, a "house with oratory and productive property of about 6 hectares price 25,000 pesetas"; and another in Just Sant, for 170,000 pesetas.[74]

The most expensive house in Barcelona was a single-family residence in the Putxet, in the exclusive Sarrià-Sant Gervasi district, an area in which Amelia Barleycorn had settled, as we know from her death certificate dated 3 January 1920.

Amelia Barleycorn's choice of residence in Sant Gervasi was consistent with her social status in Santa Isabel and maintained her lifestyle from Africa while in Europe. Indeed, many other Krio Fernandino would settle in Sarrià-Sant Gervasi or other exclusive areas of the city, including the Rambla Catalunya. However, other Equatorial Guineans with less purchasing power, and who made shorter trips, would stay in guest houses and pensions elsewhere in Barcelona, sometimes in places recommended by family and friends, or by locating pensions advertised in the magazines published in Santa Isabel. For example, in 1916 the La Africana pension in carrer Tamarit and the Hotel Beausejour in Passeig de Gràcia were advertised in *La Voz de Fernando Poo*.[75]

The closeness of Barcelona to the African colony was also manifested in the fact that alms were even collected among the wealthy Catalan bourgeois to meet the educational needs of the missionaries in the colony, as can be seen in the news article "Alms of Barcelona to Claretians for education" from 1905.[76]

Thus, we can conclude that Barcelona and Santa Isabel enjoyed many close links in the first third of the twentieth century.

Table 26. Causes of mortality in Barcelona in December 1920

Causes of death (selection)	Total
Heart disease	219
Pulmonary tuberculosis	136
Ordinary smallpox	132
Syphilis	78
Cancer and other tumours	76
Diarrhoea and enteritis	25
Diphtheria	9
Typhoid fever	18
Flu	13
Measles	1
Pertussis	1

Source: Compiled by the author. *Gaceta Municipal de Barcelona*, 52, 30-12-1920, p. 1048.

City services

Barcelona had a large enough budget allocated for the city to grow and bolster its position. Expenditure was directed to the security and police services, public education, charities and health, although the largest budget item was for public works. The development of Barcelona was not comparable with the nascent city of Santa Isabel, either in terms of services or in terms of infrastructures of all kinds.

Among the services of the city, one of the most important for the community Krio Fernandino was healthcare. I will not expand here on this issue as it will be addressed in the next section, but it must be said that Barcelona was a safer environment than Santa Isabel because many of the diseases of the early twentieth century were reduced according to healthcare improvements. Furthermore, some of the diseases that were commonly found in Santa Isabel had been eradicated in Barcelona, such as malaria, according to the lists consulted (see Table 26).

A further attraction that Barcelona offered was leisure. As will be revealed in the next section, certain news items reported on the fun-filled events and parties that the Krio Fernandino diaspora would threw luxurious Barcelona hotels such as the Inglaterra, the Majestic or the Ritz, from the beginning of 1920. Since then that the cultural and recreational options that Barcelona boasted, was indeed widespread: it offered theatres, operas, concert halls, hotels, restaurants, cinemas, musicals and much more. As an example, the Liceu, as well as hosting concerts and operas for its select audience, also organised costume dances for carnival, competitions of the Real Cercle Artístic de Barcelona and charitable events for colonial causes, such as raising funds for those wounded in the African War (in Morocco in 1860), as noted by Brufrau (2015). There was also no shortage of audiences at the Palau de la Música Catalana with the Orfeò Catalá and its symphony orchestras. In 1911, the leisure options on offer were considerable. For theatres, there were the Teatro Principal, the Romea, the Tivoli, the Gran Teatro Español, the Soriano, the Novedades, the Imperio, and the Poliorama on carrer La Rambla 8. As for cinemas, these included the Kursaal cinema, the Diorama, the Cine Bohemia, the Walkyria, the Ideal on Gran Via de les Corts Catalanes 607 and the Belio-Graff movie hall on carrer de La Rambla 36–38, to name a few. In addition, the Sala Ramblas staged *zarzuelas* (Spanish light operas), the Sala Mercè had variety shows, and the Palacio de la Ilusión, the Gran Salón Doré, the Gran Café Restaurante del Tibidabo, the Gran Café Restaurante de Novedades and the Royal Restaurant were all options for an outing.

We can imagine that on some occasions the Krio Fernandino women and men, who were so wealthy and attracted by luxury, also visited the Liceu, the Palau de la Música and the other theatres, cinemas and variety halls of the city. For example, in the Gran Salón Doré numerous shows were held that were announced in *La Voz de Fernando Poo*, presumably attended by both Krio Fernandino and Catalans. Certain Fernandino citizens also showed their more eccentric side, such as Jorge Dougan who, in 1961, in a popular discotheque on the Costa Brava (Vilassar de Mar), was reported to have performed his "exotic and coloured dances", an indirect way to imply that the dancer was black and that his performance was able to captivate spectators.[77]

Logically, access to these shows was not afforded to everyone. The Equatorial Guineans who had arrived from the mid-1940s to study or receive training in certain professions had much more limited purchasing power, meaning their leisure outings would consist more of meetings with friends and long strolls through famous Barcelona neighbourhoods.

There were also well-known photography houses that took portraits of people and families for posterity, a luxury service that few could easily access, including most Spaniards. As an example, Rafael Areñas, who was the photographer of the Spanish kings and the Royal Order, but who also worked on commission, photographed the Barleycorn family in Barcelona, as stated on the card that Amelia Barleycorn's descendant, Amalia, has kept and treasured, the only evidence remaining of the photo that was attached to it. It is proof of the high standard of living and circles in which Amelia mingled alongside other Fernandino during her stay in the city.

Furniture manufacturers also offered pieces made from noble woods such as walnut at high prices. For example, in 1911 the manufacturer La Permanente sold dining tables at 20 pesetas each, at 30 pesetas a dozen chairs, mirrored cabinets at 110 pesetas and upholstered saddles with support at 80 pesetas. There were also popular establishments trading in silks and other kinds of fabrics, such as the Las Indias warehouses on carrer Canuda.

Still in Barcelona, tension remained in the air. A research of *La Vanguardia* allows us to see that robberies and altercations were commonplace in the city. The few Africans who lived there, mainly the Krio Fernandino at first, were more often the targets of theft than altercations, as can be ascertained from a news report on the robbery of two Fernandinos who were visiting Barcelona published in *La Vanguardia* in the early 1930s.

3.4. The Krio Fernandino: trade, health and social life

The Fernandinos' arrival in Barcelona from the end of the nineteenth century came about due to diverse reasons. In all likelihood, the main stimulus was related to economic issues, both those related to the trading of their agricultural production, alongside the control they very probably wished to exercise over their fortunes deposited in European banks, since it would be highly likely that British, Catalan and Spaniard merchants paid for part of the agricultural products through bank transfers or transfers to banks in their vicinity. Yet, beyond these compelling reasons, there is no doubt that Barcelona opened to the door to another lifestyle for them, since the healthcare and education systems of their homeland had major shortcomings, not to mention the great opportunities for leisure, recreation and socialisation that the bustling metropolis offered them.

The perks afforded by Barcelona were similar in the 1940s, when Equatorial Guineans of other ethnicities, such as Bubis, Fangs, Annoboneses, Ndowes and Bissios, gradually began to arrive on the mainland. They were able travel to mainland Spain thanks to the aid established by the Spanish government for the training of civil servants and the missionary networks that welcomed students into their congregations throughout the peninsula. Of course, this group also included those Equatorial Guineans who, as a reward for the services granted to the colony, had been issued with a letter of full emancipation that offered them widespread mobility and new opportunities, as had happened with the Krio Fernandino community, by improving the rights that were automatically recognised after the establishment of the colonial regime, in their status as African Spaniards.

Next, I present what their social life in the city was like, focusing specifically on commercial issues, studies and health, as well as on the meetings that were generated around life there and their insertion in Barcelona.

Barcelona: trade, studies and health

The Barcelona of the late nineteenth and early twentieth centuries extended wide-ranging opportunities to newcomers, from both an economic and a socio-cultural standpoint, in addition to boasting a wide-ranging health and educational network. In the Fernandinos' case, as with other Equatorial Guineans who arrived later, information has been gathered that links them closely to the trading, student and healthcare fields, which will be outlined below through a series of examples that represent the majority of Krio Fernandino who went to Barcelona for any one of these reasons.

The wealthiest Krio Fernandino maintained commercial activities related to the production and export generated by their agricultural farms. In this regard, although Amelia Barleycorn had offloaded some of her properties in 1914, she continued to lead one of the wealthiest families trading in palm oil and cocoa, which can be seen from promotional materials advertising her products in Spain[78]

It is likewise worth noting that Amelia Barleycorn was one of the few women who advertised her company in the magazines (like Collins' widow). Amelia was the only woman to keep her first name and maiden name in a public-facing context, alongside the label "de Vivour" or "widow of Vivour", which was a clear proof of her vitality and strength, as recalled by her descendant Amalia Barleycorn (2021). It is more than likely that her stance influenced other Fernandinos because, in 1918, three of them travelled to Barcelona to engage in some probable commercial activity. They were the granddaughters of the landowner Maximiliano C. Jones: Mabel, Juana and Raquel.

The transnational connections between Barcelona and Santa Isabel were constant. An example was the numerous advertisements that were published in *La Voz de Fernando Poo*, a magazine published entirely in Catalonia, in which the Krio Fernandino and Catalans promoted the most standout agricultural estates on the island. To highlight only a few advertisements from 1914, mention should be made those of Rolando Barleycorn (Owner and Exporter of Fruits of the Country, Santa Isabel, Fernando Poo) and of the Widow of Collins and Son (Harvesters and Exporters of domestically produced fruits, Santa Isabel, San Carlos, Concepción, Fernando Poo). Certain Krio Fernandino, namely José W. Dougan, diversified their interests, offering not only agricultural products and their trading, but also clothing or products for personal use, most of which were presumably bought in Barcelona and shipped to Santa Isabel.

A resounding exception among the advertisers was Maximiliano C. Jones. He represented the most outstanding member of the first generation of his lineage, an influence that remained until his death, and was a figure who undoubtedly took over from Amelia Barleycorn de Vivour as holding the greatest Fernandino fortune since the 1910s. Over the years, specifically from 1950 onwards, other farmers, both of Fang and Bubi origin, would visit Barcelona or Madrid to maintain commercial contacts, although the great fortunes of Spanish Africans had by then lost the opportunity to enrich themselves further, since big business was already inexorably in the hands of Spaniards.

It should be said, unreservedly, that one of the Krio Fernandino most committed to extending their commercial activity to Barcelona since the early twentieth century was Manuel Balboa. Proof of this is that twenty-five years after founding Casa Balboa in Santa Isabel, the business announced it would be opening its commercial headquarters in Barcelona: "Manuel Balboa (House Founded in 1890), Exporter of Domestically Produced Fruits, Cocoa Plantations... Office in Barcelona Modolell 47."[79]

Regarding the education system, it is of the utmost importance to note that many Krio Fernandino families sent some of their sons and daughters to Barcelona from the end of the nineteenth century onwards, as other Equatorial Guineans would later do from the 1950s. In many cases the students were sent to Madrid, but also to other cities, including Barcelona, as will be touched upon further in the coming section.

The first Krio Fernandino family to send descendants to study in Barcelona at the end of the nineteenth century was the Barleycorns. As I have already mentioned, Amelia Barleycorn's brother, William Napoleon Barleycorn, studied there in 1884 and 1889, after enrolling in England and elsewhere. This choice must have been triggered by the change of hegemony on the island of Fernando Poo, which shifted from English to Spanish. Other members of the family would also study in Barcelona, as was the case of Ricardo Barleycorn Macfoy, son of Rolando Barleycorn and Isabel Macfoy, who obtained his bachelor's degree at the Salmerón Institute of Barcelona in 1934.

The study of the documentation also corroborates the schooling in Barcelona of different members of the Jones family since 1910. It is known that in November 1915 Eduardo Jones returned to Santa Isabel after having completed his studies in Barcelona, where, in addition, three more daughters were studying. Amongst the nephews of Maximiliano Jones, Adolfo Jones Welah, born in San Carlos in 1903, was sent to Barcelona for secondary school in 1918, when he was fifteen years of age. He ultimately completed his studies of Industrial Engineering at Terrassa. Adolfo also played hockey for the Terrassa local team and won the Spanish championship, alongside making the odd foray into boxing.[80] Adolfo Jones Welah ended up becoming President of the Council of the Province of Fernando Poo.[81]

Another of the families who relocated to Barcelona for study purposes were the Dougans. For example, Teófilo Dougan Kinson completed his baccalaureate studies in Barcelona in 1924, as stated in the list of graduates published in a news item in *La Vanguardia*.[82] Teófilo Dougan returned to Santa Isabel in 1930 and was appointed Secretary of the first and only court in the colony. Also noteworthy is Teófilo Jorge Dougan Kinson, eldest son of José Dougan and Mariana Kinson, who, having studied in Barcelona since his youth, went on to read law at the University of Barcelona in the mid-1950s, becoming the first Equatorial Guinean to practise law in Santa Isabel. He died in Barcelona in the early 1960s.

Certain members of the Collins family also studied there. For example, Eddy Collins Jones is a highly eye-opening case since it shows that some Krio Fernandino still in the 1960s chose Barcelona as their destination. In an interview (Merino, 2011), when asked about what memories he kept of his childhood in Africa, Eddy Collins Jones answered "summers in Malabo, in the big house, and the wild landscape. During the colonial era, my parents were wealthy, meaning my four brothers and I came to study in Barcelona."

Among the other Fernandino who studied in Barcelona or other Spanish cities was Trinidad Morgades, who, as Bolekia (2019, p. 94) recalled, was "one of the main intellectuals of Equatorial Guinea with a lengthy teaching tenure at the National University." Morgades was born in Santa Isabel in 1931 and studied for her baccalaureate in the Canary Islands and Barcelona, graduating in 1945. She entered the University of Barcelona in 1954 and graduated in 1958, returning to Spanish Guinea in 1959 to join the School of Teaching of the Ministry of Santa Isabel. After independence, she was appointed first secretary of the Embassy of Equatorial Guinea (Bolekia, 2019, p. 94).

The Fernandino citizen Juan-Manuel Davies also deserves a mention, who whenever he could, made the trip to Barcelona.

> Davies was born in Lubá in 1948, studying in Santa Isabel and the university students at the INEF in Madrid, where he qualified as a teacher of Physical Education [...] studying a master's degree in Spanish Literature at Setton Hall University in New Jersey (USA) (Bolekia, 2019, p. 100).

Still, undoubtedly the benchmark references is Juan Balboa Boneke, the writer and former politician, who was born in Rebola in 1938 and who passed away in Valencia in 2014. As Bolekia explains (2019, pp. 240–241): "He was a student at the Social School of Granada [...] In 1969 he returned to Equatorial Guinea [...] After the first elections [...] with Francisco Macías Nguema [...] Juan Balboa Boneke (returned) to Spain."

The cases discussed above show that many Krio Fernandino went to Barcelona for their studies, allowing us to demonstrate their ongoing presence in the city, which, although in all likelihood barely exceeding 1,000 people, was highly significant from the end of the nineteenth century. This shifted in the 1950s, when certain Fernandinos began to choose other cities on the peninsula, such as Madrid or Valencia, as the destination for their studies (see Table 22).

It is worth highlighting, however, that the information regarding which of the Krio Fernandinos studied and when does not allow us to capture their level of comfort or integration in Barcelona. In this regard it is of major interest to understand the daily life to which certain Krio Fernandino students were exposed.

Due to the foregoing, it is of great interest to consider the narrative of a young Fernandino, Guillermo, recovered from a letter he wrote in 1898. Guillermo sent a letter to John Thompson and, in turn, responded to a letter from him. In the letter, without stating his surname, Guillermo explained that he had been welcomed by a family from Barcelona, and although there was no direct criticism, the term he used to refer to his host – "master" – was completely hierarchical since he transferred from Santa Isabel to Barcelona the domination of the white population over the black African.

From reading the letter, it appears that the boy's father had asked the Catalan family not to unsettle his religious beliefs, questioning his Protestantism, since one of the issues that most bothered the Catalan family was that the young man had still not converted to Catholicism. Part of his narrative is reproduced in a letter dated 25 February 1898 from Barcelona, which was not published until 1918.[83]

With regard to a different sphere of life, namely health issues, the chance to travel to Barcelona to receive medical care or surgery, or to simply enjoy another climate that could improve their health, aroused the interest of many Krio Fernandino. The importance of this topic is clear if we compare the causes of death in Santa Isabel (see Table 13) with the causes of mortality in Barcelona (shown in Table 25).

In this regard, it is known that on 20 February 1906 José Walterio Dougan filed a petition requesting that a substitute member of the Consejo de Vecinos of Santa Isabel be sought so that he could travel to Barcelona (AGA, box 81/07956). This was so that he could make a trip to the mainland for six months with a view to the change improving his strength and health.

It is also known that one of Maximiliano C. Jones' three daughters, who had been studying in Barcelona since the early 1910s, had been receiving medical treatment there too. She died in 1914, as recorded in a news clipping: "The wealthy owner and renowned Fernandino citizen Maximiliano Jones laments the death of one of the three daughters enrolled in Barcelona educational establishments."[84] Seven years later, in 1921, the death of another descendant of a wealthy family in Barcelona was announced.⁸⁵ Months later it was reported that Mass had also been said for Juliana in Santa Isabel: "In the Cathedral of Santa Isabel solemn funerals have been held [...] in loving memory of Miss Juliana Dougan who died [...] in this county city [Barcelona]."⁸⁶

However, it must be said that the Krio Fernandino diaspora sought medical care and had operations not only in Barcelona, but also in other European countries. That was the case of Francisco Wilson, who went to England for treatment: "Our good friend Francisco Wilson who is shortsighted [...] has entrusted his cure to one of the greatest medical accounts in England to see whether his sight can be returned to its normal state. We hope to celebrate [...] his cure."⁸⁷

The relationship between Barcelona and Santa Isabel also took shape through football. At the beginning of the 1930s, a friendly match was held between the teams from Santa Isabel and Barcelona, photographic records of which still remain, a match that surely was planned by the Krio Fernandino who lived in Barcelona. Similarly noteworthy is that, after the 1950s, certain Fernandinos stood out in the field of sport in other Spanish cities, such as Miguel Jones, who was a footballer who played at Atlético de Madrid for the 1959–1960 season, or a minor figure such as Guillermo Jones Mookava, also a footballer at the school of Escolapios de Logroño in 1946 where he was studying.

Weddings, baptisms, recreation and into Barcelona life

The shifting of Krio Fernandino residents between Santa Isabel and Barcelona had the effect of making it easier for some of the most important social events in the community to be held in the city. Weddings and baptisms were some of the occasions on which the encounters between Krio Fernandino and Catalans became more evident, leaving behind photographic proof of the guests who attended the event in some of the great religious buildings and hotels of the city, such as the Cathedral of Barcelona or the exclusive Majestic, Inglaterra or Ritz hotels. The news reports of the time explained the exclusive nature of the *amuse-bouches*, the luxury and the undoubted renown of the guests.

One of the major events involving the Krio Fernandino diaspora of the 1920s was the joining in matrimony of Esteban Rhodes and Mabel Jones. The wedding took place in the Royal Basilica of the Cathedral of Barcelona on 15 September 1921. *La Guinea Española* described it as an "aristocratic wedding" and explained:

> On 15 September, at 11 a.m. in the Royal Basilica of the Cathedral of Barcelona, the marriage of the daughter of the wealthy Fernandino Maximiliano C. Jones with the distinguished young Fernandino Mr Esteban Rhodes was held. As these were people who held a lofty position in society and were highly cultured, with whose friendship the main trading houses in Fernando Poo are honoured, the most outstanding religious ceremony in Barcelona was attended by guests that maintain or have had a relationship with our Colony of Guinea. The newlyweds delighted their friends with a hand-picked lunch served with exquisite taste [...] in Barcelona.[88]

La Guinea Española published an interesting photograph that displayed the economic power and distinction of the families joined together through this union.

The Rhodes and Jones wedding was also picked up in an item in the *La Vanguardia* society section that reported that their marriage had coincided with another wedding and that together they had assembled the most select elites of the city, making it clear that the racialisation of skin colour was of scant import when the class variable intervened. The magnificent wedding banquets were held in the halls of a famous hotel, at which the two new couples presented themselves – the newlyweds Esteban Rhodes and Mabel Jones, and Gastón Negre and Josefina Gotzens – who imprinted a character of remarkable brilliance and distinction to such distinguished links.[89]

La Voz de Fernando Poo also offered numerous details of the wedding of Esteban Rhodes and Mabel Jones,[90] pointing out that the marriage had taken place in the Cathedral of Barcelona, with celebration in a renown hotel. The report gave details of how the ceremony had gone, highlighting that Consuelo Balboa had been singing theatrical *cuplés*:

> The bride and groom then invited all their friends to a sumptuous banquet in the luxurious and aristocratic Hotel Inglaterra and in the end several toasts were made that were warmly applauded. The young people danced beautifully and even Mrs Consuelo Balboa took part in the festivities as she sang some *cuplés* admirably, showing perfect pitch and above all with a vibrant voice that aroused the admiration of those gathered there that who enthusiastically applauded. The party drew to a close at 8:00 p.m. Our congratulations to the

lords of Rhodes, a charming couple we wish in their new lives together all manner of adventures and congratulations.[91]

These three news items prove undoubtedly that the racism or contempt for Africans due to their skin colour was absent from the ceremony, since the Krio Fernandino couple was accompanied by the Fernandino community that was in Barcelona and by the standout elite of Catalan society in Barcelona holding business interests in Equatorial Guinea.

The Krio Fernandino's next big event in 1930s Barcelona was a wedding between the Jones and Dougan families, which ran similar to the Rhodes and Jones liaison. The news reached the pages of *La Vanguardia*, which did not hesitate to include it in its photographic summary of 13 May 1932.[92] The newlyweds were Susana Dougan and Alfredo Jones Níger, surrounded by the Catalan *haute bourgeoisie*. The caption of the photograph was highly illustrative: *"Boda colonial"* (Colonial Wedding).

The wedding feast was held at the Hotel Ritz and because of the photograph taken at the ceremony, all the guests, both Catalans and Krio Fernandino, wanted to pose to preserve the moment for eternity. For many of the Catalans, it must have been quite a surprise to see an African couple surrounded by upper-class Catalans, including the maids of honour. Dougan and Jones were a clear example of how intersectionality could overcome the race biases grounded on skin colour that were highly relevant at that same time in another place, Santa Isabel.

Alfredo Jones Níger took the opportunity to explain his cherished relationship with Barcelona on the occasion of the homage to him at the Hotel Ritz on 17 June 1963. In addition to Alfredo Jones Níger and his wife Susana Dougan, other Fernandinos, such as Alfredo Jones and Maximiliano Jones (their sons), Aurora Jones, Daniel Jones, Trinidad Collins and Manuel Morgades, had been invited to the hotel. Among the attendees, mostly from the Catalan bourgeoisie, were the Chair of the Spanish Guinea Foundation, Juan Domènech Viñas, with other Catalans such as Francisco-Javier Pérez Portabella, Deputy Chair of the Spanish Guinea Foundation, Enrique Roselló Pons, Primitivo Ruíz de Villa, Francisco Recasens Musté, Rev. Joaquín María Girvent Canet, Manuel Gallego Prats, Teresa Ràfols Teixidó, and the widow of Jover, amongst others.

Photographs of the meeting showed the diners seated at a banquet, African Spaniards alternating with the rest of the guests, all elegantly dressed.

Figure 5. Report on the Tribute to Mr Alfredo Jones Níger together with Susana Dougan in the Ritz Hotel in 1963. Open Source Guinea.

In Alfredo Jones Níger's speech, he recalled the Krio Fernandino diaspora of the past before an audience that knew perfectly the role they had played and what they had meant for the colonisation of Spanish Guinea: "Maximilian, Dougan, Balboa, Kinson, Collins, etc., are in the memory of many of you."[93] The Hotel Ritz was the establishment in which Alfredo Jones Níger was married, and which was often frequented not only by the wealthiest Fernandinos, but also by Catalan businessmen of the Casa de la Guinea Española (House of Spanish Guinea) to host celebrations of all kinds. That day, Alfredo Jones Níger recalled that some of his children had been born in Barcelona, and that two of his sisters had lived and died there as well. His words reflected what many other African Spaniards of Krio Fernandino origin living there felt about in the city:

> This affection and constant relationship had its reciprocity in the natives of my land. The few who have so far achieved academic degrees of different rank – doctors, lawyers, etc. – here they studied and here they were trained for their struggle in life, without at any time being made to notice their difference in colour as an unavoidable defect. As far as I am concerned, I must say that if I did not study in this city, this was due to the fact that at the time my profession

was lacking a School that issued the corresponding official titles of Agricultural Experts; but my affection for Barcelona I have shown in a resounding way: here we were wed, in this same hotel – odd coincidence –; here one of my daughters was born who has honoured in the confines of our home and between as the relatives "the Catalan", and here were educated others [...] Here also two of my sisters paid due tribute to the earth, who in their last moments were cared for as if the carers were treating their very own.[94]

Like weddings, burials also took on the role of other social events. Starting with our main character, I must point out that there is no record of the events that were organised surrounding the death of Amelia Barleycorn de Vivour on 3 January 1920 in Barcelona. Her death certificate states that she had died in the city of Barcelona, in the district of Sant Gervasi, at 10.30 am and that the certificate was issued before Mr Enrique del Puig i Jorda, Municipal Judge, and Javier Millas i Horta, Secretary, also citing Mr José Genodia, a native of the city, whose registered address is given as carrer Menéndez Pelayo 133, as owner of the rented house in which "Mrs Amelia Barleycorn, a native of Santa Isabel, Fernando Poo, had died as a result of cardiac arrest while at home." The death certificate also stated that:

> the deceased was the widow of Mr Guillermo Vivour, a native of Sierra Leone, with whom she had a daughter named Isabel, a child who was the legitimate daughter of Guillermo and Amelia, deceased, natives of Santa Isabel, of whom it is unknown whether she left a will and that her body should be buried in the cemetery of Les Corts (Barcelona).

The document was signed by the five men present, and it was recorded that her neighbours, "W. Enrique Piferrer, married, and W. Federico García, residents of this city, employees, of legal age", had acted as eye-witnesses. Regarding the servants under Amelia Barleycorn's employ, there was no mention to them, meaning it is not known whether it was actually her neighbours who provided all the personal information on the deceased, since the officials surely would never have known this. One hundred years later, the Barcelona tomb in which the mortal remains of Amelia Barleycorn lay must have ceased to be occupied by her, since the non-payment of municipal taxes in Barcelona always entails the process of withdrawal or seizure of property, whether rented or owned, to be deposited in a mass grave. It is therefore a shame that nowhere in the city is there any evidence of her time in Barcelona.

In February 1920, *La Guinea Española* announced the death in Barcelona of "the aristocratic Amelia Barleycorn de Vivour" in which the condolences were given to the family and their companies,[95] the editor acknowledging he learned of her death through the obituary published in *La Voz de Fernando Poo*. With her death, the heiress to the greatest fortune of Spanish Guinea in 1890 had ceased to be.

Although remembered by the descendants of her brothers, especially William Napoleon, no monument was erected in her memory in Fernando Poo like the one she had erected to her late husband William Allen Vivour.

Many decades later, other Barleycorns would make their way into the Barcelona press. As an example, we can recall the two Barleycorn Boricó brothers, George Armando and Ricardo Emilio Barleycorn Boricó, who died in a car accident in August 1988 and whose funeral rites and burials were held jointly. Other deaths of prominent members of the Krio Fernandino diaspora were some Dougans. We can highlight in particular the death of José Walterio Dougan McCarthy in 1947, because, although it occurred in Santa Isabel, it was stated that a Mass would be held in his honour in Barcelona. The obituary remembered his children Lorenza, Theophilus, Joseph and Susana.

However, the deepest interaction with the Catalan community came from a Balboa. Manuel Balboa During admitted to living in Barcelona when *La Guinea Española* published its potted biography in 1928. That same year, the regulation on the letter of emancipation of the Equatorial Guinean population had finally been approved. The Claretian missionary Ruiaz (1928) devoted a biography to him. Ruiaz believed that having a flat in the city gave grandeur his country, although he recalled that Balboa's success was due to his "indigenous activity", showing the reader that no matter how Spanish he was by birth, all those born in colonial lands would remain Africans in the eyes of the Spanish population. Certainly, the Balboas had their home on the emblematic calle La Rambla de Catalunya 26. Manuel Balboa was married to Isabel Arkins Bruch, who was born in Santa Isabel (1873–1933). His son, Abilio Balboa Arkins, was born in Barcelona in 1906 and died in Barcelona in 1967. His sons were also Consuelo and Manuel Balboa Arkins. Abilio Balboa Arkins is remembered for being elected mayor of Santa Isabel in 1961, replacing Jones Níger, and as Procurator in the Spanish courts during the Franco regime. Among some of his descendants based in Barcelona and other Spanish cities, we can highlight Armando Balboa Dougan, son of Abilio Balboa Arkins, who was born and died in Santa Isabel (1931–1969) and was a famous politician and footballer who spent some years in Barcelona studying at the prestigious La Salle Bonanova. We can also mention Armando Balboa Dougan, who married the Catalan Núria Mercè, with whom he had five children in a mixed marriage that was popular in the city. Armando Balboa Dougan's brother Norberto was also the grandfather of footballer Javier Balboa.

Certain news reports in the 1960s praised the relationship between Barcelona and Fernando Poo, as well as the knowledge of the Catalan language shown by the Krio Fernandino:

> I remember with satisfaction that in the field of sports [...] I started to speak in Catalan with several *moreno* Fernandino players who, in a way, feel the nostalgia of the happy years that they spent in the Barcelona. There was Theophilus Dougan! This is Mr Abilio Balboa, mayor of Santa Isabel! Mr Luís Maho, Minister of Finance of the Autonomous Government! [...] Fernando Poo's coconut trees are as welcoming as the old trees of the Barcelona Rambles.[96]

3.5. Barcelona, missionary actions and student intake aimed at Equatorial Guineans

The first missionary expedition arrived in Santa Isabel in 1856. The missionaries were slow to establish themselves since the mortality of the Jesuit fathers who were then deployed was particularly high and did not allow for widespread evangelising and scholastic expansion. The first Claretian mission was in 1883 and the first expedition of women missionaries was of the Daughters of the Immaculate Conception in 1884. It was explained that they "would be the first Spanish women who made their residence on such deadly soil [...] with the conquest of so many souls who in the space of 35 years we have won for God."[97] The most influential Catholic missions in Fernando Poo were Catalan and male, specifically the Claretian order. Among its objectives was to educate the population in order to spread the Catholic faith, along with Spanish language and culture. The Claretians were the first colonial agents to engage in the Hispanisation of the population (Fernández-Moreno, 2018). In 1905, the Claretian missionary connection between the island of Fernando Poo and Barcelona led them to receive alms from Catalan "benefactors" so that the missionaries could admit "indigenous children" as students in their Fernando Poo schools and thus educate them. The trips made by the Krio Fernandino and other Fernandino citizens to study in Barcelona, as discussed above, bore no relation to these missionary channels that were activated between Spanish Guinea and Barcelona.

Equatorial Guineans studying in Barcelona

The missions and select individuals took the initiative to move Equatorial Guineans to the Iberian Peninsula from the mid-nineteenth century, either to work for them or to study under their protection. The Spanish state facilitated these trips from 1930 but with a reduced offer of scholarships that, over the years, gradually increased, since the cases prior to that decade were merely anecdotal.

In the documentation consulted, one of the first cases on an Equatorial Guinean who was taken to the peninsula with an evangelising mission has been unearthed. It was a fifteen-year-old Bubi boy who missionaries brought to the mainland in 1888 in order to baptise him. The missionaries were the Sons of the Immaculate Heart of Mary and explained after finding him "in the Fernandino forest" in a state of "utter savagery", they "picked him up and instructed him", having decided to take him to the mainland (Matas, 1890, p. 74). He was baptised as Mariano Cristino Santiago. The young man was sponsored by the Queen Regent herself, who appointed the Marquis of Quintanar to be her representative at the ceremony officiated by the Herald of His Holiness in Madrid on 25 June 1888. In the news report, it was explained that the Church of Saints Justus and Shepherd was overflowing "with a multitude of people of all social classes, who crowded to contemplate an event so seldom seen in this court" (Matas, 1890, pp. 73–74), which was said to be good proof of the exceptionality of the occasion. This version of events has great similarities to the exotisation of Africans in colonial propaganda, as the boy was torn from his family to be taken to the mainland where he suffered a public exhibition similar to that of the Senegalese in the Tibidabo Park in Barcelona in 1913. Other cases of Equatorial Guineans brought to Spain occurred from the first decade of 1910 under missionary auspices.

Certainly, the colonial authorities were gradually raised that the civilisational rhetoric of Africa should be accompanied by facts. Awareness of this led to an arrival route being set up to promote the academic training of select Equatorial Guineans, using ecclesiastical routes and remaining under the responsibility of the Spanish missions.

An internal note of 1915 illustrated this concern about the first experiences of the transfer of young Equatorial Guineans to the mainland to embark upon educational training. It was proposed that the implementation of scholarships should consider the basic needs of clothing, health and supplies, proposing that they be accommodated in private homes, if the option of student residences was not possible.

Below, an extract from the internal note is reproduced to gauge the type of issues that the colonial authorities feared in relation to encouraging Equatorial Guineans to study in mainland Spain:

> The first consideration that I had to have with the indigenous people [...] to avoid physical disturbances due to the abrupt change of climate [...] To avoid moral responsibilities [...] as soon as they arrived, it could be observed that it was absolutely necessary to provide them with interior and exterior clothes to protect them from the cold because the clothes they were wearing were much more appropriate for tropical countries. In due time, the necessary steps were taken to install them in the most appropriate centres and schools [...] [including] a private home that offered all the guarantees for good treatment and proper supervision. Newly arrived at the Court [...] it was observed that one of the girls was unwell [...] a fatal outcome was feared. Thanks to the effective assistance of the Sisters of Charity, the sick woman was able to recover and devote herself fully to her studies. Due to this circumstance [...] there was a need to cover the most essential expenses such as travel, clothing, pensions to the Colleges, doctors, medicines, and sundry items that are detailed in the attached account of 4,123 pesetas (signed on 31 December 1915).[98]

The cases disclosed in this note were followed by others. For example, a document dated 13 May 1918 gave an account of four indigenous people whose studies were funded by the colony.

For this book, I have focused especially on the dossier of Pilar Momo, as she studied at the School of the Sagrada Familia in Barcelona. As will be seen, one of the major concerns of the missionary orders was who was going to bear the students' expenses. It would seem that the missionary channels were activated since they were financed by the Spanish state, as happened with their missionary work in Africa that was always charged to the budgets of the colony.

Thus, as stated in a letter dated 20 April 1925 from the Secretary of the Ministry of State addressed to the Authorising Officer of the Colonial Section, it was said that:

> Given the accounts submitted by the College of the Sagrada Familia established in Barcelona, where she is enrolled on a Teacher Training Course [...] a native of Fernando Poo, Pilar Momo, corresponding to the last quarter of the current economic year funding needs 932.50 pesetas [...] The remaining amount available to meet the aforementioned account amounts to 484.50 pesetas, therefore 447.05 pesetas are missing [...] It is perfectly understood that the amount of the credit has been exceeded since both the girl and the *moreno* who receive instructions in [...] this Court [...] and who also are also studying [...] for their National Master's [...] have completed their high school education in two years [...] Pilar Momo will definitely finish her studies in this course, meaning that in July at the latest she will embark for her native country, and there will be no other expenses to be paid (AGA, box 81/07032).

The documentation also makes it possible to reconstruct the details of the expenses incurred by the student Pilar Momo in June 1924 in Barcelona (see Table 27). Her monthly pension was 300 pesetas, which had to cover absolutely everything she needed in terms of clothes, change of sheets, doctors, etc.

Over the decades, the presence of Equatorial Guinean students in Barcelona increased. In addition to the cases already mentioned, certain others who were trained in Barcelona returned to Spanish Guinea to occupy positions of greater responsibility. Such was the case of Pilar Momo, who would become a symbol for the Equatorial Guinean population after her studies in Spain; Gaspar Gomán, a professor at the School of Fine Arts of Santa Isabel; and Manuel Morgades, an official of the Spanish Guinea Regional Government.

At the beginning of the 1960s, Equatorial Guinean students still had no space of their own for meetings and information in Barcelona despite the pleas they had made to the Spanish Guinean Foundation, which were disregarded since its interests were purely commercial, "rather than social or cultural".[99] Founded after the Civil War, its mission was to promote Catalan and Spanish investments in the colony, not to provide meeting facilities and help to the Equatorial Guinean population who studied in the city.

Table 27. Annual study expenses of an Equatorial Guinean girl in the Sagrada Familia College in Barcelona, 1921 (in pesetas)

Enrolment fees (course)	30
Monthly pension (quarter)	300
Monthly wash	22
Monthly class	80
2 uniform aprons	34
6 sheets	30
4 pillowcases	12
2 white bedspreads	21
Fleece blanket + 1 cotton blanket	30
6 towels	12
6 napkins + 2 napkin holders	13
1 blanket	12
4 shirts at 7 pesetas each	28
4 pair of stockings at 3 pesetas each	12
4 underwear at 7 pesetas each	28
4 T-shirts at 6 pesetas each	24
2 underskirts at 6 pesetas each	12
6 handkerchiefs	6
3 round-trip second class tickets and other expenses in a 24-hour journey for two people and return for 1 person	298.75
Total	1,004.75

Source: Compiled by the author. Informe en Madrid del 5 de octubre de 1921 AGA, box 81/07032 "Gastos de indígenas en la metrópolis, 1916–1925."

A news story published in *La Vanguardia* of 30 October 1966 reported on the visit to Barcelona of three illustrious Equatorial Guinean figures. The clipping hints at their roots in the city and the fact that some of them had studied there years ago. The article talks of Luís José Maho Sicachá, and says: "Mr Maho is linked to Barcelona for many reasons, he was here for ten years. He completed his baccalaureate and law degree in our educational centres, while his brother, now director of Health of Guinea, studied medicine."[100]

3.6. Krio Fernandino intersectionality: class, gender and race

The application of the concept of intersectionality to Fernandino women explains that belonging to a social class could neutralise the gender and race variables that encouraged the marginalisation of black women, since both racialisation based on skin colour and the sexual hierarchy that reduced women to the family sphere were deactivated. In all truth, racialisation and sexism were a constant presence on the Iberian Peninsula and in the overseas colonies, although it was unknown that there had been African women who in the late nineteenth century subverted stereotypes in certain Iberian cultures, such as the Catalan, through their stays in Barcelona.

In the next section, I will consider how Krio Fernandino women were viewed in the colony in order to demonstrate the shock that their image generated with respect to colonial rhetoric. I will then review a selection of examples of their presence in Barcelona and the encounters that arose between the Fernandino and Catalan bourgeoisie during the first third of the twentieth century.

Fernandino women as a counterpoint to colonial rhetoric

During the late nineteenth and early twentieth centuries, Spain was clearly androcentric, resulting from its sexual expectations that placed men above women, on the basis that the latter were confined to the family sphere (Nash, 1983). Leadership, decision-making and power were understood to be eminently male (Rosaldo, 1979; Maccormack, 1998). These androcentric standpoints were also standard in other European countries (Stolcke, 1996). It should be noted that these stereotypes did not consider that a middle- or upper-class European woman could have more power and autonomy than a man of the same or a lower social class (Creshaw, 1995). The assessment was even more complicated for African women, because in addition to sexism, there was the impact of colonialism (Walsh, 2018) that detracted from the significance of the African collective, all without considering that the authority of many African women – whether due to matricentric preferences, wealth or community leadership – was not in question in African communities (Amadiume, 2018).

Reviewing the references that have been preserved of Krio Fernandino women with this deeply male-focused grounding is indeed eye-opening. The scant travellers, military servicemen and explorers of the nineteenth century who made any mention of them failed to comment on anything beyond their sumptuous dresses, their elegance and their polite manners.

With regard to the missionaries, no account was written about them, although they did appear in some of the social news clippings of colonial times, as well as in the news that thanked them for their generosity to the Catholic orders with missions in Fernando Poo or for the odd donation they made of money or objects, as was the case, for example, of the words they dedicated to Amelia Barleycorn.

This shortage in terms of direct descriptions of the Krio Fernandino women brings us to the similarities that were dedicated to Fernandino men, praise that voiced their qualities as approaching those of European cultures. To illustrate this issue, I will use the note published by Father Ruiaz (1928) in *La Guinea Española* about the Fernandino Joaquín Salomé. Ruiaz was eloquent in his description, making it clear that, even for the missionaries destined for the colonies, the ways of the Fernandinos constituted an exception among the African populations, and this despite the animosity they had towards those who had not yet replaced the Protestant religion with the Catholic one.

For Ruiaz (1928, p. 84), Salome was "the kind of honest gentleman, good Christian, humanitarian and serious, of which the Europeans of his time said, that their moreno went no further than their colour", a way of explaining that the only thing "African" about them was their blackness . As can be seen, the Eurocentric narratives grouped chivalry, honesty, Christianity, humanitarianism and seriousness as European values, suggesting that the antonyms would be defined by the values that summarised the rest of Africans. These people, viewed as "savages" and "atheists", were stripped of those qualities with an orientalist perspective that, as I have explained, inverted the qualities of the European ego in the defects of the African otherness. It was clear that the colonial rhetoric that they had put into circulation to justify the occupation and that denigrated the African did not apply in the same way to the Fernandinos.

These issues related to European androcentrism and Eurocentrism are vital for understanding how disturbing the power and authority held by Krio Fernandino women was for many Catalans and Spaniards, both in Santa Isabel and in Barcelona, since some Spanish should not be able to easily hide their impotence in the face of the inferiority complex that the encounters with the Fernandino had to cause them. In a general sense, they proved to be somewhat self-reliant in their transcontinental movements, with their multi-sited residence and with their continuous contacts with the transnational family located in other countries of Central and West Africa. In addition, their social class was very high and became highly visible both in the way they dressed and their livelihoods, and in the fact of travelling to other continents alone or with their own domestic servants.

As we will see in the next section, their very existence was a real counterpoint to discourses that undervalued African women on the grounds of race or geographical origin.

Encounters between the Krio Fernandino and the Catalan bourgeoisies

An example of the transcontinental mobility, independence and wealth of Fernandino women in Barcelona can be seen in the local note published by *La Vanguardia* on 3 March 1911. The text explained the theft inflicted on two Fernandino women, one from the Balboa family and one from the Joneses, of a significant sum of money during their stay in Barcelona. The status and wealth of both must have surprised the editor of the newspaper, but not so much the readers, who would have gathered from the surnames, one denoting Cuban heritage and the other English, that the unfortunate persons involved were foreigners, given that the editor highlighted the skin colour of their servants, but not theirs, as he probably considered it an unsavoury detail. The note explained that the robbery had been perpetrated by one of the women's own servants in the upper area of the city:

> Two ladies named Isabel Balboa and Raquel Jones, both of legal age, married and residents in a house on carrer Ballester, reported yesterday to the authorities

that during the previous night two squat black men had disappeared who had been employed as servants in their house, taking 1,100 pesetas in bank notes. They only know that one of them was named Soke and the other Fidel, aged 20 and 11 years old, respectively.[101]

It is likely that the robbery of these two great heiresses was supplemented by the solidarity of other Fernandinos in the city or of the Catalan bourgeoisie with whom their families had business in Santa Isabel. The two "servants" of these Krio Fernandino, one a minor, were described as "two little black" lads, although we do not know whether this was the description of the editor or the Fernandino. This detail cannot be disregarded, since it shows the complex process of racialisation or de-racialisation of people that can occur in a given context and simultaneously. If that was the literal description provided by the women, it would show that racialisation incorporated the class variable, since the Fernandinos were also black, but they excluded themselves as such, leaving blackness as a label for those who were in a situation of dependence and belonged to an inferior social class. If the news report was written by a journalist, in contrast, it would show that, for him, the Krio Fernandino women were aristocratic and as such should not be considered "black", unlike their servants.

The aim of including this anecdote is to summarise the major challenge of class, race and gender posed by the presence of the Afropolitan Krio Fernandino women in Barcelona at the beginning of the twentieth century. Their status as women, African, black and rich synthesised a means of understanding and moving around the world, in a process of (de)racialisation through skin colour that would vary depending on who was the issuer of the message and the purpose behind it: they would racialise the servants, or the journalist would de-racialise the Krio Fernandino by racialising the servants. As proof that it was not typical to de-racialise those appearing in the stories if they were lower-class blacks, we can quote from another news item from 1909, in which it was explained that the police had arrested "a black accused of being the perpetrator of the wounds inflicted a few days ago on an individual."[102]

Besides the above, the high standard of living of the Krio Fernandino community who visited or lived in Barcelona led them to reside in upper-class neighbourhoods, as recorded in many of the postal addresses they had since the early twentieth century. It should borne in mind, merely as an example, that the two Fernandino women who had been robbed during their stay in Barcelona were housed in carrer Ballester, located in a very exclusive area of Barcelona, near the Putxet Park, an area that constituted the über-elite and well-to-do outskirts of the Catalan bourgeoisie. This inescapably linked neighbourhood brought together many Fernandino and Catalans with evident interests in Spanish Guinea, both in Barcelona and in Fernando Poo.

In this regard, certain details of Amelia Barleycorn's death certificate of 1920 are highly illustrative, since she lived in the exclusive district of Sant Gervasi at the time. Just as an example, it can be mentioned that the company La Barcelonesa in San Carlos, which was very close to the landholdings she ran in Fernando Poo and which was owned by Sebastián Torres, had its registered office at Passeig Sant Gervasi 42. It was also a significant detail that, on the death certificate, the witnesses who signed it were "two residents" who had been called, as stated in the document, and not any direct family member who was at home, nor any Fernandino who resided at that time in Barcelona, nor even the domestic servants that surely accompanied Amelia and could attest to her being at home. This fact suggests, on the one hand, that the death of Amelia was clearly unforeseen, because otherwise she would have been accompanied by family and friends, and that, on the other, these two residents would have exchanged visits with Amelia in their homes as contained in the personal details that were included in the aforementioned document. Also, in this regard, note that the judge who drafted the certificate decided to exclude the testimonies of the very likely African domestic servants who were by her side. Thus, they sought out Catalan citizens, despite the fact that there were numerous cases of Krio Fernandino families who travelled to Barcelona with domestic servants.

All these data bring us closer to a reality in which Eurocentric racism and European androcentrism expressed through skin colour and the African condition and the female gender of our central characters were neutralised by the variable of social class.

That said, an essential question is how Krio Fernandino women were perceived by Catalan society. Although the answer is uncertain, it is very likely that in the first third of the twentieth century the Krio Fernandino men in Barcelona consolidated their relations with Catalans with greater stability and speed than the women, and that, therefore, the variables of class, gender and race benefited them compared to Fernandino women.

I labour this point because, as I have explained, the demands of Catalan women to attain equal rights to those enjoyed by men were notable at the beginning of the twentieth century, gaining the right to vote in 1932, in addition to the fact that businesses and family businesses were spearheaded by the male head of the family, rather than their women, something that was also happening among the Krio Fernandino families. These indications allow us to suppose that the most conservative Catalan families may have felt very uncomfortable at the prospect of their daughters being influenced by the young Fernandinos, and that these Catalan families may have been opposed to their sons socialising or even marrying such autonomous Fernandino women, who, no matter how wealthy Spanish Africans were, had it working against them that they were of African origin, and either *moreno* or black, as per by the vocabulary used at that time in both mainland Spain and the colony to denote the non-"white" population.

These aspects would encourage the Krio Fernandino women to bolster in Barcelona a core of closer relations with other Fernandino women, rather than Catalan women, not to mention that the Fernandino community was particularly inbred and that, aware of their class, they neither sought nor planned the union of their daughters to young members of the Catalan bourgeoisie. In this regard, it should be noted that, of course, there were mixed unions such as that of Manuel Balboa or George Armando Barleycorn Boricó, but that these became more common with the passage of time and as the Krio Fernandino become more established in Barcelona, not at the peak of their power in Santa Isabel. That is the approach also developed by the Annobonese Ávila Laurel (2022) in his novel, because its protagonist interacts with the Krio Fernandino and not so much with the Catalans.

On the other hand, the more formal meetings between the Fernandino and Catalan communities remain to be briefly explained. In previous sections, I have already pointed out that the Fernandino bourgeoisie maintained close economic and commercial ties with the Catalan bourgeoisie, which fostered their interaction in Santa Isabel and Barcelona.

I examine these issues concerning their mutual commercial interests to recall that the links between the Krio Fernandino and Catalans were expressed both in Spanish Guinea and in Barcelona. Therefore, it is no surprise that numerous events were held in the city combining the two geographical contexts, although when news reports mentioned "the Equatorial Guinean colony" they referred to the Catalans who had interests and businesses in Spanish Guinea and not to the Fernandino people who visited or resided in the city.

The issues reviewed here allow us to see that the elite status of the Krio Fernandino as Spaniards allowed them to travel to Europe before the letter of emancipation of 1928 was approved, leading a very comfortable life. It was thus the class variable that limited the effects of racism that they may have suffered in Barcelona. Fernandino women, therefore, broke through the barriers of the time in terms of class, gender and race. This advantage was lost with the decline of the economic status the Krio Fernandino enjoyed, meaning their arrival in the city at the end of the nineteenth century merged with the rest of Equatorial Guinean groups arriving on the peninsula in the 1950s.

3.7. Spain's collective amnesia post-1968 and the onset of racism during the 1990s

Gilroy (2004, p. 109) claims that modern histories of European countries such as Spain could be used to construct arguments "amid the rubble of their colonial expanses" that gave consistent responses to immigration, as their difficulties in acknowledging the sorrow "left by their imperial conquests and adventures were becoming" evident.

Certainly, after the colonial independence of Equatorial Guinea, the Spanish state did not activate mechanisms to recognise and repair its colonial past in Africa, instead plunging into a deep colonial amnesia. The Krio Fernandino and Equatorial Guinean imprints were erased from Iberian peninsular history, just as they disappeared from Catalan society which forgot the intercultural coexistence that made its presence felt in Barcelona for more than a century.

Below reasons that explains why the connection between Barcelona and Santa Isabel was forgotten, alongside the upsurge in racism that took place during the 1990s.

Clean slate and colonial memory

As we have seen throughout this book, the settlement of African Spaniards in Barcelona was constant since the late nineteenth century. The period between 1890 and 1940 was marked by the arrival of the Krio Fernandino diaspora, but from the mid-1940s, with some exceptions, Equatorial Guineans also began to arrive to study or enrol in ecclesiastical institutions. From the mid-1950s until the colonial independence of Equatorial Guinea in 1968, communities such as the Fang, the Annobonese or the Ndowe had a more modest presence in Barcelona, although not the Bubis, who settled both in Barcelona and in Madrid, Valencia and Bilbao, partly due to their proximity to the Fernandino. The arrival of Equatorial Guineans further increased a few years before decolonisation for study, work or to visit the country. Barcelona had ceased to be the standout destination and other cities in the Community of Madrid, the Valencian Community, Galicia, the Basque Country and Extremadura became more popular.

Colonial independence completely changed the relationship that until then had been maintained between Equatorial Guineans and Catalans and Spaniards. The island of Fernando Poo, renamed Bioko, and its capital, Malabo, had been the main link. Once the perks that allowed the Catalans and Spaniards to enrich themselves at the expense of colonisation, through landholdings that did not belong to them, paying wages and salaries that represented a miniscule percentage of what the whites received – whether Catalans, Spaniards or other Europeans had come to an end (see Table 10) most had decided to leave.

The newcomers to Spain had to settle in a country that had been disseminating colonial rhetoric against the African populations for more than a hundred years. This, together with the colonial memory that led Spain into what Rizo (2012) has labelled state-promoted amnesia, had the effect of propelling the Krio Fernandino collective into irrelevance, and therefore the Equatorial Guineans faced the same fate, encountering the racism that began to emerge strongly at the end of the 1980s.

The Spanish situation was not far removed from that of other old European countries. A process was triggered that authors such as Balibar and Wallerstein (1992) have described as racialisation of immigration, something that Taguieff (1987) also questioned in the French context when he pointed out that prejudices were hindering the integration of the African and Muslim population, problems very similar to those that also occurred in Great Britain (Baumann, 1999). As Blanchard and Bancel (1998) pointed out, with postcoloniality the status of Africans changed, moving from the category of "indigenous" to that of "immigrants".

Spain shifted from declaring Equatorial Guinea a *materia reservada* (reserved matter), an information restriction that extended from

January 1971 to October 1976, prohibiting any information about the country (Iyanga Pendi, 2021, p. 690; Rizo, 2024), to maintaining a complete silence on its colonial past in Equatorial Guinea, while the former colony fell into irrelevance in the history of Spain under the yoke of the respective dictatorships of Macías Nguema and Obiang Nguema. The first swept the country and the second survived thanks to a corrupt and kleptocratic system that revolves around oil extraction.

The consequence of the lack of interest in reviewing the past in Spanish Guinea was to make Equatorial Guinean voices known.[103]

Therefore, so it is that the contrast between the testimonies of African Spanish men and women who lived in Spanish Guinea and voices of the Equatorial Guinean women and men are being revealed. This directly affects Euro-African cultural heritage since it is observed that the memories of Spaniard and Catalan settlers continue to conform to the historical justification that the Spanish empire put in place to defend colonisation in Africa.

These facts show that Africa's colonial past has neither been updated nor is it being influenced by renewed postcolonial memories. This is a sign of the colonial debts that states such as Spain have to face in the twenty-first century, and it is also a symptom of the continuities existing between European imperial logics and their cultural stereotypes, since the lack of self-criticism has consequences for the consideration that many African communities in Europe receive. In the end, receiving European "nationalities" in colonial times did not help Africans, nor does it seem to help them today to be considered fully European citizens, even though this time they do have citizenship rights.

Coexistence in Barcelona: blissful ignorance

Despite the conciliatory words of Alfredo Jones Níger's speech on the day of his homage at the Hotel Ritz, in 1963, his concerns already highlighted the racism that with the passage of the time would settle in Barcelona: "in this tormented world with its problems of decolonisation on the one hand; racial discrimination on the other, generators of others as serious as in current times afflict the people of my race", although he added that "[in Spain] they have always considered the indigenous [...] as *potentially* possessors of equal duties and rights."[104] His clarification was significant. The Spanish nationality status that was granted in colonial times to the African populations was worth no more than the paper it was written on unless it went hand-in-hand with the letter of emancipation, a perk that for decades had signified the advancement of many in the Fernandino community.

Racist incidents in Barcelona began to emerge in the 1980s, although during the 1970s there had already been news of the xenophobic backlash that the Moroccan community was experiencing. *La Vanguardia* collected reports on some of the attacks, sometimes perpetrated against Africans, or people simply described as "black", and other times perpetrated by "blacks", in a stigmatisation that would ultimately encourage the criminalisation of people based on their skin colour, something that, it should be remembered, we already saw had occurred in Santa Isabel to justify a colonial order that was hierarchical, unfair and unequal. Fewer articles would be devoted to ascertaining the problems faced by migrant groups from diverse backgrounds that were already, from the 1970s onwards, multitudinous and varied.

It would be in the late 1980s that the expulsions of foreigners began in Barcelona, an episode reminiscent of the events in Santa Isabel that led to the two great mobilisations of 1920. These deportations, along with the emerging xenophobic and racist violence, resulted in a large citizen demonstration in February 1992. A news report about the demonstration pointed out that it was the first major united and massive reaction against racism in the history of Barcelona and it took place a few months before the celebration of the Olympic Games in the city. The key to the mobilisation was the involvement of organisations such as SOS Racisme, which were aware that the first Aliens Law in Spain needed urgent improvements to recognise greater rights to foreigners (Organic Law 7/1985 of 1 July on the Rights and Freedoms of Foreigners in Spain).

The resounding success of this demonstration, and of others that followed it that same year, was to offer a forceful response to a racism that did not go unchecked in the city and that was discernible in graffiti and aggressions. As an example of the initiatives to combat it, citizen institutions had reported the removal of a graffiti against "blacks" that had appeared in the district of Horta-Guinardó in 1990. In the news it was reported that several "black race" families who had settled there "had integrated very well into the borough", with some of their children playing in the Sant Genis team.[105]

One of the racist aggressions that is of particular significance for this book due to its major symbolic content occurred in the early 1990s. It was the attack on a descendant of two of the most important Krio Fernandino families in Spanish Guinea, the Balboas and the Dougans, both of which had

Table 28. Total population of Barcelona, Catalonia and Spain and proportion of resident foreigners, 1996

	Total population	Foreigners	%
Barcelona	1,508,805	43,214	2.86
Catalonia	6,090,040	114,264	1.87
Spain	39,669,394	538,984	1.35

Source: Moreras (1998, p. 59).

been established in the city since the late nineteenth and early twentieth centuries. The writer and essayist Ávila Laurel (2022) decided to start his novel with this reference as a memoir, since the work begins in a police station where its Fernandino protagonist, Valerina Vivour, a character he dreamt up between fiction and reality, is making a complaint about the racist attack inflicted on a Krio Fernandino friend of hers. Valerina's indignation is about the height of ignorance shown by a Barcelona society that does not know that this community had been hugely prestigious and influential in the past and had been living in the city for more than eighty years.

The attack that inspired Ávila Laurel's book was reported in the newspaper *La Vanguardia*. The first account was of an attack on "a black man" in September 1992, where it was reported that some young people had "left a man of African race half dead",[106] and the second attack on 5 June 1994 was on a man of Guinean origin. The prosecutor sought fifty years for the Lesseps Square skins.

The reports in the press highlighted Barcelona's poor memory: no one knew who the Balboas or the Dougans had been, nor that Spanish Guinea had had a close relationship with Barcelona and Spain in general, nor that these citizens had been Spanish Africans. The 1994 aggression indicated that no one remembered that the Krio Fernandino had been a highly respected and valued community in the first third of the twentieth century, nor the sumptuous parties and banquets they organised or to which they were invited.

In the 1990s, the administration put in place mechanisms to quantify what was considered a large influx of immigrants, which, in reality, remained very low as it did not reach even 3% of the total population (see Table 28).

Table 29. Foreigners residing in Barcelona, Catalonia and Spain by nationality, 1996

Barcelona	Catalonia	Spain
1. Peru 9.2%	1. Morocco 25.8%	1. Morocco 14.3%
2. Morocco 8.9%	2. France 6.8%	2. United Kingdom 12.7%
3. France 7.6%	3. Germany 6.8%	3. Germany 8.5%
4. Philippines 6.7%	4. United Kingdom 4.9%	4. Portugal 7.1%
5. Italy 6.5%	5. Peru 4.9%	5. France 6.1%
6. Germany 5.9%	6. Italy 4.7%	6. Italy 4%
7. Dominican Republic 5.8%	7. Dominican Republic 3.7%	7. Argentina 3.4%
8. United Kingdom 4.7%	8. Argentina 3.5%	8. Peru 3.3%
9. Argentina 4.3%	9. Gambia 3.5%	9. Dominican Republic 3.3%
10. China 3%	10. Philippines 3%	10. United States 2.9%
30. Equatorial Guinea 0.5%	30. El Salvador 0.4%	30. Poland 0.6%
35. Denmark 0.4%	35. Equatorial Guinea 0.3%	35. Austria 0.5%
38. Bolivia 0.3%	38. Iran 0.2%	38. Equatorial Guinea 0.4%
Total: 43,124 (100%)	Total: 114,264 (100%)	Total: 538,984 (100%)

Source: Moreras, 1998, p. 78.

The year 1996 saw the beginning of a great increase of foreign migrations to Barcelona (see Table 29), which constituted the point of departure in the Euro-African memory of the city that essayists such as Sipi (2004, 2010) fight with the circulation of migrant experiences rooted in the city from an African and women's perspective.

In the Barcelona of the late 1990s, there was no longer any trace of the historic settlement of African Spaniards, whether Krio Fernandino or Equatorial Guineans (see Table 29). The neglect of the state, the disinterest of the church and the scant data available about their stay in the colonial metropolis or the city of Barcelona, which even the experts on migrations to Spain managed to overlook, led to an unforgiveable oblivion that erased the traces of entire generations of Equatorial Guineans, while the current migrants seem to have to beg for rights of residence and nationality that decades before had marked them as if it were a property.

Nothing remained of the cordial atmosphere breathed by the wealthy Krio Fernandino in the bourgeois circles of Barcelona. The institutional and social racism that was so useful in oppressing Africans in the colonies reappeared, this time in seemingly democratic systems that had not put in place mechanisms to combat racialisation.

3.8. Conclusions

Regarding Amelia Barleycorn, it is worth pointing out that she travelled frequently between Africa and Europe from the end of the nineteenth century until her death in 1920, a death that was unforeseen due to a heart condition, which does not allow us to ascertain whether her wish was to die in Spanish Guinea or in Barcelona. Her mobility from Santa Isabel to Barcelona and London, and vice versa, encouraged the trips of other members of the Barleycorn and Vivour families to Barcelona to study, trade, socialise, care for their health, attend social events or simply enjoy leisure and shopping in a European city. And not only did the Barleycorns and Vivours begin that route, they were followed by the Balboas, the Dougans, the Collinses and the Joneses, families who also took Barcelona as a reference city on the mainland.

Life in the city showed that racial segregation and racialisation in the colony did not have the same daily effects as in Santa Isabel, since there was no state legislation that prohibited access to premises or services because of their skin colour, nor was the population registered with this variable, since skin colour was not what defined people's rights and duties. In this sense, life in Barcelona was less racialised and with fewer effects at the level of everyday racism than in Santa Isabel.

The choice of Barcelona was not accidental, due to the major trading interests that were forged between the two cities after the loss of the British influence on the island of Fernando Poo. Barcelona offered many advantages over Santa Isabel, however it was Amelia's connection to Africa that inspired her to build her stunning mansion in San Carlos. This fact is not a minor issue because she was not known to have owned houses either in London or in Barcelona, but instead she rented villas, which indicates that her lack of interest in owning property in Europe was inversely proportional to her Afropolitan Africanism that prevailed in its constant multilocality, transnationality and translocality.

Life in Barcelona must have been surrounded by the same luxury that she enjoyed in the colony, because in the end the privileges stemming from her emancipated status were the result of her great estates and wealth. It was precisely Amelia's empowerment in colonial times that would show the darker side of power Krio Fernandino and likewise certain excesses that the Fernandinos had in the control over labourers to increase the necessary authority. Surely Amelia also found some Protestant church among the many existing in Barcelona to attend a Sunday service, as she would also do in the small Methodist church near her home in San Carlos. Regarding her social life in Barcelona, there were no more testimonies than those provided by the neighbours who signed her death certificate.

Still the chapter has also shed light on other, more general aspects. The most relevant was that Barcelona became the arrival point of the Krio Fernandino diaspora from 1890, some of whom would establish themselves in the city, as other Equatorial Guinean ethnic groups, especially Bubis, later would in the 1940s.

This chapter has also analysed the intersectionality of women in terms of class, gender and race, because this allowed us to address the chameleonic integration of Krio Fernandino women in Barcelona, regardless of the variables of sex and race. Thanks to their high social status, they mixed with the Catalan bourgeoisie at events related to trade between Santa Isabel or Barcelona, and at social events such as Fernandino weddings.

Finally, Madrid's air links with Santa Isabel would bolster the change of metropolitan capital that until then was held by Barcelona, even though the historical networks of relatives and friends had already been woven in that city.

The connection between Santa Isabel and Barcelona highlighted the Fernandinos' multilocality, transcontinental nature and Afropolitanism, given their dynamism and ability to integrate into the contexts they visited. Subsequently, the reason for the Spanish forgetfulness after the colonial independence of Equatorial Guinea has been analysed, as well as the unforgivable Catalan oblivion regarding their coexistence with the Fernandinos. These aspects have been put in context with the rise of racism of the 1990s, which brought to an end any remaining shade of Krio Fernandino exceptionalism in Barcelona.

CHAPTER 4

Decolonising the African past from a gender perspective

In previous chapters, the social reality of the Krio Fernandino and Equatorial Guinean community has been addressed both in Santa Isabel and in Barcelona. However, this work has not yet delved into different aspects that defined Fernandino women and that, raised from a decolonial perspective, allow us to decipher certain keys regarding their social practices. To achieve this, Amelia Barleycorn, Vivour's widow, will be taken as a benchmark, along with other Fernandino women who exerted widespread influence. The aim is to recognise their socio-cultural influence while presenting them as dynamic and active subjects who enjoyed different levels of authority and power, albeit under Spanish colonial androcentric pressure.

There are characteristic aspects of the Krio Fernandino women that explain their capacity for action and influence. A paradigmatic case of their capacity for action and influence was the claim that Amelia Barleycorn lodged against the Spanish colonial government in 1911. The chapter also raises how the elite status of the Fernandino promoted their women's rights. It considers how their use of domestic servants contributed to class racialisation, and looks at how the lifestyle and social presentation of the Fernandino women's bodies had an influence on their identity. The chapter concludes with an analysis of the impact the Spanish colonies had on Fernandino decadence.

4.1. *Amelia Barleycorn de Vivour v. Spanish Government* (1911): marriage, nationality, gender and religion

Spanish Guinea was the reluctant subject of a legal transplant by the Spanish state. After decades of effective colonisation, services of all kinds were implemented very slowly, which had serious legal knock-on effects for the population, as the Spanish authorities applied rules demanding documents without having yet created the centres and infrastructures for processing them or having sufficiently advertised them to an illiterate population. A standout example of the consequences of poor implementation can be seen in the civil registries.

In the following, we look at the claim lodged by Amelia Barleycorn, much to her chagrin, before the Ministry of State in 1911, in which this Krio Fernandino lady submitted significant claims on issues of marriage, nationality, religion and gender, thereby contextualising the defence of the rights of Spanish Africans and the Krio community in the colony.

The document sent to her, in response to her request to register her marriage, revealed some of the hindrances that Amelia Barleycorn chose to face, which had resulted in the non-recognition of her marriage to William Allen Vivour. Amelia Barleycorn was one of the thousands of Equatorial Guineans affected by Spanish ineptitude.

Missionary work to spread Catholicism throughout Spanish Guinea had been rather unsystematic. Conversion to Catholicism could be requested to formalise legal perks, such as semi-emancipated or emancipated status, but for decades the faith did not have an extensive loyal following. As an example, the data on Catholic marriages show a rather low number for all the marriages that were performed nationwide: just ten unions in 1942 (Resúmenes Estadísticos del Gobierno General de los Territorios Españoles del Golfo de Guinea, 1945, p. 37).

The low number of Catholic marriages reflected the scant follow-up that took place in the 1940s, with those registered likely to belong to the Spanish or European population, thereby excluding from the statistics the African population that did not follow this faith.

During a similar period, it is observed that the inadequate follow-up of marriage rites did not equally affect Catholic deaths (752 in 1943, according to Resúmenes Estadísticos del Gobierno General de los Territorios Españoles del Golfo de Guinea, 1945, p. 38). In that sense, Christianisation would seem more settled in this context among Equatorial Guineans. It is likely that adherence in this sphere was down to the population fearing that not making use of the Civil Registry implied through failure to register the deceased might thwart procedures as timely as inheritance matters.

This aspect should not be overlooked, as the Catholic Church and the Spanish authorities had voiced their concern about the Protestant settlement that had existed since the mid-nineteenth century. They devoted strident efforts to eradicate it, since they considered that the native populations would finally accept Catholic conversion provided that they did not already belong to another branch of Christianity.

These aspects allow us to gain a closer understanding of the valuable argument submitted by Amelia Barleycorn in 1911, since she was the largest landowner in Santa Isabel in 1890, largely thanks to her husband's inheritance. And given that she had married him in a Protestant ceremony, and not the Catholic rites that Spain tried to impose at all costs, the non-recognition of her Protestant marriage thereby called into question her bond with William A. Vivour, the legitimacy of their daughter Isabel, along with the vast inheritance she received as his widow.

Amelia Barleycorn's plea for equal rights in colonised territories, beyond religion, gender and race

Amelia Barleycorn's application to the Spanish government was dated 26 September 1911 and allows us to see first-hand the problems faced by the Fernandino population in relation to the recognition of Protestant unions, which, due to the English influence, were the most common form of marriage until the beginning of the twentieth century, after common-law marriages. The rejection of Protestant unions in favour of the promotion of Catholic marriages had perverse legal effects on the legitimacy, or not, of Krio Fernandino children, alongside the acceptance, or not, of their inheritance rights.

All the documentation consulted, alongside the quotations, is part of the file that the Archivo General de la Administración of Alcalá de Henares houses on this initiative inspired by Amelia Barleycorn de Vivour. The file is entitled "Acción promovida por Amelia Barleycorn sobre la inscripción de una certificación en el Registro Civil de Fernando Poo" (Action lodged by Amelia Barleycorn on the registration of a certification in the Civil Registry of Fernando Poo), with the notarial files and other documents available ranging from 1911 to 1912. Proceedings began with a handwritten notarial document dated 8 February 1911, addressed to the Minister of State in Madrid and signed by Amelia Barleycorn.

The case was one of immense importance since, if Amelia Barleycorn's marriage to William A. Vivour had not been legalised, she could not have been, as she was, his heiress to his large fortune. Hence, in the document, she discussed the irreparable damages:

> to consider applicable to my marriage the precepts of the Civil Code and those of the Civil Marriage Law is a legal absurdity that causes me moral and material

damages of unimaginable importance; this criterion not being able to prevail such damages to my person, and in damage to many families and many interests that the State must protect in its actions as protector (AGA, box 81/06340).

The document expounded on the legal and moral issues related to civil registers and the application of the law of the Spanish mainland in the colony, the rights of Spanish Africans compared to the rights of foreigners, the recognition of the Protestant religion as well as the Catholic one, the treatment of women for not professing Catholicism, and inheritance rights. All these issues will be presented through the arguments that Amelia put forward in her writing.

In summary, the legal arguments lodged against the Spanish state were that:

> 1. In the year 1882 in which I had to wed, the Civil Code that governs today was not in force [...] I know well that those of its provisions that favour me are applicable to the case before us; 2. The Civil Marriage Law was neither applicable to these Territories in the above-mentioned year of 1882. Article 28 of the Royal Organic Decree of the Administration of this Colony [...] dated 11 July 1904, is to be interpreted as meaning that marriages held in the Methodist Church with the solemnities and according to the rites of the Protestant Christian Church, are useless by transcription of the appropriate certification of their Pastor in the Civil Registry of this Colony (AGA, box 81/06340).

Regarding civil registers and the application of the law of the Spanish mainland to the colony, Amelia pointed out that:

> in wishing to exercise certain rights coming into being as civil purposes through my sole marriage I have discovered: the lack of prior registration in the Civil Registry of my aforementioned union with Mr Guillermo A. de Vivour is an obstacle to doing so. In view of this fact, I have tried to remedy the fault by registering the certification issued by the Pastor of the Methodist Church [...] under whose auspice it was held [...] yet encountering further hindrance [...] to judge these authorities as in force in the year 1882, in which our nuptials took place, under the Civil Marriage Law of 1870 (AGA, box 81/06340).

As she pointed out, neither the population nor the Protestant pastors had been notified of the need to register the marriage in the registry:

> See [...] the enormity [...] of considering the Civil Marriage Law in force in the Territories [...] without it having been arranged beforehand for it to be made public in the official newspapers of this Colony; and even by personal notification to the Protestant pastors, so that they would make it known to their numerous believers here (AGA, box 81/06340).

Similarly of the utmost importance was her complaint that Spain's obligation was to protect colonised populations and remove them from primitivism, not to plunge them into the chaos that meant the non-recognition of their marital ties or their descendants. In this regard, Amelia said that:

> [T]he State in its standout mission to realise their right, exercises a guardianship over its citizens and this guardianship is closer to parental authority or paternal action as those same citizens, either because of their age, or because of their race status, or, finally, because of the lack of culture in the peoples that due to their primitive social state the State actually civilises, meaning moreover they must need it (AGA, box 81/06340).

This argument led Amelia to defend that the action of tutelage of populations, who must be "civilised", was what justified there being different laws in the colonies than on the mainland:

> Therefore [...] to exercise certain professions, certain knowledge acquired or proven in the educational centres; [...] to hear that tutelary action regulates in its laws legal institutions such as tutelage and even grants testament for its caregivers in the intestate succession and finally for that tutelary action protects and defends in its Colony those who were born in it, teaching them, civilising them, and even governing them, by special laws, different from those of mainland Spain (AGA, box 81/06340).

In this regard, Amelia argued that only those who had been civilised should obtain full emancipation "until acquiring the necessary cultural standing to declare them emancipated and in the fullness of their rights" (AGA, box 81/06340).

Regarding the rights of the Spanish Africans with respect to the rights of the foreigners in the colony, she stated that:

> applying the laws of the Peninsula to these Territories with the same criteria with which they are applied in the case subject to this appeal, it turns out that the foreigners who live in this Colony, and I refer to those of Ethiopian race, enjoy more favourable conditions than those of Spanish nationality (AGA, box 81/06340).

She was referring to the legal inequality in which the said law was applied to the African Spaniards over the rest of the Africans who lived in the colony.

To return to the issue of the non-recognition of their Protestant marriage on the part of the Spanish state, she recalled that the colonised territories also implemented an international norm that protected the rights of the population in respect of issues related to marriage, parental authority or the rights of wives:

> It is known that [...] the Civil Codes of civilised missions devote a preliminary title to deal with the principles of Private International Law [...] to determine what kind of legal acts are within the generic denomination: indicate that the legal rules govern [...] marriage, parental authority, guardianship, marital authority and the rights of married women [...]We therefore understand this generic phrase "state and capacity of persons" to include aspects such as marriage and the legitimacy of offspring (AGA, box 81/06340).

In this regard, Amelia displayed boundless energy regarding the conflict that caused other Krio Fernandino who maintained English nationality to be allowed Protestant marriage whereas she was not, because in the end the foreigners had more rights than the Spaniards:

> Article 9 of our Civil Code [...] establishes that marriage is regulated, by the law of the nation to which the spouses belong. Thus, Protestant marriage, or the marriage of the Anglican Church, is the only legitimate one for the English. Then my brothers of race who have English nationality and contract marriage according to the rite of the Protestant Church have contracted legitimate marriage, while I am Spanish by birth and by will, entering into the same marriage was not legitimate for lack of the mere formality of registration in the Civil Registry. Ergo if such doctrine prevails, the foreigners in these Territories are of better condition than the Spaniards (AGA, box 81/06340).

Regarding the sanction of Spanish laws that were later intended to be applied in the colony without making this publicly known, Amelia made her stance very clear:

> Article 28 of the Royal Organic Decree of the Administration of these Territories in relation to Article 10 of the Royal Order of July 23, 1902 [...] must be interpreted in the sense that the religious marriage of the Protestant Christian Church celebrated with the rites or solemnities of the Methodist Mission [...] in these Spanish Possessions is legitimate (AGA, box 81/06340).

Furthermore, it should be stated that the claim of the Spanish state to apply laws that were not even recognised on the mainland by the Spaniards themselves generated a comparative grievance of such dimensions that Amelia herself reproached them in her claim.

She was likewise forceful regarding the non-recognition of the Protestant religion alongside the Catholic one, since she pointed out that:

> I do not consider fair speaking, it is clear, in terms of defence and saving all respect the indicated obstacle and therefore I come to you in plea of legal precept that defines my marital status; and, by the way, that of many more families that in the same situation are found (AGA, box 81/06340).

For Amelia, the injustice of not recognising her marriage was straightforward:

> I have tried to prove [...] that the Civil Code was not in force in 1882 [...] that the precepts of said Code [...] are not applicable to me as soon as they harm me though become so as soon as they favour me (AGA, box 81/06340).

Amelia was forceful on the point that they could not apply a law retroactively when it was not yet applied in the colony, proof of the slow Spanish colonisation:

> I believe, therefore, to have shown that neither the Civil Code, nor the Civil Marriage Law, governed in this Colony [in] the year 1882, nor during the years in which my late husband lived and the lack of registration could be corrected (AGA, box 81/06340).

Regarding the Civil Marriage Law, Amelia recalled that it was not in force in Spanish Guinea:

> [T]he Civil Marriage Law of 1870 has not only not been published in the *Boletín Oficial de los Territorios Españoles en el Golfo de Guinea*, but even the most important of its precepts have not been fulfilled; since neither the Municipal Judges were in charge of it, nor were there any books in form, nor was any registration made until the year 1892; therefore, the aforementioned law did not govern in these Territories (AGA, box 81/06340).

Regarding the treatment of women for not professing Catholicism, Amelia was relentless:

> If here we judge whether the Civil Marriage Law of 1870 is in force, it will be evident: that the Methodist or Protestant Christian marriage that is not registered in the Civil Registry [...] will not be legitimate marriage and therefore the women who had to enter into it believing it to be holy, since this religion is that of many civilised nations, we will not be for the Law of the State the wives of our husbands, rather their concubines; and the State that must be our father for its tutelary mission, instead of honouring us as good daughters, prostitutes us by ruling our marriage illegitimate (AGA, box 81/06340).

Vis-à-vis the injustice created by the Spanish state, Amelia highlighted the contradiction that civil marriages were required to be registered when the population did not know of their existence: "if the Civil Registry existed in 1882, in these Territories the same thing would happened as happened with the Roman calendar until Imco Flavio took it from his lord to teach it to the plebs." As she recalled, "no law can be applied, without prior publication or promulgation" (AGA, box 81/06340).

She also seemed to feel a great indignation that the Spanish state was illegally applying a law in the colony when because the various changes it introduced it was not applied in Spain itself until 1899:

> To prove that the Civil Code was not in force in these Territories the year of 1882 in which I contracted the marriage [with William A. Vivour] which I intend to legalise few reasons are needed. It is more than enough to state that it was not enacted on the Spanish mainland until the year 1899 [...] Therefore, in the year 1882, this could in no way be in force in this Colony (AGA, box 81/06340).

After the submission and argumentation of the claim, Amelia requested a legislative change that would affect all the territories and islands throughout the colony, which would mean that other Protestants like her could register their marriages, legalise inheritances and recognise their offspring as legitimate. For this reason, Amelia concluded her statement saying she:

> PLEADS that if it is deemed timely, a provision of a general nature be issued, in which taking into account the state of the previous and present culture of these territories, it is arranged that until the date that VE [you] deems prudential, the marriages held in accordance with the rites of the Protestant Church will be registered in the Civil Registries of Santa Isabel, Bata, Elobey, San Carlos, Annobon, Corisco and other peoples that have been appointed Delegate of the General Government, issuing thus an irrefutable document for registration, the certification certifying the celebration of the marriage issued by the Pastor or Missionary in charge of the aforementioned Church and which must be transcribed (AGA, box 81/06340).

The resolution of the conflict with Amelia Barleycorn adopted in the Council of State

The request of Amelia Barleycorn was of such importance that the Ministry of State decided that it should be resolved by the Council of State (Consejo de Estado), which, on 9 January 1912, testified to the reading of the request of Mrs Amelia Barleycorn, Vivour's widow. However, they responded to her request in the negative (AGA, box 81/06340).

In addition, the Council of State demanded documents that would allow Amelia's request to be processed:

> the Commission understands that the documents that justify the aforementioned extremes must be added to the file, in order to be able to appraise the requested consultation with complete conviction the matter deserves. Which I have the honour to bring to the attention of you for the appropriate purposes (AGA, box 81/06340).

The Council of State had thus decided not to deny Amelia's arguments, but rather continued to request that she send them her husband's marriage, nationality and death documents in order to process them.

This ruling was answered by Amelia, which gave rise to a new Report of the Permanent Commission of the Council of State signed in Madrid on 26 September 1911, which on this occasion did indeed review her substantive argument in greater detail (AGA, box 81/06340).

The text recognised that the aforementioned legal principles were worthy of study and lawful, but that the Council of State believed that the main issue was that her husband, William Vivour, had already died and that it could not be verified that the marriage had actually taken place, nor could it be corroborated that she had obtained Spanish nationality due to the simple fact of being born in the colony. It was also critical of Amelia's assertion that by holding the marriage in Fernando Poo it should be automatically recorded because being a Baptist and not being recognised by themselves that the Protestant pastors exercised in the Spanish possession, at least it should be verified by the colonial power to which the pastors belonged, in this case the British Empire. However, although the letter continued to set out other obstacles to respond affirmatively to her request, the Council of State ended up recognising that Spain could not leave so many people who were in the same predicament in a situation of helplessness, since, having been unable to register them owing to a shortfall of judges before the aforementioned date, it had to give "a solution to the applicant" (AGA, box 81/06340). For this reason, the Council of State considered that a transitional period covering these cases should be enacted until 1 January 1912 to recognise all previous Protestant marriages.

In the document's conclusions, the Council of State recognised that Amelia's initiative would entail a substantial change for the entire Protestant community of the Spanish Territories in the Gulf of Guinea from the period that comprised the effective Spanish colonisation, until 1 January 1912.

It is understood that Amelia Barleycorn submitted the requested documentation of her husband William A. Vivour, since it is not known that she experienced further problems with her husband's inheritance or any claim since his death in 1890.

On 26 February 1912, the Council of State processed Amelia Barleycorn's request once the supplementary documentation to support the request had been submitted.

In fact, the effects of Amelia Barleycorn's lawsuit could be extended beyond those years by another interesting document archived in her own file. In the background of the document there was reflection on whether the Krio should be granted Spanish nationality because, even if they had been born in the Spanish Territories in the Gulf of Guinea who preferred to classify them as simple immigrants.

Yet, it was the Spanish government that was faced with the need to clarify the procedures to obtain Spanish nationality. This situation was reflected in the report "On the desirability of adopting a simple procedure for acquiring Spanish nationality dated 4 July 1927" (AGA, box 81/06467). This document was signed by the Governor General Núñez del Prado, Director General of Morocco and the Colonies, and it recognised the problems of documentary management and registration occurring in Spanish Guinea and that the procedure for acquiring nationality to avoid the abandonment of the inhabitants of the colony. Núñez de Prado concluded by recognising that "it is necessary to establish a simple procedure by which the African foreigners who wish to become naturalised could easily achieve this provided that through their conduct they become creditors of such mercy" (AGA, box 81/06467).

Miguel Núñez del Prado's document openly recognised that the adoption of nationality for having attained resident status in any Spanish territory was *inapplicable* due to the lack of necessary documentation to endorse this claim. The document did not mention the scarce implementation of civil and consular records that Amelia Barleycorn had already decried in 1911, although it was activated as a solution to start a simple procedure that

> could be reduced to the request of the interested party, informed by the General Government, which would ensure [...] the honesty and good conduct of the applicant, to avoid the introduction of disturbing or dangerous elements [...] Once the request is returned and nationality granted, the applicant would go to the Registry to waive their previous nationality and take the oath of the Constitution (AGA, box 81/06467).

It is of great interest that, upon winning the lawsuit, Amelia managed to make the colony recognise that the Protestant pastors had arrived before the Catholic missionaries and that the marriages they had performed should be legalised, that is, until a date that would end their recognition if they had been granted the status of Spanish Africans rather than foreigners. It is clear that her intermediation was fundamental to the recognition of marriages performed by the Protestant church.

That said, the case of Amelia Barleycorn served as a legal basis for granting Spanish nationality to all Krio who requested it, with a simple procedure from 1928. There should therefore be no doubt that her defence of Krio Fernandino rights put an end to the cataloguing of the Krio as "eternal foreigners", a view that still persists among certain Equatorial Guinean populations in post-independence times, as demonstrated by Iyanga Pendi (2021, pp. 41–42).

Amelia Barleycorn's claim is of extraordinary worth from a social, legal, political, cultural and gender standpoint, since, although we cannot know from primary sources her thoughts regarding her status as a Spanish African and a Euro-African, we are fortunate to have this long letter that she drafted to the Ministry of State in 1911, a text in which she made a resounding defence in light of her African origin of English influence, Spanish nationality, Protestant religion, letter of emancipation, and above all, her female status. It is therefore a document that reflects the complexities of being a Protestant, cultured, black and wealthy woman at the Spanish colonial margins.

4.2. Fernandino women: between bourgeois elitism and colonial power

The select and minority Krio Fernandino group constituted a powerful African elite that exerted its influence both in the colony and in the metropolis, although very little is known of the influential Fernandino women. This did not mean that wealthy and energetic women had not excelled in the community, but that beyond oral transmission, especially by women, there are no extensive accounts or texts devoted to them.

In the next section, the different spheres of power of Fernandino women will be reviewed to show their areas of influence and decision-making capacity in very diverse social areas.

As will be shown, elitism and Fernandino privileges are the cornerstones that enabled this Krio minority to position itself with greater rights and advantages than the other African populations that lived in Spanish Guinea, which had a direct impact on the women of the community.

Fernandino privileges and women's empowerment

If the African matricentrism studied by Amadiume (2018) was characterised by motherhood being the factor that conferred prestige and power to African women, facilitating their visibility and decision-making at the social, economic and even political level, in the case of the Krio Fernandino it had an even more tangential role.

The social relevance of Fernandino women was determined by the elite status of a privileged African minority that recognised the equal rights of men and women and, therefore, accepted their full autonomy and ability to manage their wealth. In this context, Amalia Barleycorn (2021), explained that her great-aunt still remained a very powerful woman despite losing her husband and only daughter:

> She was an economically independent woman, not only as a result of what she had achieved, but also due to what she had inherited and for the estates she had received [...] Amelia had to weave her magic. All of the above shaped her character.

Amelia Barleycorn, like other Krio Fernandino women, exercised her power and authority within her particular religious, economic, political, commercial and social framework. Part of this influence was exerted by her proximity to groups of initially British and then Catalan settlers who supplied the agricultural products that would later be exported to the mainland. This made her even more of a contradictory figure since African women like her running their own businesses clashed with the deep-rooted European androcentrism and Eurocentrism.

And in fact, it is necessary to remember that Amelia was neither the first nor the only Fernandino woman to manage her fortune independently. When Muñoz y Gaviria (1871a) reported on the commercial activity of M. Enry Materos's widow in the last third of the nineteenth century, he described her as an educated and wealthy woman. In his description there was no hint of racism or androcentrism, biases that were widespread at the time. On the contrary, it would seem that Muñoz y Gaviria (1871a, p. 4) was dazzled by her:

> the widow of M. Enry Materos, a singular black woman who, with her daughters, dark mulattoes, received in England a careful education, conversing

fluently English, French and Spanish. She runs the business of her homestead herself, and often also goes into the woods to deal with the rural inhabitants. Instruction is not peculiar only to this family, as many parents of noted fortunes have sent their children to the schools of Sierra Leone to be educated. This means that the status of certain *moreno* people of Santa Isabel is such that they solely hold African nationality.

A further example of a rich and self-reliant Fernandino woman was provided by Hall (1874). Although we lack the detail of her name, he explained that an extremely wealthy African woman from Santa Isabel had ended up assassinating an English captain in 1869. Hall (1874, pp. 154–155) said that the deceased was one Captain Robinson and that it was the price he had paid for not wanting to yield to her charms because he was a god-fearing and married man. It was then that the African woman had decided to take revenge, bribing one of his servants to poison him. It is a rather long narrative that probably sought an explanation for a sudden death, while casting doubt on those powerful African women of Santa Isabel. As will be made clear, there were other cases, but these two examples allow us to illustrate how, long before the Spaniards managed to colonise the island of Fernando Poo effectively, the Krio women enjoyed autonomy.

It must also be said that the influence of many Fernandino women in the religious and socio-political sphere was remarkable. A significant number would have stood out as benefactors of Catholic and Protestant religious groups. Regarding this support for Catholic missions, it must be stated that their collaboration coincided with the beginning of the decline of Protestantism on the island of Fernando Poo, which ran parallel to the expansion of Catholicism. This fact was reflected in certain Fernandino families deciding to openly adhere to Catholicism as they knew that this would improve their socio-political influence with colonial authorities. This is known from the constant praise they received in magazines such as *La Guinea Española*, which simultaneously published lists of the most generous contributors to the works on the cathedral, the vast majority of whom Krio Fernandino, while explaining their presence at Sunday masses or celebrating family rituals in local notes. Among the most renowned families would probably be the Joneses and the Dougans, since both had converted to Catholicism and constituted an Equatorial Guinean example to be promoted by colonial and ecclesiastical structures.

That was not the case of Amelia Barleycorn, who kept her Protestant faith until the end of her days, maintaining regular contacts with Methodist pastors. They even looked after the keys to her mansion in San Carlos when she travelled to Barcelona or England, or were the one who were asked about Amelia's whereabouts if she was required. Moreover, there is no doubt that her plea for the recognition of Protestant marriages in Spanish Guinea in 1911 was the greatest proof of her fidelity to the Methodist Church.

That said, Amelia Barleycorn, like other Fernandinos who were not willing to convert to Catholicism, but still wanted to maintain good relations, gave regular aid to the missions. This collaboration responded to the Church's requests for donations, but also to their interest in maintaining a cordial relationship with Catholic ecclesiastical structures. Therefore, the numerous gifts that she, like the rest of the Fernandinos, made during the construction of the Cathedral of Santa Isabel should come as no surprise. Among the gifts, it was stated that they had donated items ranging from an organ to different ornamental elements, in addition to financial aid for the works. One of the thank-you notes published in 1903 was addressed to Amelia and was titled *"Precioso regalo"* (Precious Gift).

> The wealthy Amelia Barleycorn, Vivour's widow, has returned in the mail steamer *San Francisco*, after a happy journey to England undertaken as the just desire to view her daughter's progress. Upon return to Fernando Poo, she has pleasantly surprised the Spaniard Missionaries of this city by gifting them a charming harmonium, as a reminder of her trip and as proof of the affection and sympathy with which she has always distinguished them. It is an artistic object [...] everything is made of primordial carved walnut [...] May heaven more than reward Madame Amelia's generosity while we Missionaries remain deeply grateful.[107]

Therefore, this aid must be considered as a way of displaying her support for Spanish colonisation and the mission of Catholic conversion, an attitude that was highly valued by colonial structures. What is more, in fact, the needs of the orders were well known, as in the missions in Fernando Poo (1890, p. 87) numerous details were forthcoming regarding the appeal for the congregations to maintain their activities, as well as the boarding school for African schoolchildren, which was maintained, so it was said, with the help of "charitable and affluent people".

Therefore, to summarise, it is worth stressing that gifts and philanthropy were given by Amelia Barleycorn and a good part of the Krio Fernandino community to the ecclesiastical structures, even going so far as to give land on which to build a Protestant cemetery, as a means of protecting all those who professed the Protestant faith and because it urgently needed a new location. This is reported in a 1911 news clipping that testified to the gratitude the missionaries offered to Amelia for having given them land, together with Maximiliano Jones, to create a cemetery. The cemetery would have a section set aside for Catholics and another for non-Catholics, in other words Protestants.

The economic and commercial field has been extensively reviewed in the chapters devoted to Santa Isabel and Barcelona, where numerous data were also offered one the export and import of products. In these paragraphs, the influence of Krio Fernandino came to light and was similarly expressed in the privileges they had acquired owing to their participation in these areas. Therefore, it should not be overlooked that their wealth came from the ownership of land and farms engaging in agriculture. Their influence in the colony emanated precisely from their great fortunes. Amelia Barleycorn had not been the first wealthy Fernandino woman, yet she was undoubtedly the richest of the entire colony by the end of the nineteenth century.

This trading leadership of the Krio Fernandino community, including women, presupposed a capacity for decision-making and promotion of initiatives, which was demonstrated in how they managed their money and rented their properties. They were also the plaintiffs when there was any legal conflict, since no male representation was necessary, something that was more typical of the Spanish mainland. An example of this is provided by a document in which a handwritten authorisation appeared from Susana Barleycorn to Jeremías Barleycorn to withdraw the money she had deposited in the Administration by Pascual Sepa.

It should also be noted that certain Fernandino subjects, such as Amelia Barleycorn, had responsibilities on their estates, meaning they had to monitor the work of their foremen and issue orders to improve the progress of their crops and plantations. In that regard, Amelia's life must have been quite different from that of the wife of her brother William Napoleon, Dorcas Fanny de Barleycorn, who played a major role in the Protestant community, as, like other missionary wives, she had a role in the mission, especially among women converted to Protestantism, and not so much in the commercial oversight of the family lands. What is more, Amelia had to oversee her fortune and her business in a highly masculinised colonial framework dominated by Spanish structures and that gave such little visibility to women. Amalia Barleycorn's words make sense when she explained the strength and authority with which her great-aunt had to impose herself. In Amalia's testimony (2021) she highlighted her ancestor's effort to overcome all the men around her since, after all, she was a very rich and powerful woman who had to impose herself on her foremen and *braceros*: "She had an obligation, you have to impose yourself! She was the boss of men; all the workers were men."

Perhaps that is why legends have circulated detailing the brutality of Amelia Barleycorn in demanding her *braceros* increase the yields, something that, regardless of whether or not it is based in actual fact, still manages to confirm that image of an energetic and powerful African woman.

Additionally, the mistreatment of labourers was not an isolated characteristic of Amelia Barleycorn, though this has been difficult to prove since in the numerous complaints that were filed in the Spanish archives, I found few from her farmlands, although a larger amount from other members of the Krio Fernandino community, specifically Fernandino men. For the colonial authorities these complaints by labourers against the landowners were unjustifiable, because if the foremen gave "a blow or a slap to a labourer", it was only because they had deserved it "because they were insolent [...] because of their striving to avoid work [...] because of one of the thousand examples of glibness", because all these were the excuses that "the *braceros* find ways not to work", as stated in the Law of 17 July 1912 on Native Work (Miranda Junco, 1945, pp. 392–395).

Indeed, on all the plantations, management was not devoid of conflicts and the foremen's assessment was always imposed over what they considered inadequate attitudes of their *braceros*, whether of Equatorial Guinean or foreign origin. The foremen's assaults against the *braceros* were not always reflected in the documentation of the colony, despite being habitual. One example, however, can be found in a file describing "the aggression of the native foreman against a *moreno* who showed him his hand" on an estate of Joseph Dougan on 28 April 1920, in which it is explained that he was transferred "immediately to the hospital" (AGA, box 81/07189).

With regard to Amelia Barleycorn's plantations, there were strict rules for the *braceros*. Some Fernandinos, like she, Dougan or Collins, had complaints made by their workforces, a situation that was the same or worse on the Catalans and Spaniards' plantations. Amelia was therefore not an exception; among the documentation consulted, certain documents have been found concerning the complaints that were filed on a property run by Amelia. However, as in all cases, these represented a very small figure when compared to all the conflicts that occurred in all the plantations and they were not processed.

Indeed, there is abundant documentation on *braceros* and farms, which Martino (2012) has studied in detail. Certain documents show harsh punishments, which would soften over the decades. As an example we can take the list of punishments imposed by the Delegation of Conception of 30 April 1921, in which twenty lashes were given equally to those who refused to work and to those who "slept with the boss's wife without his permission and in the absence of the latter" (AGA, box 81/07190).

The documentation also allows us to imagine the attitude and ingenuity that a Fernandino woman had to have in order to impose her authority on the estates, although on other occasions they prioritised mutual respect. In fact, Amelia Barleycorn showed large amounts of diplomacy in relation to the colonial authorities, as can be ascertained from certain files, since she sought reciprocity to resolve conflicts in which family members such as Carlos G. Vivour had been embroiled.

This brief review has described various areas of influence of Fernandino women in the religious, socio-political and commercial spheres, power that they enjoyed thanks to the privileges that the Krio Fernandino had as an elite. These data also show the differences how their spheres of influence changed between the colony and the metropolis, because, as we saw in the chapter dedicated to Barcelona, their influence was more limited in Europe, since, after all, it was in Africa where they had their workers and the basis of their businesses.

Female autonomy, associationism and social dynamics

It is difficult to summarise what Krio Fernandino women were actually like, but perhaps what defined them the most was their self-reliance. These women were characterised by their authority, self-sufficiency and independence, characteristics that were quite different from those valued by Spanish and many European women. This was an effect of an androcentrism that, incidentally, Catholic missionary orders were trying to implement in the colony under the doctrine that women should be mothers and lovers and wives, pledging obedience to their husbands.

Amalia (2021) recalled her great-aunt noting that they were "very wealthy women, very much in tune with their social status." They made their own decisions, often taking advice, but they had great authority to impose their own wills. Amalia (2021) said that Amelia Barleycorn was "a woman with oodles of dignity, a woman leader. Almost all Barleycorn women go beyond mere leaders, even, such is the dominance we have over ourselves, that there are men who cannot stand it. They either stay or they leave."

But the overall context of women throughout the colony varied widely. In Fernando Poo, Krio Fernandino women were very socially, economically and culturally empowered – which did not always prevent the sexual abuse by Krio Fernandino men of other Equatorial Guinean and African women. In turn, Bubi women enjoyed a certain autonomy and social recognition in relation to men due to matrilineality, their prestige due to maternal descent and the cult of ancestors (Fernández-Moreno, 2018). But in the Spanish Guinean mainland, other Equatorial Guinean women, such as the Annobonese, and especially the Fang, Ndowe and Bissio, suffered some sexual discrimination, both due to patrilineal filiation and polygynous marriage. Furthermore, there were also those Africans from West and Central Africa who arrived in Santa Isabel after the *braceros,* who had an undefined and precarious status, and were also raised by the Fernandino and occasionally forced into prostitution. These women lived under the most restricted rights due to the precariousness of living in a country that was not their homeland, far from their family networks of mutual aid. Research has revealed copious documentation in which the perilous position of some of these African women was observed, not only because they were abused by Europeans and Colonial Guards,[108] but also because of the excesses that the Krio Fernandino, some Equatorial Guineans and African labourers of other origins had with them. Some examples are a complaint about the sale of girls under ten years of age, reported in Santa Isabel on 10 February 1932; the notice stated that "there were some native Equatorial Guinean women" who were prostituting themselves when "the labourers request this service" but who had also suffered serious vaginal infections (AGA, box 81/08156, file 5); or the notice from the prison in Santa Isabel of 12 July 1868, releasing Mulato Godhech, "who was detained in this prison […] for the mistreatment of a lady from this city" (AGA, box 81/07958).

The Krio Fernandino women's dynamism can be seen in their ability to mobilise and organise themselves for what they deemed important.

It is particularly notable that what could be claimed to be the first demonstration against Spanish colonial power in the city of Santa Isabel was spearheaded by Krio Fernandino women, especially by Sara Collins, who, of course, sat in a hammock to distinguish herself from the rest. This mobilisation took place in 1915, with the lowering of taxes and tariffs as its demands. As a news item reported:

> On the 20th of the past month [...] *a female demonstration* of the population was organised which, after travelling along several streets and the Plaza de España, presented itself to the residence of the General Government, *going to the front in their hammocks three renowned mamis* as the vulgar and enlightened people also call them [...] These were Mrs Collins, Mrs Pratt and Mrs Orgill, whose purpose with the demonstration was to request the Governor General to submit his validation before the Government of the Metropolis [...] to reduce the type of urban and territorial tax [...] The demonstrators were welcomed very respectfully: by our first Authority promising take heed of what they requested, for which purpose a series of reforms would then be proposed to the tariffs that have governed imports and exports in recent times.[109]

Of similar relevance is the responsibility assumed by both Krio Fernandino women and men in defending the just causes of other Equatorial Guineans. In this type of conflict, the surname Barleycorn was again prominent, specifically in Mabel, Susana and Rolando Barleycorn's cases, although there were also Joneses, Collinses or Dougans with the same conviction. This means that certain Krio Fernandino stood up for the weak when they were witnesses to an injustice or a reprehensible attitude, a convention that was probably due to the desire to keep the Fernandinos' reputation high among the Equatorial Guinean and also the African population as a whole, and that served to divert attention away from their own abuses.

For example, I would highlight the criminal case of Mabel Barleycorn against Paulina Okara and Adama Añau. The conflict was resolved with the imposition of a fine of 50 pesetas on Paulina Okara for beating the pregnant native woman Adama Añau, who was admitted with symptoms of imminent abortion because of the blows she received in the public market of Santa Isabel on 14 July 1947. Mabel Barleycorn went to the police headquarters to report the events, and stated that "she saw that the also native Paulina Okara slapped the so-called Adama Añau, who caused her to fall; and that when the aforementioned Paulina Okara called her attention, she slapped her without justified cause" (AGA, box 81/08556).

That said, not all Fernandino women were entrusted with the running of their estates, like Amelia Barleycorn or Collins' widow were at the time. In these cases, women engaged in other activities. For example, Mariana Kinson, who was married to Samuel Dougan, participated in different initiatives, including the Cathedral choir, since in 1913, Mariana Kinson acted as vocalist, together with superior reverends in the Choir Committee of the archdiocese, being vice president of the same together with her husband Joseph Dougan.[110]

Furthermore, it is worth commenting that the Krio Fernandino women showed such boundless energy that they also founded different associations. According to news reports, María Kinson, along with Eva Barleycorn, Julia Barleycorn and Mariana Dougan, founded an association of women, mostly Krio Fernandino, called Constancia in 1914, the headquarters of which was in the Dougan house. The association was presented in a news item, which said that "to the three Associations of which we realised, we must add the Constancia, Association of Native Ladies that has as its object the mutual beneficence in time of illness."[111] This association published some advertisements with assiduity, especially between 1913 and 1916.

Fernandino women also created the Sociedad Hijas de África (Daughters of Africa Society). In this association, in which the Fernandino community and members of the Bubi community participated, in addition to some Spaniards, including some Catalans, theatrical performances were prepared that were enlivened with cocktails and appetisers. In 1921, an article about the association, with the headline "El arte teatral de Guinea" (The Theatrical Art of Guinea), explained that in the performance of the work *La casa de los milagros* (The House of Miracles) the society gave "a highly sympathetic note of Hispanisation that has earned the association the appreciation and consideration of the European element of the Colony."[112] The Bubi Elena Boneque performed the work, replacing the Fernandino Ana Watson, alongside Equatorial Guinean Isabel Lebu and the Fernandino Samuel Kinson. After the performance, tasters had also been performed by the Fernandino Luís Lolín. Certain performances also featured Catalan actors.

Other societies founded by the Krio Fernandino women's collective in the 1920s were the Sociedad Mariana (Marian Society) and the Sociedad Caridad y Amor (Charity and Love Society), both dedicated to "sickness and burial" within the framework of the Protestant religion. In *La Voz de Fernando Poo* in 1924, it was detailed that "the Sociedad Caridad y Amor relief association", with statutes based on those of another similar Sierra Leonean society, had on its Board of Directors such Sierra Leoneans as José Robinson, Esicalla Cole, Francisco Fockne and Blandavo Davis, and Fernandinos including Mercedes Smint, Orgiana Macoli, María Braun and Samuel Kinson.

In 1928, the Claretian Ruiaz (1928, pp. 87–88), took the opportunity to express serious accusations and reproaches against these Krio Fernandino associations. He began by pointing out that, except for those associations of a charitable nature, such as the Sociedad Mariana and also the Sociedad Caridad y Amor, which were of a religious nature and overseen by women, the other Fernandino associations, "rather than appreciable endeavours, have embarked upon more or less reprehensible works, although it has not been all their fault since they lacked guidance." He even added that "our Fernandino society has participated in this decline [...] Today it is undergoing a truly acute crisis" (Ruiaz, 1928, p. 87). In his opinion, owing to the fact that "truly prestigious families are disappearing, the things that remain we see in perfect decay [...] To this has contributed the ignorance of family life: drinking, together with frankness and misspending and disorder and economic disarray" (Ruiaz, 1928, p. 87). Father Ruiaz's contempt was certainly not shared by others, as in another magazine it was said that these initiatives prove "that it is the *morenos* who set the example for European whites in the foundation of such groups, and also extend their action to cooperatives".[113]

To summarise, it is worth stressing that the autonomy of Fernandino women in terms of decision-making, social mobilisation or the creation of associations showed widespread dynamism and a desire to influence society, which did not detract from the management of their farmsteads in which the women at the helm showed the same defects as Fernandino men and the Catalan settlers and Spaniards themselves.

4.3. The domestic service used by the Krio Fernandino community or how to (de)racialise class from intersectionality

Domestic servitude was widely used among the Krio Fernandino, both in Santa Isabel and in Barcelona. It was also common among Spanish settlers, who received as a reward for their establishment in the colony a "boy who would serve them at home (Aixelà-Cabré, 2021). The main difference between the two is that the Fernandinos often employed servants of various African origins. In contrast, the Catalans and Spaniards tended to hire local people as servants. This practice was influenced by the fact that the local people, classified as African Spaniards could be tried and convicted more easily.

Below, a selection of the idiosyncrasies is offered on the relationship and treatment, in order to reflect on the racialisation of the domestic servants of the Fernandinos, as well as the conflicts that emerged in the Krio Fernandino community regarding the treatment that servants were to receive. The purpose is to review some of the more extensive practices to show how class was more important than race, as well as the rudeness with which some Fernandino treated their servants.

Africans working for Africans and Europeans in colonial times: the racialisation of servants

I have already explained in previous sections that the official discourse of the Kingdom of Spain in Africa was that of a supposedly civilising mission. This narrative had permeated the ways of seeing the world of some Catalan settlers and Spaniards, who enjoyed enormous advantages over the native population in a coexistence that turned out to be highly segmented and racialised, and where the colour of people's skin defined their rights, duties and opportunities (Aixelà-Cabré, 2022a). These issues were not equally valid among the Krio Fernandino community, which, when emancipated, could enjoy all the benefits of the colony despite the segregation on the basis of skin colour, although this was more evident and notorious on the continent than on the island of Fernando Poo.

The documentation consulted has brought to light a considerable amount of travel between the mainland and the colony of people going to perform domestic labour, accompanying both Spaniards and Europeans, as well as Fernandinos. Indeed, the Regulations for the Immigration of Spaniards to the Spanish Territories of the Gulf of Guinea of 1 August 1934 specifically mention those who "perform domestic services and accompany their masters" (Article 8) (AGA, box 81/06467).

The research shows that domestic service was mostly black and consisted of both men and women. This data is available because in the list of passengers travelling to Santa Isabel, Barcelona or one of the ports where the Spanish steamships docked in West Africa, the African origin of domestic servants was specified, only stating the first name of the Africans who carried out subordinate tasks, this constituting a perverse and effective way of minimising them as their surname did not deserve to be mentioned. These people were listed as "servants", unlike Spanish women in similar roles, who were often called "maids.

It should be said, although it is not the subject of this section, that some of the first Africans the Spaniards brought to Spain in the mid-nineteenth century after their travels in Africa were brought to serve them in their homes as cooks, nannies or servants, as shown by the revised documentation of travellers or missionaries of the nineteenth century, the passenger lists of the first third of the twentieth century, and the visa applications of the mid-1950s (see Tables 22 and 23). The travel of domestic servants in the passages was a constant from the mid-nineteenth century until colonial independence.

Yet it was the case that in Barcelona a sizable number of Fernandino women and the community in general journeyed with their own servants. This is shown by a news article that appeared in *La Vanguardia* of 1911, in which the names of two servants, Soke and Fidel, twenty and eleven years old respectively, were mentioned, although there were other cases, such as Raquel Jones, who travelled with "Regina, Servant" in 1916. The influx of servants and servants accompanying Fernandinos and Spaniards would continue from 1920 to 1968, although with the passage of the decades all the personal information would be included.

It must be added that the movement of servants between the colony and mainland Spain can also be seen in the type of passage with which they made their trips, since it would often be in third class, as we saw with other Equatorial Guineans, and not with the Fernandinos, who travelled mostly in first class, proof of their elite status. Thus, the passenger record allows us to see that the practice of taking servants from Fernando Poo to the peninsula was commonplace, as a way of guaranteeing certain comforts according to African cultures, such as their gastronomic skills, customs and, of course, speech in the Pichi language.

Likewise, it is important to specify that social class strongly defined the relationship between "masters" and "servants" as one that was distant and paternalistic. The relationship was also marked by blackness if they worked for the Spanish population, and not so much among the Krio Fernandino.

This latter issue is of particular interest in clarifying the relationship that Fernandino women maintained with their servants, since if for whites having Africans in domestic service reinforced the superiority of their supposed white race, it is pertinent to consider whether the Fernandino community, and specifically their women, racialised the social class of their servants to affirm their superiority. As can be seen in the documentation of trials, complaints and lawsuits, the answer would be that the Fernandinos did not racialise their servants, although the treatment that some stopped was extremely harsh in Santa Isabel. As we will see in the next section, although some abuses that occurred within some Krio Fernandino families were controlled, such as the case of Rolando Barleycorn regarding Susana Macfoy, the time that elapsed between the abuses and the resolution of the conflict was too long to think that the Fernandino people attached too much importance to the treatment of the servants.

It has also been found that the Fernandino community often had in their service people who came from their original countries, such as Sierra Leone, Nigeria or Liberia, who they could also take on their trips to Europe. However, for their stays in Barcelona the wealthiest, such as Amelia Barleycorn, surely also hired Catalan domestic servants because they were more easily accessible.

That said, if we reverse racialisation, in the sense of whether the Fernandinos were racialised by Spaniards and Europeans, just as they racialised their African servants and the Equatorial Guinean population in general, the answer would be in the negative. According to the descriptions of the Fernandino by soldiers, missionaries and explorers consulted for this research, the racialisation process took place in the opposite direction, as the Catalans and Spaniards in general de-racialised the Fernandino collective and of course their women, with their constant comments that "they had no more brown [*moreno*] than their colour" (Ruiaz, 1928, p. 84) and as an excuse to also include them in select events and social meetings that they held both in Santa Isabel and in Barcelona.

I would likewise add that in neither of the two cities did a racialised solidarity between Fernandino and servants seem to emerge, but instead a relationship adhering to social class rather than by racism. In this regard, if a certain racism did emerge among the Krio Fernandino community with respect to their servants or even some of the Equatorial Guinean population, it is likely that it was because mixing with the Spanish and Catalan bourgeois colonial structures made the racialisation of Spanish

Africans difficult to avoid. At the end of the day, justified inequalities in terms of race were what underpinned the abuses of all European colonial regimes, a socio-economic and political framework from which the Fernandinos benefited as plantation owners. While it seems contradictory, the possible occasional racism that might emerge against Africans coexisted with Fernandino pride in their African, multi-ethnic and transcontinental origin, meaning it would channel more class issues than race.

Therefore, it could be said that, in their relationship with other Africans, the Krio Fernandino were more marked by class than by race, and that in their relationship with Europeans the colour of their skin was de-racialised for reasons of class.

This aspect is fundamental to suppose that the Krio Fernandino elite would hardly position themselves against Spaniards' and Catalans' comments that racialised the Equatorial Guinean population, which could become very visible in their meetings with the cadres of the colony, the Colonial Guard or the Catalan bourgeoisie.

From all these arguments, it could be concluded that among the Krio Fernandino class seemed to be more significant than race in their relations with their domestic servants, although the treatment that they sometimes gave to them was similar to the abuse that more than one Spaniard inflicted on their "boys".

Conflicts in the Krio Fernandino community over domestic service rights

As I have just explained, the relationships that the Krio Fernandino community maintained with their domestic servants show an established hierarchy in terms of class and not race. To show some of its specificities, a case study will be provided that highlights the opposition to certain excesses that some Krio Fernandino demonstrated, although the delay in resolving the conflict in such a small city calls into question whether the actions of the majority of the Fernandinos was free of abuse in relation to schedule, work tasks and even physical and sexual abuse.

It is likely that the sluggish correction of certain abusive situations was affected by the fact that the Fernandino community tended to prefer endogamy, since complaints and reports on the treatment of servants affected families related to each other, who often may have preferred to resolve complaints diplomatically so as not to create greater issues within their families.

In our example, a Barleycorn, Rolando, raised his voice against Susana Macfoy, the sister of his wife, Isabel Macfoy, to prevent the violence against a maid who was suffering sexual abuse, severe mistreatment and long working hours from continuing. Interestingly, this case reached the courts, unlike on many other occasions, where the conflict would either not be resolved or would be resolved internally. The truth of the matter was that the maid was denounced for leaving the home, and the conflict was resolved in the colonial courts. The case exposed both the precarious situation of the maid in the charge of a Krio Fernandino woman, along with the flexibility of many African common-law marriages, the responsibility that women had for their offspring, and sexual abuse as an issue that probably many maids had to put up with on a regular basis.

The case corresponds to File 4, "Complaint lodged by Susana Macfoy Taylor in 1919" for "disobedience, and abandonment of the home of those with whom she lived as a member of the family" (AGA, box 81/08022). The complaint was signed in Santa Isabel on 11 July 1918 and contained numerous statements made before the judge by Susana Macfoy and her maid Lucy Cole, whom Susana Macfoy said she treated as if she were family, whereas Lucy Cole had affirmed that they kept her as a slave and a maid, cleaning and cooking for the family. Susana Macfoy claimed to have brought her from Calabar because she was asked to do so by Lucy's husband and who promised that he would shortly return to her in Fernando Poo. In the complaint it was stated that the husband of the maid had ultimately embarked on another boat that made a stopover in Victoria and that he disembarked to join another woman, proving he did not plan to visit Santa Isabel. Almost three years had passed since Lucy Cole had complained that she was subject to ill-treatment because she was whipped or beaten with a stick and that she even "played the wife" of the son of "her mistress", Susana Macfoy, named Benito, since she was forced to sleep with him. Lucy explained that:

> as these scandals and mistreatments were continuous the owner of the house told her that as the house was close to the General Government she did not want any nasty surprises, that she should look to live elsewhere, and that in view of the foregoing they sent her to the house of Mr Rolando Barleycorn whose mistress is the sister of Susana Macfoy [her name was Isabel Macfoy] (AGA, box 81/08022).

Lucy Cole went on to explain that:

> in this new house the mistreatment continued, with the sister of Rolando Barleycorn, Mrs de Barleycorn, having to bring a stop to things on many occasions. Finally [she had] to have words with her husband [...] [She said] that she thanked Mrs de Barleycorn because she gave her massages and dressed the shoulder that Susana Macfoy had injured (AGA, box 81/08022).

When Susana Macfoy was asked whether her son had had sex with Lucy Cole, she said that she did not know anything about it and that it was the first she had heard of the affair, since Cole resided with her "as if she were a member of the family" because "she was given the same food that they ate and was dressed as when she was with her parents, also being granted medical assistance for her and her young son" (AGA, box 81/08022).

During the trial, the judge questioned Rolando Barleycorn as a witness and husband of Susana's sister, who said he knew that Susana Macfoy mistreated Lucy sometimes and that he did not deem it tolerable. There was also the account of another witness, the Fernandino Daniel Knox, who said that if the Macfoys did not want to have Lucy at home, it would be best for them to send her and her son to Victoria to be with her husband.

The result of reading the testimonies of this trial indicates that not all Krio Fernandino mistreated their servants, let alone with such violence. Nor do the testimonies prove that the sexual abuse of maids was widespread, although it is a scenario that might have occurred. In fact, it would seem that the intercession of a Fernandino of prestige, as mentioned in the documents, cited as "the mistress of the house" in which Susana Macfoy resided, asked that she move out of anger at the scandal, which could have been Amelia Barleycorn herself, since she was directly related to Rolando Barleycorn.

At the trial, the Kinson's widow also appeared as a witness, as she had given Lucy Cole lodging one night on one of the occasions she escaped from the house. However, she explained that she let her sleep on the couch until clarifying the truth of her complaints about Susana Macfoy, saying that the next day, early in the morning, the Colonial Guard arrived to take Lucy back to Susana Macfoy.

The judge concluded that it was proven that Lucy Cole went to Santa Isabel in the company of Susana Macfoy and that there were contradictions in Lucy's account because she said she thought that her husband was there and not that he would arrive soon. The judge said that Lucy left the house because of the constant mistreatment she received from Susana Macfoy and her son Benito and that, despite Susana saying that she beat her only moderately, the witnesses – Rolando Barleycorn, Isabel Macfoy and Daniel Knox – said that the mistreatment was constant. The judge considered that Susana Macfoy's son Benito had "used her as a woman [prostitute] without paying her anything" (AGA, box 81/08022), and Benito did not want to give more explanations than those he previously provided. The judge thought that Susana and Benito had committed an abuse of trust in relation to Lucy, considering above all the bad faith of Benito's acts that "if he let Lucy go he would be left without a woman" (AGA, box 81/08022).

In addition, the judge stated that:

> under the guise of protection, Susana and Benito wanted to dispose of the right of freedom that Lucy has as an adult [...] disposing free of all the services that she provided (AGA, box 81/08022).

Therefore, the court ruled that:

> This General Government agrees that the *moreno* lady Lucy Cole be deposited in the house of Mrs Cristina Raguel [...] until the arrival of her husband who is in Victoria, also agreeing that Susana Macfoy hand over her son to her and whichever other effects she had in her possession (AGA, box 81/08022).

A later note confirmed that "on this date Lucy Cole embarks for Calabar aboard the English steamer *Accra*, its passage being paid for by the State, which is signed in Santa Isabel on 17 March 1919" (AGA, box 81/08022).

As the case study shows, the precariousness of maids and domestic servants in the heart of Krio Fernandino society was considerable. If Lucy had not been taken to court, there remains a reasonable doubt whether she could have returned to her country with her son, escaping both sexual and physical abuse. In this regard, it is positive that figures such as Barleycorn and Knox offered testimonies in support of the maid, although the delay in resolving the conflict, after three years of mistreatment, shows that their actions should not have been exceptional because, in a population as small as Santa Isabel was in the first quarter of the twentieth century, there were no secrets. The relationship between the maid and the Krio Fernandino women may best illustrate the indifference exhibited by the Fernandinos toward the unjust status of their servants which did not allow them to escape. Only a few Krio Fernandino showed empathy in circumstances that took place in the public sphere.

4.4. The status and social presentation of the body as a formula of distinction Fernandino

The Fernandinos' high standard of living made their elite status evident. Luxury was an effective way of demonstrating that they were in the upper echelons of African society. Their estates and mansions aimed to convey their greatness and wealth, which is why their houses were always described as the most beautiful and luxurious in the descriptions given by missionaries, military servicemen and European explorers of the nineteenth century, something that lasted until the economic and commercial decline that pushed them to sell off from some of their properties.

However, examining the distinction also involved adopting a social presentation of the Europeanised body, both in Santa Isabel and in Barcelona. In fact, dress, along with language, religion and education, was the most commonly mentioned aspect of how the Krio Fernandino presented themselves in the descriptions by travellers. The texts defined the Fernandinos as Europeanised Africans of great elegance and finesse.

Below are some details of the status and standard of living of Amelia Barleycorn and the importance of dress in relation to the elite status of the Fernandino minority.

Amelia Barleycorn's status and standard of living

The previous chapters have offered a good account of the high status and standard of living of the Krio Fernandino in terms of their consumption, recreation and leisure activities both in Santa Isabel and in Barcelona. The estates of Amelia Barleycorn in Fernando Poo were a symbol of the first fortune of the colony in 1890.

In Fernando Poo, she had her house in Santa Isabel and one in San Carlos, plus another that was built overlooking the beautiful bay of San Carlos in 1905. The building was made of stone at a time when this material was not yet commonly used for the construction of homes, together with the fact that the cement that reached the colony was limited until the 1920s. The news reports speak of a spectacular house filled with luxurious furniture. In *La Guinea Española*, under the headline "Solemn Inauguration", details of the mansion were printed:

> On 1 February, in San Carlos, we were treated to the solemn inauguration of the beautiful building that Mrs Amelia de Vivour has erected there. Amongst the numerous attendees was the same Mrs Amelia and her manager José Dougan who were expressly from Santa Isabel. The whole building of carved stone and of grave and severe style is without dispute the finest on the whole island.[114]

The geographer Enrique d'Almonte (1908, p. 155), who had moved to the colony in 1906, also devoted a few lines to the mansion that housed him in San Carlos, which he described as "a beautiful house of artificial stone very well built and comfortably furnished. There we were given a hospitable welcome by the Vivour family and their representative, Mr Dougan."

The sumptuousness of the building was portrayed in the postcards issued by the Spanish Post Office that aimed to encourage the arrival of Spaniard settlers and publicise the colonised territory.

With that in mind, proof that the Fernandinos did not accept intruders on their properties was the beating that Africans received for walking along the beach of San Carlos on which Amelia Barleycorn would build her mansion. According to the Communication of the Delegate of the General Government in San Carlos, Juan Brown, of 19 August 1895, Collins and others ended up claiming that the wounded men had already been warned by Mrs Vivour's brothers that they could not walk on their beach and that was where the aggression came from.

La Voz de Fernando Poo published under the headline "Los cacos en Santa Isabel" (The thiefs in Santa Isabel) a news story about the robbery of Amelia Barleycorn's mansion in San Carlos, months after her death, in September 1920. The account included some details about Amelia's home and way of life that convey the luxury that always surrounded her. The author noted that:

> the Chief of Police was notified [...] that the house owned by Mrs Amelia Barleycorn, Vivour's widow, was open and the furniture was in disarray, indicating that it had been robbed. Immediately he came [...] and could immediately verify that the looting had been carried out, but he could not immediately

calculate the importance of what had been stolen, since the only person who could provide information on what existed in the house had recently died in Barcelona and her heirs were also absent.¹¹⁵

He went on to describe in great detail the luxurious furnishings, gold and clothing that were in the rooms:

> [I]t could be verified from the first moment that from a bureau and in a secret drawer of the same [...] they had stolen money in gold, because they were still left in it, undoubtedly as a sample, some discs of golden metal; a trunk showed unequivocal signs that it had consciously filled the functions of saving that which had been entrusted to it, because its lock resisted with strength the attacks that were launched upon it with a file; ancient and very expensive outfits left for a moment the wardrobe to go to air on the armchairs of the room.¹¹⁶

The article ended by noting that the thieves had been "two natives of Kamerun called Fain Boy and Abad", that they had been found with "ten pounds sterling [...] in gold", and that they ended up confessing where they had hidden the loot of gold and jewels:

> finding themselves wrapped in a handkerchief of very fine English lace, one hundred and eighty-six pounds sterling and nine Spanish ounces with the symbols of Carlos III, Carlos IV and Fernando VIII; two gold rings with diamonds and rubies; four pairs of gold earrings; gold and ninety pesetas in cash.¹¹⁷

It is not difficult to imagine that Amelia's travels between Santa Isabel and Barcelona were made dressed in exclusive dresses and precious jewels, accompanied by fine trunks that carried her silk clothes and lace, hats and umbrellas, as well as cash in various foreign currencies and gold. This standard of living was by no means what the vast majority of the Equatorial Guinean population had, nor indeed a good part of the Fernandino families.

African women à la European: dress as a status symbol and social class marker

The social presentation of the human body was a determining factor in distinguishing the Krio Fernandino from the rest of the Equatorial

Guinean and African community of the city in which artisans and servants also lived, as well as Europeans. Their attire set them apart from the rest of the Equatorial Guineans, yet also from other Krio groups. For the Fernandino community and also for the European community, dress was an expression of culture.

Thus, the Fernandinos became swiftly aware that dress would constitute one of the most visible elements of their distinction, able also to distinguish them from the Europeans and Spaniards who, as a general rule, were always less well kempt. In this regard, Saavedra (1910, p. 110) stressed that the dress of the Fernandino community was so exclusive "that the European colony neither surpasses nor attains the same level".

In Barcelona, certain prestigious tailoring firms were commonly used that the majority of the population could not dream of purchasing from due to their high cost. These specialist establishments were highly prized and many wealthy Fernandino citizens commissioned their suits and dresses there. One example was the outfitters Los Tres Regalos (The Three Gifts). Fashion news spread like wildfire in Santa Isabel via the magazine *Le Chic* was advertised in *La Voz de Fernando Poo* since the 1910s. The Ministers of Justice and Finance of the Republic of Liberia dressed in clothes from Los Tres Regalos in 1919. The news clipping on this explained that the Africans

> had visited everything remarkable that is in Barcelona, including the outfitters Los Tres Regalos (carrer Pelai 6), where they have been ordered to tailor fine and rich suits, not only for themselves, but also for their cabinet colleagues. They are highly satisfied and more than impressed.[118]

As an anecdote, it should be noted that the Riffian leader Abdelkrim from Morocco also tried to order uniforms from this famous tailor's shop in 1921. However, it was during the time that a major Spanish defeat was predicted in the Battle of Annual, meaning the tailor considered it better to reject the commission, "for patriotism" so they claimed,[119] given that at the time the Spaniards were still trying to conquer the Spanish Protectorate of Morocco.

If the issue of dress had a special relevance at the time, it was because in the mid-nineteenth century, while the Fernandinos wore elegant clothing and fine fabrics of lace imported from England and Spain, much of the Equatorial Guinean population of the island of Fernando Poo and the rest of the islands and the territories of Spanish Guinea bustled around semi-nude. Góngora Echenique's (1923, pp. 25-26) description of Equatorial Guinean nudity was in line with other accounts that had been published in previous decades: "the Pamue who live on land, are the prototype of savage [...] They wander about completely nude and like the Bubis when they are adults, tapping only their sexual organs."

The claim is made that nudity was an issue that from a European point of view demonstrated supposed African savagery, since culture demanded the body be covered in clothing. For the Spaniards, seeing the inhabitants of the colony naked was interpreted as proof of their primitivism and a justification of the Africans' inferiority. As a result, they decided to encourage the use of European-style clothing, especially in urban environments or on plantations that were within their sphere of influence.

Usera y Alarcón (1848) recounted a somewhat whimsical anecdote that, in reality, was a fierce criticism of the carefree African ways. In it, Governor Lynsleger lent a slave who was a cook (in a place where slavery was supposed to be frowned upon), explaining the hardship the slave felt because he only wore a loincloth:

> This Joseph was a slave of Lieutenant Governor Mr Lynsleger, who had lent him to us for our service. Young [...] lean and tall in size, he was a black man, who in certain lights was ugly [...] His entire garb consisted of a rag, which hung between his legs [...] I had to warn him [...] to stop scratching, even while serving us at the table; because while we ate, he used to scratch his calves, and even worse. I tried to cover his flesh, so I gave him a good piece of percale (Usera y Alarcón, 1848, p. 63).

Thus, certainly, the social presentation of the Krio Fernandino body was bound to contrast greatly with the nudity that was widespread in the second half of the nineteenth century. Proof of this can be found in the various testimonies of people who, either as part of the colonial authorities or as visitors to the colony, observed the Fernandino clothing and exquisiteness with curiosity. It is understandable that the encounter of the Spaniards with the English Fernandinos was marked by their careful dress and elegance, always following fads and trends with the latest European innovations, which aroused more than a sense of inferiority amongst their interlocutors.

Guillemar de Aragón (1852, p. 27) described the distinction of certain Fernandinos in Santa Isabel thus:

> The black ladies with black satin dress and French-style hats resemble in dress the whites of Europe. In the villages they work as hard as they can to clothe themselves in European clothing, and it is astonishing to see women on Sunday attending services.

In his descriptions, Guillemar de Aragón (1852, pp. 32–33) called the Fernandino way of dressing "aristocratic", since it was similar to that of Freetown.

Years later, Muñoz y Gaviria (1871a, p. 6) would also recount his surprise upon seeing the Fernandinos' Sunday strolls in Santa Isabel, with a gait that would vary little when they visited Barcelona, except that they would adorn themselves even more:

> Among these buildings that we have described [...] a beautiful promenade begins [...] that runs until the sea and that serves as a public thoroughfare, where on holidays and good weather, black women flaunt with great affection the European fashions and their exaggerated hopp skirts.

The descriptions of Fernandino women's clothing would also be echoed for Fernandino men, because like the women, they always took care of their clothes and appearance: "The blacks residing in Santa Isabel dress almost all European, and are highly politicised and civilised, except the Krumanes, who preserve the character of their people and their primitive nudity" (Muñoz y Gaviria, 1871a, p. 5).

At the start of the twentieth century, Saavedra (1910, p. 110) offered some details of the Fernandinos, noting that in addition to being practising Protestants, the men and women dressed very opulently:

> The site of the Methodist Mission, where the *moreno* population from English possessions especially attends [...] is not cheap. When they leave their religious offices [...] it is to see the luxury which they lavish upon themselves, and the taste that presides over their clothing. Some of the families from the clique to which we refer amassed considerable fortunes that allowed them to visit the capitals of Europe, London especially, there not overlooking for a second the chance to fit in with court and to satisfy the demands of fashion.

In the same vein, Ramos Izquierdo and Navarro y Beltrán (1912, p. 26) defined the Fernandino as an educated and respectful population, who dressed in the European style, including their children.

Góngora Echenique (1923, p. 21) explained that:

> there are numerous families of Fernandino *morenos* [...] illustrious in appearance and boasting grounded culture, they have learned from Europe and have acquired customs of good taste and civilisation that, as expected, are sadly lacking in those who have just left the jungle.

What is more, the little confidence that Arija (1930) would transmit was part of the detachment that Spanish colonial structures had from the Fernandinos, which was particularly evident in the 1930s. It comes as no surprise that Arija (1930, p. 136), after a description of the Fernandinos' values and merits, ended up reproducing in detail a Fernandino ritual with all kinds of macabre and scabrous details, since probably the only purpose was to sow reasonable doubts about the supposed Europeanness of the Fernandino.

Fernandino elegance is one of the symbols of the Krio Fernandino community of the late nineteenth and early twentieth centuries. Although there are not many paintings and photographs portraying the Fernandino in their full splendour that have been saved from travel, dictatorships or fires, these constitute true visual testimonies of the Krio Fernandino's way of living and being.

4.5. Fernandino women mixing cultures and continents (Africa, America and Europe)

The Krio Fernandino was an African group of multi-ethnic origin formed in Fernando Poo from 1827. Several decades later, they mixed with Cubans and West Indian and Jamaican ancestors of Sierra Leonean origin, merging African with American roots. In the first half of the twentieth century, they mixed also with Europeans in Barcelona: a few of Krio Fernandino married with Catalans, such as that of Consuelo Balboa Arkins with Fausto Ruíz Espuñas (Gargallo & Sant, 2021, p. 89). In Spanish Guinea a minority of unions of Equatorial Guinean women with Spaniards would have to wait for the end of colonisation to consolidate, since practically all of them were abandoned (Aixelà-Cabré, 2022a). The theme of mixed marriages was part of Lucia Mbomio's 2017 novel "Las que se atrevieron" (Those who dared), which tells the story of those who married in Spain. Rubiés (2001, p. 50) recalls that long ago interracial marriages were "highly frowned upon by the authorities and by all Spanish civil society."

Indeed, the interracial experience in the colony entailed sexual abuse, but this was excused since, according to the Spaniards, on many occasions it had been the African men who offered their women. This is explained by Muñoz y Gaviria (1871b, pp. 139–140), who told how they offered him two black virgins in Lagos, whom he had to accept so as not to offend the host, but for which he felt a deep repugnance.

Thus, the alliance of European men with African women as rich and powerful as the Fernandinos was atypical until the late twentieth century. However, it must be said that this type of marriage was not part of the main aim of the Krio Fernandino elites.

Within the framework of kinship, the process of consolidation of the Krio Fernandino community passed through combining endogamic marriages, as a means to strengthen their Sierra Leonean, Liberian and Nigerian roots, with exogamous marriages that would add Cuban roots to the Fernandino culture, with surnames such as Moreno, Castillo and Balboa. It is clear that the Fernandino elite understood endogamy as the route to bolstering their great fortunes while reinforcing the privileges they had acquired through their trade with the Europeans. Aranzadi (2016, p. 259) agrees with the diagnosis that "this group was constituted and developed by maintaining a certain endogamy among the groups originating from their different countries during the nineteenth century."

However, at the beginning of their decline as a wealthy elite, a certain amount of exogamous marriages with other Equatorial Guinean groups began to reappear, specifically with the Bubis, although they were a minority, such as the Boricó or Maho. These links did not bring with them the advantages of the large economic consortia of the past, as these ethnic groups had not enjoyed the same privileges as the Krio Fernandino, like a letter of emancipation. These circumstances led to the Fernandino decline that was already very clear in the mid-1950s, since a majority of Fernandino fortunes had already been exhausted, leaving only the great landowners of yesteryear.

In this rise and fall of the Fernandinos' elite status, the Krio Fernandino women were those who mixed cultures and continents with their marriages. This will be discussed below through a review of the most renowned endogamous marriages, and by examining how certain Fernandino – and also European – men wished to take advantage of Fernandino privileges either by marrying Fernandino women or accepting their surnames.

Between endogamy, mixing and Fernandino Creolism

The Krio Fernandino's roots were complex. Africans who came from countries like Sierra Leone or Liberia already had their own mixed-race roots, since as Guillemar de Aragón recalled (1852, p. 26) in Sierra Leone this colony had been "formed to shelter in its bosom the blacks that are extracted from the slave ships, there are in it races of more than thirty African tribes." Likewise, Aranzadi (2016, p. 55) explains the enormous social stratification that the Krio Fernandino minority left as its imprint in the mid-nineteenth century, since the thirty or so communities that Guillemar de Aragón pointed out were missing the recaptured slaves, "the American blacks of the Caribbean and natives of the Gold Coast (Ghana) [...] [and] the Krumanes or the Isuwu hired by the Western Company."

The constant mixing within the Krio Fernandino group would eventually highlight their classism, as it was their class privileges that they tried to safeguard through endogamic marriages that allowed them to seek a certain isogamy (marriage between equals). As Aranzadi (2016, p. 256) recalls according to sources: "The evolution of this social structure in Fernando Poo would continue to generate great fortunes."

Needless to say, one of the main arguments in the academic literature that labelled the Krio in Africa as "un-African" started from the cataloguing of these groups as extremely Europeanised (Sundiata, 1996), aligning them more with European cultures than with African ones. However, factors such as their clothing, knowledge of European languages, access to education in European centres and the practice of monotheistic religions are insufficient to doubt the African identity of the Krio Fernandino. In fact, cultural diversity and Afropolitanism were also part of the Krio Fernandino spirit.

An aspect highly relevant among the Krio Fernandino was the endogamy that had the effect of guaranteeing the size of estates. Probably some Krio Fernandino marriages were agreed on because they responded to the economic interests of the families and, in the ultimate case, of the community. For example, Amelia Barleycorn's marriage to William Allen Vivour was doubly endogamic, first because it was between Krio Fernandino families, and second because the origin of their grandparents was in Nigeria (although Vivour was born in Sierra Leone).

It should be remarked that, despite the low visibility of the Krio Fernandino women in the history of the community, they played a key role in family alliances. Below, a selection of relevant marriages and baptisms has been highlighted, in which the same influential surnames appear time and time again, thereby supporting each other.

In 1908, the baptism of Joseph Dougan and Mariana Kinson's child was held, who they would also called Joseph. The godparents were Luís Lolín Camblé and the girl Juliana Dougan Kinson. In 1911, Julia Vivour Barleycorn married Samuel Kinson. Similarly, we have Mariana Kinson's marriage to Samuel Dougan. The couple took centre stage in the baptism of their twins in 1911, who would be called Theodore and Theodora. The godparents were Teófilo Dougan and Ana Wartron, thus showing the functioning of the complex networks and complicities of the Fernandino community. This example also shows how certain Fernandinos decided to act as Catholics, probably ensure greater integration into the Spanish colony and to gain the advantages of recognition and visibility in politics and business. Another marriage between Fernandinos was that of Claudio Cole Vivour to Carlota Christian Davis in 1915. Also in 1920, the wedding of Edmundo Collins to Juana Jones, daughter of Maximiliano C. Jones, was held, with a sizable age difference between the spouses probably resulting from a pact between the two families that aimed to safeguard the economic potential of both bloodlines. Furthermore, the marriage placed Juana Jones in something of a bind, as the wedding was to be Catholic and she wished to marry according to her religion, which was Protestant: "The betrothal took place in the Protestant Chapel to which the spouses are regular attendants. As a complement, a magnificent banquet was served at Mr Fita's Restaurant."[120] Their daughters were Juana Elena and Trinidad Collins Jones.

With the Fernandino decline already noticeable in the 1950s, some of the Krio Fernandino families had already settled in Barcelona with little intention to leave. An example would be the couple Rolando Barleycorn Macfoy and Trinidad Collins Jones, who lived on the bourgeois carrer de Marià Cubí. The couple had given birth to Maria Raquel Barleycorn Collins and Rolando Barleycorn Collins.

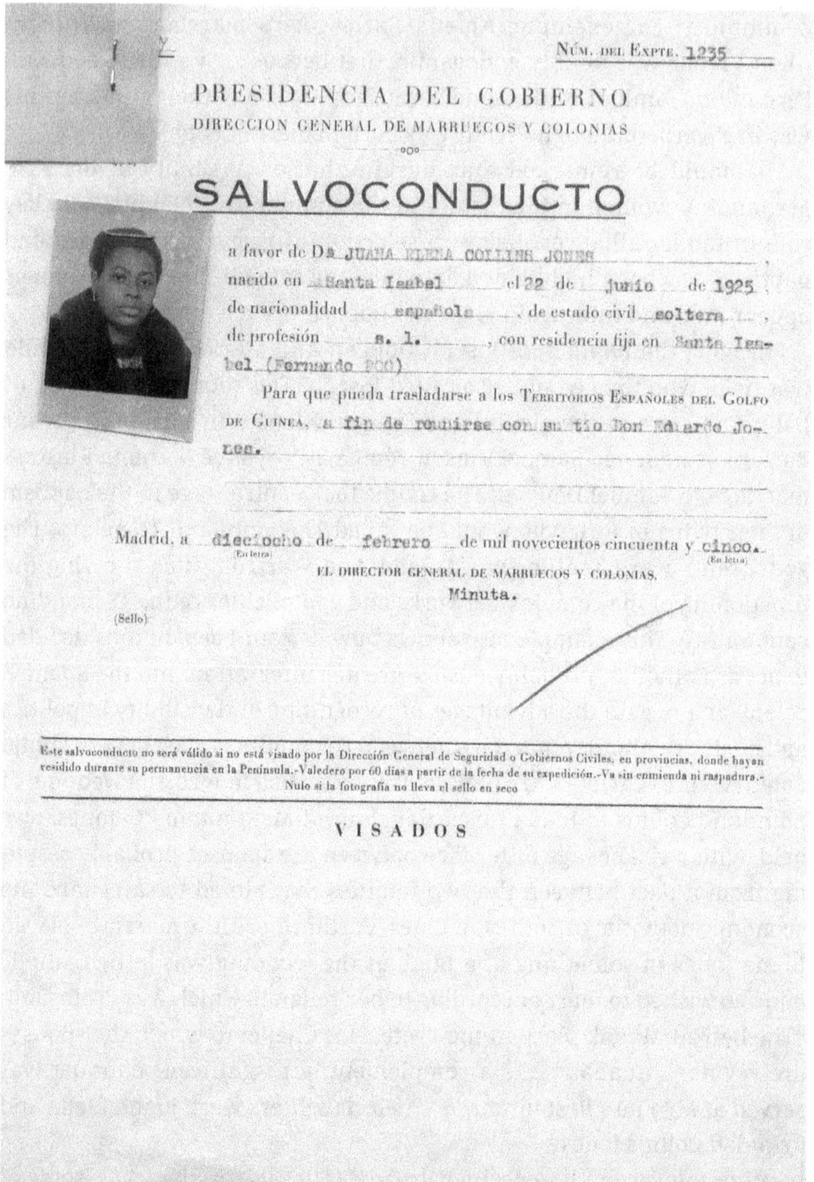

NÚM. DEL EXPTE. 1235

PRESIDENCIA DEL GOBIERNO

DIRECCION GENERAL DE MARRUECOS Y COLONIAS

SALVOCONDUCTO

a favor de Dª JUANA ELENA COLLINS JONES,
nacido en Santa Isabel el 22 de junio de 1925,
de nacionalidad española, de estado civil soltera,
de profesión s. l., con residencia fija en Santa Isabel (Fernando POO)

Para que pueda trasladarse a los TERRITORIOS ESPAÑOLES DEL GOLFO DE GUINEA, a fin de reunirse con su tío Don Eduardo Jones.

Madrid, a dieciocho (En letra) de febrero de mil novecientos cincuenta y cinco. (En letra)

EL DIRECTOR GENERAL DE MARRUECOS Y COLONIAS,

Minuta.

(Sello)

Este salvoconducto no será válido si no está visado por la Dirección General de Seguridad o Gobiernos Civiles, en provincias, donde hayan residido durante su permanencia en la Península.-Valedero por 60 días a partir de la fecha de su expedición.-Va sin enmienda ni raspadura.-
Nulo si la fotografía no lleva el sello en seco

VISADOS

Figure 6. Letter of safe passage for Juana Elena Collins Jones. General Archive of the Administration, box 81/08349.

Certainly, an appreciation of the endogamy practised by the Krio Fernandino could clearly be seen in a wedding celebrated one hundred years after their emergence as an African multi-ethnic group. The meeting was the symbol of an endless array of renowned families who watched their fortunes dwindle as the Spanish government hindered their commercial development. The well-publicised marriage of Edmundo Collins Jones to Lucrecia Jones Dougan took place at Santa Isabel's Cathedral in 1956. The newspapers at the time recounted the family ties that the spouses had with the most illustrious Fernandino families:

> Ms Lucrecia is the legitimate daughter of the spouses Mrs Lorenza Dougan Kinson and Mr Eduardo Jones Bishop. Her grandparents were Mr José Walterio Dougan, Mrs Mariana Kinson, Mr Maximiliano C. Jones, Mr Samuel Kinson and Daniel Kinson. The niece of Mr Jones, Mr Teófilo J. Dougan and Mr José Okori Dougan, we related her to the Castillo house by the marriage of her uncle Mr Wilbardo Jones Níger with Mrs Susana Castillo, daughter of Mr Pablo Castillo who passed on to a better life. He is also related to the brothers Mr Armando Balboa Arkins, Norberto Balboa Arkins and Abilio Balboa Arkins. The Fernandinos congratulate with all their heart such illustrious newlyweds on the occasion of their wedding and all their relatives from the following houses: Balboa, Barleycorn, Castillo, Collins, Dougan, Jones, Kinson and Vivour.[121]

Fernandino endogamy, by marrying each other, maintained their properties, surnames, power and influence. Yet for Amalia (2021), a descendant of Amelia Barleycorn, the advantages accrued to the Fernandino women themselves, since it was not so much a question of group safeguarding as of the freedom of the Fernandino women themselves:

> In order not to skip the rules of life, they were looking for someone within the same range. Now I understand a lot of things about why. That these women protected themselves in this way so as not to fall into certain forms of life that were not for them. Maybe we, the following Barleycorns, follow those brands and lines, because many of us are so independent that they can't have a partner either, because many of them didn't work.

Amalia (2021) concluded that, viewed from the historical standpoint, the legacy of Fernandino women like the Barleycorns was that they could not marry anyone, owing to the fact that current Equatorial Guinean society is notably marked by the Fang androcentrism that today is widely represented on the island of Malabo, formerly Fernando Poo:

> Men are now more dominant and now we have joined with a patriarchal society, without voice or vote for women, since many women of Barleycorn are left without men. Maybe they have a lover, but that is not how it works. Maybe it's our DNA.

As Amalia (2021) stressed, Fernandino women "did not marry anyone. There are women, even my aunts, who were only three sisters and only one married, because the other two did not marry because there was no man at her level."

This overview has sought to put names and dates to many of the endogamic marriages that allowed Fernandino privileges to be safeguarded for several generations. Some data are relevant because they show that the marriage between the Krio Fernandino did not relegate these women to either home or motherhood, since they had the ability to choose the path they wanted to take, whether it was developing in a family environment, or in a commercial one. It has also been observed that endogamy was a community necessity, though it was also the marriage solution for women in the Krio Fernandino group who did not wish to lose their status by marrying men from other groups.

Because of all this, the marriages between the Krio Fernandino strengthened the elite status of those who were married, safeguarding their memory for future generations as, although they lost most of their farmsteads and properties, they continued to uphold the pride of a past that distinguished them from the rest of the population, an influence still recognised in the current generations of Equatorial Guineans.

The adoption of Krio Fernandino methods as a blueprint for individual empowerment

The documentation consulted has made it possible to identify cases in Fernando Poo in which marriages to Fernandino women allowed Fernandino, Bubi and also white European males to thrive.

These practices proved husbands' desire to enhance their status through their wives. In the event that the spouses were Fernandino men, they could bring their family closer to the most powerful family in the union, that of the wife, through the adoption of her surname. This is the reverse (and for different reasons) of those who added the Spanish possessive "*de*" to their surnames to define who were wives, for example Mariana Kinson de Dougan. It cannot be determined to what extent the practice of taking or prioritising the surname of Fernandino women was statistically relevant, but in light of the cases found, it was not an isolated occurrence. This aspect is of interest as it again stresses the power and prestige that Fernandino women held, as well as the advantages gained by who married them despite not being part of any of the main Fernandino families.

One of the cases reviewed was that of Carlos G. Vivour. Despite the fact that he signed documents with this name, in reality he was Carlos García Vivour. As we saw, he married Sarah Vivour. Although there is no way to affirm this with absolute certainty, it is unlikely that two Vivours who were closely genetically related since the rules of the taboo of incest prohibited unions with a certain consanguineous proximity. Therefore, when he signed Carlos G. Vivour, abbreviating García, what he did was to bring himself closer to a family of great influence on the island: the lineage of the Vivours. Moreover, interestingly, his marriage with Sarah Vivour was rewarded with the support that Amelia Barleycorn provided on numerous occasions, in her claims in the colony, as has been recorded in numerous files about the resolution of conflicts in which he was the accused, for example the file opened against Carlos G. Vivour on the occasion of insults conferred on Lieutenant Joaquín Carlos Roca in 1907.

A different case would be the marriage of a Fernandino woman to a Bubi man. Amalia (2021) reconstructed the second marriage of a Barleycorn with a Bubi, explaining that the strength of the Fernandinos was overwhelming: "she had a husband who she could mould as she wanted, even forcing him to adopt the name of her late husband in order to become her husband." Amalia (2021) continued, recalling how in this case it was the man who gave in to the demands of his wife: "she knew perhaps to maintain that dignity or that something, the mentality of the time was to do things properly."

However, there were other Fernandino women who preferred spinsterhood to a marriage that did not match their status because they were not willing to use the practice of the husband adopting the surname of the wife (or of the deceased husband if she was a widow).

What is highly relevant in these two examples is that the marriage with Fernandino women allowed, or enhance the husbands position who took a more illustrious surname, or improve their family status.

We still need to review marriages of Krio Fernandino women to white men in the nineteenth century which, it must be said, were anecdotal. At that time, the most notable Krio Fernandino families were "Davis, Barleycorn, Vivour, Kinson, Dougan, Balboa, Knox, Barber, Coker and Collins" (Clarence-Smith, 1994, p. 190).

According to sources, London-born Governor James Lynsleger, an associate of John Beecroft (Dike 1956), quickly became rich and powerful in Fernando Poo thanks to his marriage to a black woman there, apparently a Fernandino. Lynsleger had arrived on the island "with just his breeches", as confirmed by Usera y Alarcón (1848, p. 25), and the liaison had made him a vastly powerful man. Muñoz y Gaviria (1871a, p. 12) recounted: "Mr Lynsleger, who [...] had been governor of the island by the Spanish government [...] [was] about forty-six years old, married to a hugely wealthy woman of that population, in which she owns a good colonial establishment."

As a matter of fact, it is known that the house of Lynsleger was the most luxurious in all of Santa Isabel, as reported by Father Usera y Alarcón (1848, pp. 19–22) when he arrived at Fernando Poo in 1845: "some of the English missionaries, whom I visited frequently, can be said to enjoy luxury that would raise eyebrows even in that country. The finest of all is the one owned by Lieutenant Governor Mister Lynsleger."

A further case at that time between a Fernandino woman and a European man was the relationship of the Englishman John Beecroft, who was born in Yorkshire, with Mrs Scott, a well-known black widow of the island, between whom there was no marriage. Usera y Alarcón (1848, p. 24) described Beecroft as

> an Englishman of around 54 years old, of a fairly regular stature, stocky and of venerable appearance, giving to his physiognomy a particular importance his grey-headed, and sparsely populated head of hair. For about 19 years he has lived on the island, always engaged in trading, in the exercise of which he has acquired a reasonable fortune. He owns his own house on the coast, and about two leagues from the capital [...] For this reason, in Santa Isabel he used to live in the house of the widow of colour "Miss Scott".

Marrying Scott would have been unlawful because Beecroft was already married in Yorkshire and had four children there when he died, meaning he would not have been able to formalise his cohabitation with this black widow, in whose house, according to Usera y Alarcón (1848, p. 24), he often stayed. Now, the fact that they did not marry does not mean that the relationship did not exist it was not known by everyone.

The cases reviewed reveal that there were situations in which the husbands of Fernandino women who were of Fernandino or Bubi origin chose to take their wife's surname for reasons of prestige or because the wife so requested to hide a non-Fernandino origin. At the same time the case of marriage with one of the Englishmen who arrived on the island, since Beecroft's was never formalised, as he was previously married in England, would bolster his intent to integrate into the community while garnering power and authority. Regardless, Krio Fernandino women appeared as the subjects who improved the status of men thanks to their family lineage.

4.6. The impact of Spanish colonialism and Fernandino decline

An example of the colonial exoticism with which African dignitaries were viewed at the beginning of the twentieth century can be ascertained from the report published in *La Voz de Fernando Poo* discussing to the visit of a Cameroonian king of Fang ethnicity to Madrid in 1919. Under the headline "The Castaways of War. The Black King of the Pamues visits *El Día*", the article described the visit of the African monarch and his entourage without sparing any details, including that at the reception of the newspaper there were "a black lord, who is king, and accompanied by other blacks".[122] The visit was classified as "odd", since at that time the black African population who visited or lived in the capital of the Kingdom of Spain was minimal and no one expected a guest of such lofty status. The editor explained that the king dressed elegantly in a suit, that he spoke decent German and English, and that, among other anecdotes which he told him, was that he always dressed in European style but that his usual king's suit was a leopard skin with elephant tusks. Surely the journalist would have been surprised at the Germanophilia of his guest, if nothing else because he had told him that he was in exile after being expelled by the French and that he expected to receive the support of Germany to regain his power: "I studied in Berlin. They view our country as civilised.

Schools are numerous and treat us with affection and respect."[123] The editor could not fail to mention in the article, to the demerit of the black king, that "like any modest bourgeois, they stay in a second-rate hotel", adding snidely "as one would expect."[124]

This anecdote serves as an introduction to understand how the stereotypes of the Spanish colonialities faced Africans boasting excellent education, financial wealth and better clothing than their interlocutors, since this was the most common profile of the Krio Fernandino men and women, both in Fernando Poo and in the mainland Spain from 1850 almost until independence.

Below are some of the key elements of the Fernandinos' slow decline, alongside the effects that Hispanisation and Christianisation had on the emergence of certain Spanish colonies that would impact the Krio Fernandino and the Equatorial Guinean population differently.

The Fernandinos' slow decline and linguistic and religious Hispanisation as a form of integration into the colony

Throughout this book Fernandino–European mediation has been addressed as the key that constituted the source of the Krio Fernandino's privileges and benefits, first with the English and then with the Catalans and Spaniards. The huge fortunes of the Krio Fernandino would not have been amassed without the fostering of this elite on the part of the British, who ended up empowering themselves to the point of controlling the agricultural and commercial trade of the entire island of Fernando Poo by the end of the nineteenth century.

Three major factors converged to a different extent in the Fernandinos' decline: the obstacles raised by the colonial authorities to maintaining their properties, the supposed squandering of their fortunes on luxury goods and high standards of living, and the linguistic and religious Hispanisation that characterised Spanish colonisation.

First of all, the Fernandinos' slow decline can be explained by the numerous obstacles that Spanish colonial authorities implemented to reverse the dominance of the Krio Fernandino, since their aim was to divert the gains that the Fernandino had obtained from agricultural production into Spanish hands.

We have reviewed some of the difficulties posed by Spanish colonisation throughout this book that led to the Fernandinos' loss of power. These have included changes in legal regulations to favour Spanish holdings and impediments to renewing or obtaining new agricultural concessions.

Claredon Smith (1994) highlights as one of the factors that led to the decline the fragmentation of large estates as a result of inheritances and the decrease in the concessions received. He notes that some Krio Fernandino still retained one-sixth of the island's properties in 1941, despite the power deployed by the Spanish colonists to eradicate all their privileges:

> The subdivision of land through inheritance may have caused a fall in the average amount of property per head, but it did not of itself reduce the total amount of land owned by the community. Concessions were frozen at 39,000 hectares in 1930, of which 21,000 were in the hands of Europeans and 8,000 (46 per cent) in the hands of African (Claredon Smith, 1994, p. 198).

The transition to decay was somewhat gradual. The Spaniards wanted to take away their power and centrality on the island and in Santa Isabel. In fact, most of the new firms that were founded either excluded them or did not involve them in any scale. An anecdote that illustrates this loss of power is the case of Jeremías Jones Mehilo, since the authorities applied unfair and disproportionate interests to him so that he lost his property in an unfair and underhand practice. When consulting the claims in court, there is documentation that says:

> Case filed by Jeremías Jones Mehilo, reporting that having mortgaged 6 hectares of a 14-hectare estate that he has in Basapo, in 1919, for the amount of 5,000 pesetas, to the Casa Sebastián Torres in Barcelona, they still claim that the debt stands at 25,000 pesetas (AGA, box 81/06340).

It is certain that the Spanish government not only wished to avoid extending the concession of the estates to the Fernandinos or transferring new ones. Furthermore, it did not want the *braceros* who had been hired to work on the estates to stay on the island at the end of their contracts. Therefore, a decree was finally promulgated in 1919 prohibiting *braceros* from acquiring land, as stated in the *Boletín Oficial del Protectorado*.

Aranzadi (2016, p. 257) concluded that "the decadence of the Fernandinos began with the immigration of the Spaniards and from the mid-1920s among the factors would be the formation of public limited

Table 30. Largest Spanish populations in Santa Isabel. Census of 1942

Origin	Men	Women	Total
Alicante	17	1	18
Barcelona	69	28	97
Cordoba	18	11	29
La Coruña	31	18	49
Las Palmas	31	16	47
Madrid	68	89	157
Murcia	31	13	44
Orense	35	2	37
Oviedo	36	16	52
Pamplona	17	17	34
Valencia	22	13	35
Spanish Territories of the Gulf of Guinea	63	58	121
Other and not stated	2,255	143	2,398
Total	2,693	425	3,118

Source: Compiled by the author. Resúmenes Estadísticos del Gobierno General de los Territorios Españoles del Golfo de Guinea (1945, p. 32–33).

companies and an accentuated social discrimination." For her, according to the Fernandinos themselves, their decline was due to the fact that when the Spaniards arrived, most of the estates belonged to the Sierra Leoneans and the credit and tax policy did not benefit them (Aranzadi, 2016, p. 257).

It should also be remembered that the loss of Fernandino power from the 1930s coincided with the decline of the influence of the Catalan bourgeoisie in Spanish Guinea, which was also taken out of agricultural and commercial production for the benefit of owners in other regions and cities of the mainland, especially the capital, Madrid (see Table 30).

The second factor in the Fernandinos' decline concerns their alleged squandering of their wealth. Suffice to say that much has been written about this as the main reason for their decline, without sufficiently appraising the discomfort of the Spanish authorities with the fact that the greatest fortunes of the island were in the hands of Fernandino who, although Spanish subjects, were actually black Africans, enjoying a greater influence than that which the white settlers themselves could exert.

The matter of Krio Fernandino consumption was related to their lifestyle and the luxuries and vast expenses they generated. The Claretian Father Ruiaz (1928, pp. 87–88) was very clear when he reproached the Fernandinos for their profligacy in Santa Isabel, in April 1928. His moral criticism conveyed a certain indignation at the high standard of living that the Fernandinos had come to acquire and, although he did not mention the issue of blackness, this was in the background of the pejorative assessment professed by many Catholic missionaries. This is because, in their day to day work, their aim was to convert "primitive and savage Africans", and not have to maintain a reverential attitude towards a black African collective of elevated socio-economic status:

> Our Fernandino society has participated in this decline: it shows strength to confess it, but today it is undergoing a truly acute crisis. The disappearance of those prestigious men, who gave it such a high name and who, if they lived, would be the channelling of forces and tendencies towards a healthy and moralising current is a fact: truly prestigious families are disappearing and if not, what will become of the old? With a few exceptions, the things that remain we see in perfect decay. To this has contributed the ignorance of family life: drinking, united to frittering away their assets, alongside disorder and economic disarray. Today's Fernandinos have found a fortune that they did not work to amass and therefore cannot comprehend the efforts needed to attain this; they do not know what is honest work and pander to themselves enjoying what their self-sacrificing parents bequeathed them, believing that this will never end (Ruiaz, 1928, pp. 87–88)

Certainly, the accusations of improvidence directed by Catalan missionaries towards the Krio Fernandino people focused on the numerous expenses incurred by their exclusive way of life, with mansions, trips, studies, jewellery and lavish parties on the island and in Europe. However, the missionaries averted their eyes, as this same community was willing to respond to the numerous requests for money they received from the missions, both Protestant and Catholic, which requested aid and alms sometimes sufficiently large to finance their activities and godly works. This was the case of the Catalan and Spanish missionaries in relation to the Cathedral of Santa Isabel, financed not so much with the money destined for its construction by the Kingdom of Spain or the Catholic Church itself, but with the aid received from the Krio Fernandino, many of whom were nevertheless still Protestants, as is proven by much of the documentation consulted.

It should also be said that certain Fernandino descendants have been displeased with the loss of their ancestors' fortunes. One of the Joneses who still lives in Malabo told me in 2008 on a visit to the centre of the city – where, as a tour guide, he highlighted all the buildings that had been owned by the family – that after independence they had practically nothing left of everything treasured by their grandfather Maximiliano. For her part, Amalia (2021) was less critical, since she did not question the lavish expenses of the Barleycorns, nor that descendants like her had not received the fortune as an inheritance, since for Amalia the family was much more than money: the past prestige was for them the guidelines of Fernandino honour and dignity in the present.

Clarence-Smith also recalled that the traveller Mary Kingsley referred to the Fernandinos in terms of extravagant spending, implying that these Africans did not know how to save. In this assessment she contrasted with the claims of the ethnographer Tessmann, who described William A. Vivour, the husband of Amelia Barleycorn, almost as a miser because of how thrifty he was. Ultimately, Clarence-Smith (1994, p. 196) concluded that, after his research, he would rely more on the assertions of a German observer than on the comments of an English traveller, since excessive spending was the result of the consumption of people "of all colours", not just a bad Fernandino habit.

Thus, either due to Spanish pressure to strip the Fernandinos of their power, or the product of their alleged profligacy, or because of the combination of both factors, the truth is that the Krio Fernandino families of Santa Isabel were finally left bankrupt, many of them having no option but to flee when the dictatorship of Macías broke out after independence, with some descendants of the most famous families returning only decades later.

What is more, the Fernandinos' decline also coincided with the decline of influence of the Protestant community, which became very evident from 1920 onwards. This third factor must be considered when appraising whether the dissipation of female influence was the result of Hispanisation and colonial Christianisation. It should be borne in mind that, until the arrival of the Spaniards, Christianisation was imposed via Protestantism and the English language, which caused part of the Fernandinos to reject the conversion to Catholicism and the linguistic Hispanisation required by colonial authorities to facilitate integration into the Spanish colony and to carry out all kinds of procedures in trials, courts, concessions, family registries, etc. The result of this colonial pressure was that those Fernandinos who agreed to convert and apparently adopt Spanish as a lingua franca – although the majority continued to speak Pichi day to day – ended up gaining greater socio-economic influence than those who continued to practise Protestantism and kept English as their lingua franca. In this regard, Maximiliano C. Jones would become the role model of Catholic conversion and linguistic Hispanisation, a successful individual who colonial authorities fostered perhaps to show the rest of the Fernandinos what behaviour they expected from them in relation to Spanish colonisation if they wished to be rewarded with its perks.

The influence of the great Krio Fernandino landowners in Santa Isabel and Fernando Poo prevented racism as an ideology from developing at the same level as it did in Bata and other territories. Racial segregation was present, but was limited to timetables and venues, since it was also not possible to hide the deep racialisation that the Spaniards had fostered towards the Equatorial Guinean populations, both in the colonies and on the mainland.

In fact, racialisation had also seeped into Spanish Catholic missions to a lesser extent than in the British orders: if the English always gave great power and visibility to black African Protestants, the Spaniards and Catalans did not empower them, nor did they dedicate the same recognition to those who collaborated in the spread of Catholicism. Perhaps because of this, Hispanisation was slow and saw limited success until the 1920s.

Colonial Hispanisation also had a bearing on how Equatorial Guinean women were viewed, with clear patterns in terms of what changes they should adopt. These aspects were negatively felt on an overall level because, unlike the Fang, Bissio and Ndowe women, the Bubi women maintained somewhat egalitarian social dynamics in terms of sex, that was not very androcentric compared to Spanish culture. Thus, it was in the early 1920s that the Church began to impose its vision of the construction of gender that prevailed in Spain through Catholicism (Nash, 1983).

Ruiaz (1928, pp. 87–88) also related what, in his opinion, were the Fernandino excesses and the place that women should occupy. His presentation, which is intentionally instructive, reflected the stubborn criticisms of the way of life of the Fernandino collective in Santa Isabel:

> Because what is viewed as decadent nowadays can be your fault, since in the race there is spirit and life; and what is convenient is to put into motion those vital energies of the spirit. Like what? Listen to me: (1) Love family life [...] (2) Work proudly [...] (3) Be frugal in your dealings [...] (5) Be religious (Ruiaz, 1928, pp. 87–88).

The Fernandinos' decline was also leaked to written sources. Their loss of power was transferred to the way of naming them, as it began to become more common to refer to the Krio Fernandino elites as "natives", without devoting as much praise or implication in news reports, comparing them in practice to other Equatorial Guinean ethnic groups that had always remained subject to colonial power.

The Fernandinos' loss of influence in the field of production and trade also meant the loss of economic power for later generations. Their commercial collaboration with other bourgeoisies, such as the Catalans, had the effect of facilitating their replacement by other large landowners, many Spaniards. The Fernandinos' decline occurred in tandem with that of the rest of the emancipated Equatorial Guineans, although the latter had not enjoyed as many privileges as the Fernandinos. That said, there was similarly no lack of efforts by the community to improve its image in the final stretch of Spanish colonisation (Iyanga Pendi, 2021). The Krio Fernandino found themselves apologising for their colonial collaborationism, while at the same time it must have been difficult to explain that the secret of their success had been the colonial system.

4.7. Conclusion

This chapter's aim has been to facilitate a decolonial reading of different aspects related to Krio Fernandino women that transmitted their authority, dynamism and influence.

The analysis of Amelia Barleycorn's claim for the recognition of Protestant marriages showed the precariousness of the rights of the African Spaniards in the colony. Her daring approach, submitting a request that had to be resolved by the Council of State, led to the recognition of all Protestant marriages in the colony from the effective colonisation in the mid-nineteenth century until 1 January 1912. This initiative was a great legal, religious and social success spearheaded by a Fernandino woman, who had also amassed the greatest fortune in Spanish Guinea in 1890. Her defence of issues relating to marriage, nationality, religion and gender make it possible to contextualise the situation of the Protestant collectives and of the "Spanish nationals" in general, as her claim resolved the latent conflict that existed retroactively for all the Protestants in the colony. Even decades later, the precedent of this action also served to facilitate the entire Krio community that had resided on the island for decades to finally be able to apply for Spanish nationality with a simple procedure, should they so wish.

Likewise, the different spheres of power of Fernandino women have been reviewed to gauge their areas of influence, on the basis that their privileged status with respect to other Equatorial Guinean women and European colonists resided in bourgeois elitism and, in particular, in the alliance they had entered into with the colonial power.

The need to have a female Krio Fernandino storyline that explains the challenges and achievements of these women, as well as their capacity for mobilisation, organisation and association, while at the same time that some were also responsible for their estates and the management of their fortunes, has also been highlighted. The Fernandino story has to be written from a feminine standpoint using relevant figures such as Amelia Barleycorn.

The chapter includes an analysis of Fernandino racialisation from the perspective of their experiences with domestic service. This theme has highlighted that the Krio Fernandino, including Amalia Barleycorn, always had servants in their employ, both in Santa Isabel and in Barcelona, many times travelling on the same steamers. The interest was to examine the conflicts that could occur in dealing with servants. It was found that for the Fernandino community class was above race.

The high living standards of the Krio Fernandino have also been analysed, which is what made their elite status more visible and evident. This has been undertaken by reconstructing Amelia Barleycorn's lifestyle in San Carlos, as it would have had little difference from the one she maintained on her trips to Barcelona and England. Likewise, the social presentation of the body has been studied as a determining factor to transmit their greatness and opulence, since their dress was the most commonly mentioned aspect in the descriptions by nineteenth-century missionaries and explorers of the great elegance and finesse of the Fernandinos.

On the other hand, the issue of the Fernandinos' mixing has been reviewed, as this was one of the elements that characterised their culture and seemed to contradict the practice of endogamic marriage. It has been established that endogamy was a way of safeguarding the privileged status of the Krio Fernandino and was useful in ensuring the continuity of their fortunes. It has been highlighted that the interracial experience in nineteenth-century Spain was stigmatised in part by all the colonial rhetoric that was circulated to justify the indiscriminate abuse of African populations for the sake of Spanish colonialism. This did not, however, prevent Amelia Barleycorn and other Krio Fernandino from feeling comfortable in cities with a markedly cosmopolitan nature that facilitated their integration. In this regard, the impact that an alliance with such rich and powerful women had on the prestige of men has been analysed, observing the effects on Fernandino and Bubi men who were interested in adopting the surnames of their Fernandino wives, or of their wives' deceased husbands, as a method to strengthen their position in society.

Finally, the effects of Fernandino–European mediation have been studied as the key that constituted the source of Fernandino privileges, but also the beginning of their end, given the loss of power and authority once Spaniards became empowered and prevented the Fernandino community from continuing to enrich itself with agricultural trade. Viewed thus, the impact that the refined and cultured Fernandinos had on the Spanish colonists, missionaries and population of the peninsula has also been reviewed, since their excellent training, exquisite manners and elegance in dress clashed with the type of interlocutors that colonial rhetoric had led to be expected from primitive Africans. Certainly, the comparison of their life in Santa Isabel and Barcelona has given us a glimpse of the profound discomfort Spaniards felt when encountering this black African collective in Santa Isabel and on the peninsula, but not in the encounters with the Catalan bourgeoisie in Barcelona, in which, less afflicted by complexes, class was placed before race for trading interests, perhaps due of their experience with colonial Cuba.

CHAPTER 5

A past forged in the present: the collective memory of Krio Fernandino women – Closing notes

This book has combined the history of Africa with that of Europe from the mid-nineteenth century to the end of the twentieth century, starting from the Krio Fernandino community that flitted between Santa Isabel and Barcelona, and specifically from the figure of Amelia Barleycorn de Vivour.

This has taken the form a journey between cultures and continents that has aimed to write a diasporic *herstory*, while making the contributions of African women in Africa and Europe visible. In addition, the focus on the extraordinary mobility of the Krio Fernandino between cities and countries has provided an axis alon which to build an emotional geography that creates a map capable of connecting common past and present, incorporating experiences disregarded by European countries under the cumbersome weight of gender, blackness and African bias that I set out to reverse. In this sense, the research contextualises the solid grounding of the Afro-European claims of the twenty-first century, which require referents and, above all, recognition.

It is likely that the *chiaroscuros* of the Krio Fernandino community, as a "black coloniser", impregnated the figure of Amelia Barleycorn de Vivour, showing the sizable cracks in issues related to social justice and equal rights, because her empowerment was possible thanks to European colonialism. However, the Krio Fernandino were part of the machinery of colonialism – basically British, since the Spanish discomfort with this group was manifest. Therefore, it should be remembered that their racial liminality was manifested in the difficulties they facing in fitting in with the group of white settlers during their rise. Their decline allowed the colonial racialisation to emerge due to their skin colour, which left them one rung below, together with the African emancipated from the rest of the Equatorial Guineans, thus rearranging a racial pyramid that the Krio Fernandino had altered with their power and wealth since the end of the nineteenth century. Yet the colonial system had other essential collaborators to support it, beyond the Krio Fernandino community, such as the indigenous Colonial Guards, who severely repressed the population, or the community leaders, who applied the repressive measures ordered by the colonial authorities. It is worthwhile bearing in mind that when the colonial authorities wanted to repress the Equatorial Guinean population that had full or limited emancipation, they offered abusive loans to those who lost their lands or withdrew agricultural concessions, rescinded emancipation letters that were theoretically inviolable, or denied the right to travel as a form of reprisal for some inappropriate attitude.

Despite all the foregoing, the figure of Amelia Barleycorn is emblematic. Amelia reveals the tenacity, autonomy and independence of many other African women who had to fight titanically to overcome Eurocentric sex and race biases between the late nineteenth and early twentieth centuries, and who also did so without forgetting their African roots or neglecting their family. It was as if their Afropolitan consciousness allowed them to be in a world made to their measure. If there were doubts about the trajectory of Amelia Barleycorn, there was the request to the Ministry of State on the mainland, living proof of her struggle for the recognition of rights, not only her own, but of all those who were in the same situation, and of the Krio community in general.

The study has found that the colonial system shaped the rights and opportunities of Africans, not only in Africa, but also in Europe. It also endorses the idea that without accountability it will not be possible to counteract the fact that the powerful reverberations of the colonial way of looking at and interpreting the African continent and its women continue to this day. In fact, we have examined how being Spanish for the purposes of nationality in colonial times was in name only because, as if they were another possession, their rights were absolutely restricted compared to the Spaniards, both in the overseas colony and on the mainland, unless the variable social class was activated, as was the case with Krio Fernandino, which had allowed them to obtain the letter of emancipation.

Next, I will briefly offer some findings on the five specific aims outlined in the book.

The first aim was to offer a herstory of Africans in Africa and Europe centering women, which has been done using the biographical reconstruction of Amelia Barleycorn de Vivour and other influential Krio Fernandino women and families of the time. The research highlighted that Amelia represented a generation that has since died out. Although her group and elite consciousness remained throughout her life, her power diminished in parallel with that of her wealth in the following generations, a situation that was common to that of all families. Amelia perfectly synthesised all the values and defects of the Krio Fernandino, both those that indicated their entrepreneurship and strength in the face of adversity, and those that denoted their harshness towards *braceros* and servants. However, their group sense of honour always emerged with pride. If the Krio Fernandino story had been written with a female focus, Amelia Barleycorn would have undoubtedly taken centre stage.

The second aim proposed to distinguish being Euro-African or Afro-European from legal issues because, as we saw, colonisation granted European nationalities without citizenship rights that disappeared after independence and left the Africans who arrived in Europe as Afro-Europeans. I have already explained that the condition of being Euro-African or Afro-European was not intended to show the different options for being and feeling Euro-African and Afro-European, but rather to highlight the unpaid historical debt of colonial Europe to Africa that "Fortress Europe" has just erased and that, however, should represent a legal basis for granting European nationalities to those Africans who demand it. Research has proven that the supposed advantages that pseudo-European nationalities should have provided to Africans did not serve to improve their legal and juridical status. On the contrary, they were given a differentiating socio-political classification, i.e. emancipated or not, that laid the foundations for the abuse of African populations while turning into the racialising rhetoric of otherness that, to a different extent, impacted Africa and Europe before and after the decolonisation processes.

The third aim was to study the impact of intersectionality on class, gender and race among the Krio Fernandino. Certainly, the legacy of Amelia Barleycorn is very much alive, because she showed herself to be an autonomous and independent woman who was not intimidated by race, sex or the social class of her interlocutors, nor by the Spanish colonial power. In fact, some documents have shown how the processes of (de)racialisation were active, it being the context and the interlocutor that would end up determining whether the balance tipped in one direction or the other. It is likely that there was a notable racism on the part of the Krio Fernandino community that expressed itself against their servants, but this did not seem to be so much due to skin colour as to by social class, since classism is not the same as racism, although it can have similar effects. Another issue was how Amelia had to cope in male environments, since her leadership on her estates and in trade was an exception in the world of rich African and European landowners who were mostly men, something that came to her by inheritance from her husband, not by paternal inheritance.

The fourth aim considered the issue of African women in Barcelona and the rise of racism. The results of the research allow us to conclude that Equatorial Guinean women suffered minimisation, racialisation and subalternisation, but not the select diaspora of Krio Fernandino women, who, since they had power and authority thanks to their status as an elite, neutralised the discrimination of race, gender and class in their favour, both in Santa Isabel and in Barcelona. It was only later that the loss of their privileges dragged them toward defencelessness and anonymity. From then onwards, these women, and the Equatorial Guinean community in general, began to suffer the daily racism in Barcelona that other groups had faced, the ultimate expression of this colonial and urban forgetfulness being the racist aggression suffered by an illustrious Krio Fernandino descendant who united the Balboa and Dougan families in 1992. However, these aspects can be balanced by the description of who these women were, what they were like and how they lived in Africa, because only by reconstructing their environment and responsibilities, and the challenges and impact of the Spanish colonisation, can we demonstrate the dynamism, power and authority they displayed in Barcelona.

Regarding the fifth and final aim relating to the survival of colonialities in the Iberian framework, it should be noted that concepts such as multilocal, transnational, transcontinental and Afropolitanism have been fundamental in classifying the Krio Fernandino elite, since their characteristics and mobility between cities, countries and continents allow us to understand how their commercial relationship with the Catalan bourgeoisie, as we have seen, also included more private and family meetings. The term "Iberian cultures" has allowed me to soften the centrality of an analysis that leaves the connections and traces between Barcelona and Catalonia with Santa Isabel and Fernando Poo at the undefined margins. It could be concluded that while the Krio Fernandino had privileges, class was more significant than race, both in Europe and in Africa. Another question was how the loss of economic status plunged them into a racialisation that previous generations had not known, a decline that occurred in parallel with the loss of Catalan influence in the colony. In the 1930s, their loss of economic power allowed the Spanish colonists to run riot. The reconstruction of the historical presence of Africans on the Iberian Peninsula could not have been carried out without the study of the existing connection between Barcelona and Fernando Poo, since colonisation built a bridge that, although only a few Africans were able to cross, laid the foundations for their arrival at the end of the nineteenth century, a trace that has been lost today.

In short, my hope is that this book will serve to reduce the cloak of invisibility shrouding these figures while combating European colonialities, as these constitute one of the great obstacles to the recovery of African imprints in the history of Europe and to the enhancement of African diasporas today.

Notes

1. This work was supported by the R&D projects, directed by Y. Aixelà-Cabré, "Africans, Maghrebis and Latins (1808–1975). Blackness, resistance and deracialization of elites" (BLACK SPAIN) (PID2022-138689NB-I00), and "Africans and Maghrebis in the Iberian Peninsula (1850–1975). A history on the margins of Spain and Portugal" (AFRO-IBERIA) (PID2019-108397GB-I00/AEI/10.13039/501100011033), both funded by MCIN/AEI/10.13039/501100011033/ and "FEDER Una manera de hacer Europa". The volume was also supported by the project "Música, patrimoni i societat" (SGR 2021 00499), directed by María Gembero-Ustárroz (IMF-CSIC) and funded by AGAUR-Generalitat de Catalunya. This book has been translated by Craig Cavanagh and revised by Rebecca Bryan.
2. The effects of linguistic Hispanisation on the island of Fernando Poo had an impact on the name of Amelia: for the following generations of Barleycorns, the Spanish version has been used – Amalia. This will allow us to distinguish between her descendant Amalia Barleycorn and Amelia Barleycorn herself.
3. Another comparison between cities was the study of the Spanish colonial legacies in Al-Hoceima and Bata (Aixelà-Cabré, 2022a).
4. For greater detail on the concept of "Afropolitan" see Wasihun (2016). In order to know more about the Krio of Sierra Leone, see Goerg (1995). For future studies regarding the Afropolitan character of the Fernandino community, see A. Caballero-Svensson (2023) who previous research focused on the women vendors in Malabo.
5. See Santana (2020).
6. It is similarly noteworthy to stress a not-insignificant detail regarding the nomenclature used in this book. As all Fernandino were Krio or Creoles, but not all Krio or Creoles were descendants of Fernandinos, as specified by Yakpo (2010, p. 12), in this book I will use the term "Krio Fernandino" or "Fernandino" to delimit the collective to which I refer.
7. Pekarofski (2021) applied the concept of racial liminality to analyse whether some African-American figures modified the conception of race in US through their own existence.
8. Other linked concepts are the decolonial turn (Maldonado-Torres, 2008) and the decolonial inflection (Restrepo & Rojas, 2010).
9. Marcus (1995) proposed multi-sited ethnography that referred to multilocality.
10. The application of the glocalisation concept to the ethnicity and the disputed heritage in Morocco and Equatorial Guinea in Aixelà-Cabré (2022a) may also be consulted.
11. In the Portuguese case, it reflected a logic of mixing due to the multiple existing representations of the mixing (Ferraz de Matos, 2013).
12. Studies of sub-Saharan migration to Spain began in the late 1990s with the works of Ribas (1999), Kaplan (2002), Fons (2002), Rodríguez (2004), Sow (2004) and Jabardo (2006).
13. On this subject Cohen (1997) is recommended. For the Nordic case, see Sawyer and Habel (2014).
14. For European statistics, see Eurostat, "Migration and migrant population statistics", March 2019.
15. Continuous Registry Statistics, Population (Spanish/foreign) by country of birth.
16. It is necessary to clarify that my work is methodologically different from Adeleke's because mine is based on lived memories (oral voices) and narrated memories (documentary voices), and not on the narratives of prominent intellectuals.
17. Ralph Austen used the term Afro-Europeans to define Creole Africans, as highlighted by Sundiata (1996, p. 65).

250   NOTES

18 For Mbororo mobility, see Enguita-Fernández (2021).
19 Note that Balakrishnan (2017) took the Afropolitan concept from artist and writer Selasi (2005), and that the term was studied by Mbembe (2007).
20 Regarding the person of the Marquess of Comillas, see Rodrigo (2000). With respect to the link between history and memory, see Pich, Rodrigo and Arnabat (2024).
21 Thus, at the end of the passenger list the rest of the Africans were grouped together. In one particular example, the list ended with "25 coloureds for Monrovia and 18 for Sierra Leone". *La Guinea Española, 18*, 1908, 144.
22 On this subject, see Plasencia (2019) and Valenciano (2022).
23 Throughout the book, I will not constantly specify the Spanish condition of the Equatorial Guinean community in colonial times, nor will I insist that when I refer to the Spaniards, I am referring to the Spaniards of the peninsula. The objective is to lighten the text without renouncing that this is my starting point.
24 The most thorough historical description of the city came from the hand of Martín del Molino (1994).
25 *La Guinea Española, 49*, 1905, 3.
26 *La Guinea Española, 4*, 1915, "Agricultura".
27 *La actualidad española*, 5-3-1959, 54.
28 *La Voz de Fernando Poo, 261*, 1921, 13.
29 *La Guinea Española, 19*, 1908.
30 *La Guinea Española, 23*, 1908, 191.
31 *La Guinea Española, 9*, 1911, 71.
32 *La Guinea Española, 6*, 1908, 47.
33 *La Voz de Fernando Poo, LXXXV*, 1913, 4.
34 *La Guinea Española, 36*, 1904, "Cinematógrafo en Santa Isabel".
35 *La Guinea Española, 83–86*, 1928, 87
36 *La Guinea Española, 23*, 1908, 191.
37 *La Vanguardia*, 23-2-1945, 8.
38 One example was Teresa's contract with Johnny 1, a native of Monrovia, on 25 April 1920. AGA, box 81/07189.
39 Consejo de Vecinos de Santa Isabel, session of 11 December 1905. AGA, box 81/07956, file 1.
40 *La Voz de Fernando Poo, 107*, 1914, 5.
41 *La Voz de Fernando Poo, 108*, 1914, 6.
42 *La Guinea Española, 19*, 1903, 7.
43 For further information on healthcare issues, we recommend reading Martínez Antonio (2009) and Brydan (2018).
44 *La Voz de Fernando Poo, 145*, 1916, 10.
45 *La Guinea Española, 3*, 1916, 35
46 *La Guinea Española, 46*, 1905, 16.
47 *La Guinea Española, 21*, 1920, 178.
48 *La Guinea Española, 21*, 1920, 178–179.
49 *La Guinea Española, 21*, 1920, 178–179.
50 Terradas (1979) offers a detailed work that has reference to the British industrial revolution, starting from the study of the industrial colonies in Catalonia.
51 *La Guinea Española, 23*, 1918, 205.
52 For example, in Catalonia the exhibition of the "Negre de Banyoles" (Black of Banyoles) in the local museum was well known, and it was finally returned to Africa with all due honours, amid great controversies about its true nationality.

53 *La Vanguardia*, 16-3-1913, 4.
54 *La Vanguardia*, 16-3-1913, 4.
55 *La Vanguardia*, 28-4-1925, 8–9.
56 *La Voz de Fernando Poo*, 217, 1919, 3.
57 On the notion of the "dis-encounter" between Africa and Europe, Merolla (2021) is recommended.
58 Regarding the European discourses on whiteness, the works of Persánch (2020) and the updated revision of Persánch and Aixelà-Cabré (2022) are recommended.
59 AGA, box 81/08156, file 5. Document available at Open Source Guinea.
60 A brief biography of Dorcas Fanny de Barleycorn written by Jeremy Crump is available, which also shows her gravestone in London, in "Barleycorn, William Napoleon (1848–1925)", see *My Primitive Methodists*. Other publications of interest about Methodists in Fernando Poo are Crump (2015, 2017a, 2017b).
61 See "Castle, 81 Holloway Road, Islington N7", from Wiki.
62 *La Guinea Española*, 24, 1904.
63 *La Voz de Fernando Poo*, 145, 1916, 10.
64 *La Guinea Española*, 16, 1919, 152.
65 These data were collected for the exhibition "Barcelona, Mosaic de Cultures", after consulting population yearbooks by districts of Barcelona, for 1949 and 1996.
66 See Rizo (2023).
67 Fauria and Aixelà-Cabré (2002) are recommended because although the book does not deal with the Fernandino case, a review is made of the different ways in which cultural diversity has an impact in Barcelona.
68 *La Vanguardia*, 25-5-1962, 37.
69 *La Vanguardia*, 25-5-1962, 37.
70 *La Vanguardia*, 25-5-1962, 37.
71 *La Vanguardia*, 25-5-1962, 37.
72 *La Vanguardia*, 25-5-1962, 37.
73 *La Vanguardia*, 25-5-1962, 37.
74 *La Voz de Fernando Poo*, 220, 1919, 13.
75 *La Voz de Fernando Poo*, 153, 1916.
76 *La Guinea Española*, 52, 1905, 64.
77 *La Vanguardia*, 7-7-1961, 33. For example, the subject of African sportsmen has been investigated by García (2024), African art by Rizo (2024) and African literature by Persánch (2023, 2024).
78 *La Voz de Fernando Poo*, 92, 1914, 12.
79 *La Voz de Fernando Poo*, 153, 1916, 8.
80 *La Guinea Española*, October-December 1968, 35–36. For more on boxing, see García (2023).
81 *La Guinea Española*, October-December 1968, 35.
82 *La Vanguardia*, 29-10-1924, 13.
83 *La Guinea Española*, 9, 1918.
84 *La Guinea Española*, 20, 1914, 237.
85 *La Voz de Fernando Poo*, 262, 1921, 9.
86 *La Voz de Fernando Poo*, 269, 1921, 9.
87 *La Voz de Fernando Poo*, 220, 1919, 13.
88 *La Guinea Española*, 507, 1921, 13.
89 *La Vanguardia*, 16-9-1921, 5.
90 *La Voz de Fernando Poo*, 263, 1921, 9.
91 *La Voz de Fernando Poo*, 263, 1921, 9.

92 *La Vanguardia*, 7-7-1961, 33.
93 Open Source Guinea: "Memoria del Homenaje a D. Alfredo Jones Níger".
94 Open Source Guinea: "Memoria del Homenaje a D. Alfredo Jones Níger".
95 *La Guinea Española, 5*, February 1920, 52.
96 *La Vanguardia*, 11-6-1965, 47.
97 *La Guinea Española, 19*, 1903, 170.
98 *La Vanguardia*, 25-5-1962, 37.
99 *La Vanguardia*, 25-5-1962, 37.
100 *La Vanguardia*, 3-3-1911, 5
101 *La Vanguardia*, 3-3-1911, 5.
102 *La Vanguardia*, 4-1-1909, 2.
103 In this regard, the works of Figueroa-Vásquez (2020) and Riochí (2018) are recommended.
104 Open Source Guinea: "Memoria del Homenaje a D. Alfredo Jones Níger". Emphasis added.
105 *La Vanguardia*, 1-6-1990, 37.
106 *La Vanguardia*, 3-12-1992, 27.
107 *La Guinea Española, 19*, 1903, 8.
108 García Balañà (2019) analysed the abuse of black women by the Colonial Guard in Cuba in a highly recommended text.
109 *La Guinea Española, 21*, 1915, 252. Emphasis added.
110 *La Guinea Española, 16*, 1913.
111 *La Guinea Española, 15*, 1914, 17.
112 *La Voz de Fernando Poo, 259*, 1921, 10–11.
113 *La Voz de Fernando Poo, 334*, 1924, 13.
114 *La Guinea Española, 46*, 1905.
115 *La Voz de Fernando Poo, 244*, 1920, 9.
116 *La Voz de Fernando Poo, 244*, 1920, 9–10.
117 *La Voz de Fernando Poo, 244*, 1920, 10.
118 *La Voz de Fernando Poo, 220*, 1919, 13.
119 *La Voz de Fernando Poo, 259*, 1921, 12.
120 *La Guinea Española, 3*, 1920, 29.
121 *La Guinea Española, 1455*, 1956, 129.
122 *La Voz de Fernando Poo, 220*, 1919, 8.
123 *La Voz de Fernando Poo, 220*, 1919, 8.
124 *La Voz de Fernando Poo, 220*, 1919, 11.

Primary and secondary sources

Primary sources

Informants

Amalia Barleycorn is Krio Fernandina and was born in 1963. Interviews online and in person in the province of Barcelona and in Madrid. The interviews took place in 2021 and 2022.

Sally Fenaux Barleycorn is Amalia's daughter, is an artist, lives in Catalonia and is in her thirties. Meetings held in 2021 and 2022.

Eduard Giménez Ferrer is Catalan. He was born in 1943. His father was co-owner of the Virgen de Montserrat Estate in Oveng, Bata, along with the other partners who were Catalans and Canarians. He has transferred all the documentation of the plantation to the IMF-CSIC, which constitutes the Fondo Giménez Ferrer. The interviews took place from 2016 to 2021.

Official reports

Barcelona Municipal Gazette. Accessed 1914, 1915, 1947 through IDESCAT where they are digitized from 1914 to 1999. Selected *1*, November 4, 1914; and *38*, September 18, 1950. Retrieved from https://www.idescat.cat/

Statistical Summaries of the Spanish Territories of the Gulf of Guinea. Available from IMF-CSIC, Fondo Giménez Ferrer. Detailed in the Bibliography (see section 6.2.).

EUROSTAT. Consultation of population statistics in Spain. Retrieved from https://ec.europa.eu/eurostat/statistics-explained/index.php?title=Main_Page

Digitalised documentary archives

Archive of the Gran Teatre del Liceu. Retrieved from https://www.uab.cat/en/libraries/historical-archive-liceu

Arxiu Fotogràfic de Barcelona. Retrieved from http://ajuntament.barcelona.cat/arxiumunicipal/arxiu-fotografic/ca

Arxiu Històric de la Ciutat de Barcelona. Retrieved from http://ajuntament.barcelona.cat/arxiumunicipal/arxiuhistoric/ca

Arxiu Municipal Contemporani de Barcelona. Retrieved from http://ajuntament.barcelona.cat/arxiumunicipal/arxiucontemporani/ca

Arxiu Municipal Sarrià-Sant Gervasi. Fund of the City Council of Sant Gervasi. Retrieved from http://ajuntament.barcelona.cat/arxiumunicipal/ca/arxius-municipals-de-districte-1/sarria-sant-gervasi

Biblioteca Nacional Hemeroteca Digital de España. Photographic material consulted. Retrieved from http://www.bne.es/ca/catalegs/hemeroteca-digital

Fondo Giménez Ferrer, IMF-CSIC. This archive constitutes the documentation of the Virgen de Montserrat Estate in Oveng-Bata (Continental Region of Spanish Guinea), established in 1927. This coffee plantation was created by different Catalan and Canary Island partners and ceased to be operational in 1965. The collection includes more than a hundred letters, as well as numerous company documents such as balance sheets, shares and notarial documents, among others. Retrieved from http://www.imf.csic.es/project/fondo-gimenez-ferrer/

Instituto Nacional de Estadística, INEbase / History. Population censuses of Santa Isabel, Fernando Poo and Barcelona were searched. Statistical Yearbooks of Barcelona. Retrieved from http://www.ine.es

Institut d'Estadística de Barcelona. Population census from 1900. Retrieved from http://bcnroc.ajuntament.barcelona.cat/jspui/handle/11703/94371

Open Source Guinea. The following documents were consulted: (1) Memory of the Tribute to Mr. Alfredo Jones Níger. Casa de la Guinea Española, Carrer Comtal 32, Barcelona, 1963; (2) Report of the governmental police dated May 25, 1933. Retrieved from http://www.opensourceguinea.org/

Physical documentary archives

Ajuntament de Barcelona. Statistical population data and Municipal Register of Inhabitants 1986 and 1991.

Archivo General de la Administración de Alcalá de Henares (AGA). Funds for Africa (15) and Culture (3) were consulted.

Archivo Histórico Nacional.

Biblioteca de la AECID.

Biblioteca Nacional de España, sede de Alcalá de Henares. Magazines, books and the Official Gazette of the Spanish Territories in the Gulf of Guinea wereconsulted.

Cementiris de Barcelona. Cemetery of Les Corts, where the book of death records was located in the city for 1920, in which the death of Amelia Barleycorn was recorded.

La Vanguardia. I directed and carried out a very exhaustive research at the Hemeroteca *La Vanguardia* for nine months in 1999 to locate news related to foreigners and national immigrants in the city of Barcelona. Emptying covered the years 1900 to 1999. Together with me worked Francesc Bailón and Enric Sánchez within the framework of the exhibition "Barcelona, Mosaic de Cultures" of the Museu Etnològic de Barcelona that I co-curated (for more information, see Fauria & Aixelà-Cabré, 2002).

Registro Civil de Barcelona. Deaths Application for Amelia Barleycorn's death certificate.

Journals and newspapers

La Guinea Española, biweekly magazine. For the research, all the issues for the years 1903, 1904, 1905, 1907, 1908, 1909 (1906 and 1910 are not available), 1911, 1912, 1913, 1914, 1915, 1916, 1917, 1918, 1919, 1920, 1921, 1924 and 1956 were consulted. The journal is available online. Retrieved from http://www.bioko.net/guineaespanola/laguies.htm

La Voz de Fernando Poo, biweekly magazine. The years 1911, 1912, 1913, 1914, 1916, 1919, 1920, 1921, 1924 and 1956 were emptied. As the magazine is partially in different archives, numbers were consulted in the Biblioteca Nacional de España at its headquarters in Alcalá de Henares.

Secondary sources

Bibliographical references

Adeleke, T. (2009). *The case against Afrocentrism*. Jackson: University Press of Mississippi.
Aixelà-Cabré, Y. (2005). *Género y antropología social*. Sevilla: Editorial Doble J/Comunicación Social ediciones.
Aixelà-Cabré, Y. (2011). *Guinea Ecuatorial: Ciudadanías y migraciones transnacionales en un contexto dictatorial africano*. Barcelona: Ceiba.
Aixelà-Cabré, Y. (2012). Equatorial Guinean Women's Roles after Migration to Spain: Conflicts between Women's Androcentric Socialization in Equatorial Guinea and Their Experiences after Migration. *Urban Anthropology and Studies of Cultural Systems and World Economic Development*, 42(1–2), 1–55.
Aixelà-Cabré, Y. (2017). Exploring Euro-African pasts through an analysis of Spanish colonial practices in Africa (Morocco and Spanish Guinea). *Canadian Journal of African Studies/La Revue canadienne des études africaines*, 51(1), 23–42.
Aixelà-Cabré, Y. (2020a). The Presence of the Colonial Past: Equatorial Guinean Women in Spain. *Itinerario. Journal of Imperial and Global Interactions*, 44(1), 140–158.
Aixelà-Cabré, Y. (2020b). Colonial Spain in Africa: Building a Shared History from Memories of the Spanish Protectorate and Spanish Guinea. *Culture & History Digital Journal*, 9(2), e017.
Aixelà-Cabré, Y. (2021). Memories of Segregation, Racism, Gender and Naming. In Aixelà-Cabre (Ed.). *Africa in Europe and Europe in Africa. Reassessing the cultural legacy* (pp. 39–59). New York: Peter Lang.
Aixelà-Cabré, Y. (2022a). *Spain's African Colonial Legacies: Morocco and Equatorial Guinea Compared*. Leiden/Boston: Brill.
Aixelà-Cabré, Y. (2022b). Geografía emocional y gestión de la diversidad en Europa. Reflexiones decoloniales desde la superdiversidad y las ciudadanías fallidas. *Procesos Históricos Revista de Historia*, 41, 61–77.
Aixelà-Cabré, Y. (2023a). African Women in Iberia. The Fernandino elite in Barcelona (1870–1992). *Ethnic and Racial Studies*, 47(7), 1382–1402.
Aixelà-Cabré, Y. (2023b). Unwritten Afro-Iberian memories and histories. Race, ethnicity and gender in Portugal and Spain. *Ethnic and Racial Studies*, 47(7), 1353–1364.
Aixelà-Cabré, Y. & Rizo, E.G. (2023). *Afro-Iberia (1850–1975). Enfoques teóricos y huellas africanas y magrebíes en la península ibérica*. Barcelona: Bellaterra Edicions.
Alcoff, L.M. (2007). Fraser on Redistribution, Recognition, and Identity. *European Journal of Political Theory*, 6(3), 255–265.
Amadiume, I. (2018). *Hijas que son varones y esposos que son mujeres*. Barcelona: Edicions Bellaterra.
Antebi, G., López Bargados, A. & Martín Corrales, E. (Eds.) (2017). *Ikunde. Barcelona, metrópoli colonial*. Barcelona: Museu de les Cultures del Món.
Aranzadi, I. (2016). El legado cultural de Sierra Leona en Bioko. Comparativa de dos espacios de Criolización africana. *Éndoxa*, 37, 237–278.
Arbaiza, D. (2023). Límites y vislumbres en el archivo: africanos en España entre 1843 y 1883. In Aixelà-Cabré & Rizo (Eds.). *Afro-Iberia (1850–1975). Enfoques teóricos y huellas africanas y magrebíes en la península ibérica* (pp. 31–46). Barcelona: Bellaterra Edicions.
Arbaiza, D. (2024). Shifting Representations, Ambiguous Bodies: African Colonial Subjects in Nineteenth Century Spain. *Ethnic and Racial Studies*, 47(7), 1365–1381.

Ares Queija, B. & Stella, A. (2000). *Negros, mulatos y zambaigos. Derroteros africanos en los mundos ibéricos.* Sevilla: CSIC.
Aris, J.P. (2021). *El gobierno securitario-humanitario de las fronteras de Europa.* Madrid: CSIC.
Armengol, A. (2015). *Els catalans a la Guinea.* Barcelona: Albertí Editors.
Atlan, C. & Jézéquel, H-J. (2002). Alienation or Political Strategy? The Colonised Defend the Empire. In Chafer & Sackur (Eds.). *Promoting the Colonial Idea. Propaganda and Visions of Empire in France* (pp. 102–115). London: Palgrave.
Ávila Laurel, J.T. (1999). *La carga.* Malabo: Editorial Palmart.
Ávila Laurel, J.T. (2000). *El derecho de pernada.* Malabo: Editorial Pángola.
Ávila Laurel, J.T. (2006). *Guinea ecuatorial: vísceras.* Valencia: Institució Alfons el Magnanim.
Ávila Laurel, J.T. (2009). *Arde el monte de noche.* Madrid: Calambur Editorial.
Ávila Laurel, J.T. (2022). *Dientes blancos, piel negra.* Barcelona: Edicions Bellaterra.
Balakrishnan, S. (2017). The Afropolitan Idea: New Perspectives on Cosmopolitanism in African Studies. *History Compass, 15*(2), 2–11.
Balibar, E. & Wallerstein, I. (1992). *Raza, nación y clase.* Madrid: Iepala.
Balsameda, F.J. (1869). *Los confinados a Fernando Poo e impresiones de un viage a Guinea.* New York: Imprenta de La Revolución.
Baumann, G. (1999). *The Multicultural Riddle.* London: Routledge.
Baumann, G. (2002). Tres gramáticas de la alteridad: Algunas antropo-lógicas de la construcción del otro en las constelaciones históricas. In Nash & Marre (Eds.). *Multiculturalismos y género* (pp. 49–70). Barcelona: Edicions Bellaterra.
Baumann, G. (2004). Grammars of identity / Alterity. A Structural Approach. In Bauman & Gingrich (Eds.). *Grammars of identity / Alterity. A Structural Approach* (pp. 18–51). New York: Berghahn Books.
Beauvoir, S. (1976). *Le deuxième sexe.* Paris: Gallimard. [First edition 1949].
Bela-Lobedde, D. (2018). *Ser mujer negra en España.* Barcelona: Ediciones B.
Blanchard, P. & Bancel, N. (1998). *De l'indigène à l'immigré.* Paris: Gallimard.
Bolekia, J. (2003). *Aproximación a la historia de Guinea Ecuatorial.* Salamanca: Amarú ediciones.
Bolekia, J. (2016). *Los caminos de la memoria.* Madrid: Sial.
Bolekia, J. (2019). *Quién es quién entre los escritores de Guinea Ecuatorial.* Madrid: Sial.
Borst, J. & Gallo-González, D. (2019). Narrative Constructions of Online Imagined Afro-diasporic Communities in Spain and Portugal. *Open Cultural Studies, 3,* 286–307.
Boturu, R.S. (2010). *Luz en la noche. Poesía y teatro.* Madrid: Verbum.
Brancato, S. (2009). *Afro-Europe: Texts and Contexts.* Berlin: Trafo.
Brancato, S. (Ed.) (2011). *Afroeurope@n Configurations: Readings and Projects.* Newcastle: Cambridge Scholars Publishing.
Brufrau, C. (2015). Ball de màscares al Liceu. Primer ball de màscares: 26 febrer 1848 – 1936. In *Enciclopèdia de les Arts Escèniques Catalanes.* Barcelona, Institut del Teatre. Retrieved from https://www.institutdelteatre.cat/publicacions/ca/enciclopedia-arts-esceniques/id1437/ball-de-mascares-al-liceu.htm?fcat_5=87
Brydan, D. (2018). Mikomeseng: Leprosy, Legitimacy and Francoist Repression in Spanish Guinea. *Social History of Medicine: The Journal of the Society for the Social History of Medicine, 31*(3), 627–647.
Caballero-Svensson, A. (2023). *Shortchanged. Elderly Women Street Vendors in Malabo, Equatorial Guinea.* Uppsala: Uppsala Universitet.
Campoy-Cubillo, A. & Sampedro, B. (2019). Entering the Global Hispanophone: an introduction. *Journal of Spanish Cultural Studies, 20*(1–2), 1–16.
Carr, M. (2012). *Fortress Europe. Dispatches from a Gated Continent.* New York: New Press.

Castillo, S. (2016). La colonización lingüística de España en Guinea Ecuatorial. *Platô, 3*(6), 6–19.
Castro-Gómez, S. & Grosfoguel, R. (2007). Prólogo. Giro decolonial, teoría crítica y pensamiento heterárquico. In Castro-Gómez & Grosfoguel (Eds.). *El giro decolonial: reflexiones para una diversidad epistémica más allá del capitalismo global* (pp. 9–23). Siglo del Hombre Editores.
Césaire, A. (2006). *Discurso sobre el colonialismo.* Madrid: Ediciones Akal. [First edition 1950].
Clarence-Smith, W.G. (1994). African and European Cocoa Producers on Fernando Póo, 1880s to 1910s. *The Journal of African History, 35*(2), 179–199.
Clark Hine, D., Keaton, T.D. & Small, S. (Eds.) (2009). *Black Europe and the African Diaspora.* Urbana, IL: University of Illinois Press.
Cohen, R. (1997). *Global diasporas. An introduction.* London: University College London Press.
Cooper, F. & Stoler, A.L. (Eds.) (1997). *Tensions of Empire: Colonial Culture in a Bourgeois World.* Berkeley: University of California Press.
Crenshaw, K. (1995). Mapping the Margins: Intersectionality, Identity Politics and Violence Against Women of Color. In Crenshaw, Cotanda, Peller & Thomas (Eds.). *Critical Race Theory. The key writings that formed the movement* (pp. 357–383). New York: The New Press.
Crump, J. (2015). Charles Booth and the Primitive Methodists. *Proceedings of the Wesley Historical Society, 60*(2), 47–63.
Crump, J. (2017a). Militant Geographers and Primitive Maps. *Livingmaps Review,* 3 September. Retrieved from http://livingmaps.review/journal/index.php/LMR/article/view/74
Crump, J. (2017b). Our Struggle in London: Primitive Methodists and the Metropolis, *The London Journal,* July. Retrieved from http://dx.doi.org/10.1080/03058034.2017.1346968
D'Almonte, E. (1908). Guinea Española. *Revista de Geografía Colonial y Mercantil, 5*(3–5), 81–160.
Dike, K.O. (1956). John Beecroft, 1790–1854: Her Britannic Majesty's Consul to the Bights of Benin and Biafra 1849–1854. *Journal of the Historical Society of Nigeria, 1*(1), 5–14.
Doppelbauer, M. & Fleischmann, S. (coord.). (2012). Hispanismo africano. *Iberoromania, 73–74,* 1–12.
Enguita-Fernàndez, C. (2021). Understanding Ethnicity as Positional. In Aixelà-Cabré (Ed.). *Africa in Europe and Europe in Africa* (pp. 113–135). New York: Peter Lang.
Enyegue, J.L. (2014). The Jesuits in Fernando Po (1858–1872). In Maryks & Wright (Eds.). *Jesuit Survival and Restoration: A Global History, 1773–1900* (pp. 482–502). Leiden: Brill.
Essed, P. & Hoving, I. (2014). Innocence, Smug Ignorance, Resentment: An Introduction to Dutch Racism. *Thamyris/Intersecting, 27,* 9–30.
Falconi, J. (2023a). A Casa das Estudantes do Império: discursos e representações de raça e género. In Aixelà-Cabré & Rizo (Eds.). *Afro-Iberia (1850–1975). Enfoques teóricos y huellas africanas y magrebíes en la península ibérica* (pp. 109–124). Barcelona: Bellaterra Edicions.
Falconi, J. (2023b). African Women's Trajectories and the *Casa dos Estudantes do Império. Ethnic and Racial Studies, 47*(7), 1403–1419.
Fauria, C. & Aixelà-Cabré, Y. (Eds.) (2002). *Barcelona, Mosaic de cultures.* Barcelona: Edicions Bellaterra/ Museu Etnològic de Barcelona.
Fernández-Moreno, N. (2018). Colonial Discourse and Native Resistance. The Evangelization of Bioko Island in the Early 20th Century (Equatorial Guinea). In Aixelà-Cabré (Ed.). *In the footsteps of Spanish colonialism in Morocco and Equatorial Guinea* (pp. 71–99). Zurich: Lit Verlag.
Ferraz De Matos, P. (2013). *The colours of the empire: racialized representations during Portuguese colonialism.* Oxford/New York: Berghahn Books.
Ferrer-Gallardo, X. (2008). The Spanish–Moroccan border complex: Processes of geopolitical, functional and symbolic rebordering. *Political Geography, 27,* 301–321.
Figueroa-Vásquez, Y.C. (2020). *Decolonizing Diasporas. Radical Mappings of Afro-Atlantic* Literature. Evanston, IL: Northwestern University Press.

Fons, V. (2002). Historia de un viaje sin retorno. Proceso migratorio de la población de Guinea Ecuatorial a España. In Ondo, Bokesa & Liniger-Goumaz (Eds.). *Misceláneas Guineo Ecuatorianas I. Del Estado colonial al Estado dictatorial* (pp. 109–120). La Chaux: Editorial Tiempos Próximos & Les Éditions du Temps.

Fradera, J.M. (2015). *Historia de dos ciudades/historia de dos países: La Habana y Barcelona, 1868–1933*. Barcelona: Ajuntament de Barcelona.

Fraiture, P.P. (2022). Thinking, Performing, and Overcoming Belgium's Colonial Power Matrix? An Introduction. In Fraiture (Ed.), *Unfinished Histories. Empire and Postcolonial Resonance in Central Africa and Belgium* (pp. 11–39). Leuven: Leuven University Press.

García, M. (2023). Boxeadores de origen africano en España: el ring como espacio de promoción social (1900–1975). In Aixelà-Cabré & Rizo (Eds.). *Afro-Iberia (1850–1975). Enfoques teóricos y huellas africanas y magrebíes en la península ibérica* (pp. 137–150). Barcelona: Bellaterra Edicions.

García, M. (2024). Black Extras and Actors in Francoist Cinema. *Ethnic and Racial Studies*, 47(7), 1420–1437.

García Balañà, A. (2019). "No hay ningún soldado que no tenga una negrita". Raza, género, sexualidad y nación en la experiencia metropolitana de la guerra colonial (Cuba, 1895–1898). In Andreu Miralles (Ed.). *Vivir la nación. Nuevos debates sobre el nacionalismo español* (pp. 153–186). Granada: Comares.

García Bravo, H. (2019). La exhibición del cuerpo nacional. Maniquíes, cráneos y tipos indígenas mexicanos en Madrid, 1892. In Pardo-Tomás, Zarzoso & Sánchez Menchero (Eds.). *Cuerpos mostrados. Regímenes de exhibición de lo humano. Barcelona y Madrid, siglos XVII–XX* (pp. 182–198). Barcelona: Anthropos.

Gargallo, E. & Sant, J. (2021). *El petit imperi: catalans en la colonització de la Guinea Espanyola*. Barcelona: Angle.

Garrido-Castellano, C. & Leitão, B. 2022. Introduction. Fictions of Cosmopolitanism, Spectacles of Alterity. In Leitão & Garrido-Castellano (Eds.). *Curating and the Legacies of Colonialism in Contemporary Iberia* (pp. 1–21). Wales: University of Wales Press.

Gilroy, P. (1993). *The Black Atlantic. Modernity and Double Consciousness*. London: Verso.

Gilroy, P. (2004). *After empire: Melancholia or convivial culture?* London: Routledge.

Goerg, O. (1995). Sierra Leonais, Créoles, Krio: la dialectique de l'identité. *Africa: Journal of the International African Institute*, 65(1), 114–132.

Góngora Echenique, M. (1923). *Ángel Barrera y las posesiones españolas del Golfo de Guinea. Su labor colonizadora, los misterios, bellezas y tesores de nuestras posesiones, política colonial, orientaciones*. Madrid: Imprenta San Bernardo.

González Echegaray, C. (2017). *Historia de la prensa en guinea ecuatorial en el siglo XX. Cien años de publicaciones periodicas*. Retrieved from https://static.cambridge.org/content/id/urn:cambridge.org:id:article:S026667311500001X/resource/name/S026667311500001Xsup001.pdf

Granda, G. de (1988). *Lingüística e Historia: Temas Afro-Hispánicos*. Valladolid: Universidad de Valladolid.

Grau-Rebollo, J., García-Tugas, L. & García-García, B. (2024). Induced Vulnerability: The Consequences of Racialization for African Women in an Emergency Shelter in Catalonia (Spain). *Ethnic and Racial Studies*, 47(7), 1510–1527.

Guillemar de Aragón, A. (1852). *Opúsculo sobre la colonización de Fernando Poo, y revista de los principales establecimientos europeos de la Costa Occidental de África*. Madrid: Imprenta Nacional.

Hall, Rev. J. (1874). *Life on the Ocean; or, memorials of Captain Wm. Robinson one of the pioneers of Primitive Methodism in Fernando Po: With an account of the manners and customs of various tribes resident on the West Coast of Africa; the introduction of Primitive Methodism into Fernando Po; and death of the pioneers*. London: F.H. Hurd.

Hochadel, O. & Nieto-Galán, A. (Eds.) (2016). *Barcelona: An Urban History of Science and Modernity, 1888–1929*. New York: Routledge.

Holt, J. (1948). *The diary of John Holt*. Liverpool: Henry Young.

Iliescu, C. (2017). Equatorial Guinean Migrants in Spain. An Analysis of Implicit Discourse. *Hispanófila*, 181, 169–189.

Iliescu, C. & Bosaho, R. (2015). Guinea Ecuatorial: una propuesta de análisis discursivo de los silencios impuestos. In Aixelà-Cabré (Ed.). *Tras las huellas del colonialismo español en Marruecos y Guinea Ecuatorial* (pp. 195–220). Madrid: CSIC.

Innes, C.L. & Stein, M.U. (Eds.) (2008). African Europeans. *Wasafiri: The Magazine of International Contemporary Writing*, (23)4: 1.

Iyanga Pendi, A. (2021). *Historia de Guinea Ecuatorial*. Valencia: Nau Llibres.

Jabardo, M. (2001). *Ser africano en el maresme. Migración, trabajo y etnicidad en la formación de un enclave étnico*. PhD thesis in Anthropology, Universidad Autónoma de Madrid, Spain.

Jones Mathama, D. (1962). *Una lanza por el boabí*. Barcelona: Tip. Cat. Casals.

Kaplan, A. (2002). Los procesos migratorios. Una motivación económica: Senegambianos en Cataluña. In Fauria & Aixelà-Cabré (Eds.). *Barcelona, Mosaic de cultures* (pp. 121–132). Barcelona: Edicions Bellaterra.

Kingsley, M. (1897). *Travels in West Africa, Congo Français, Corisco and Cameroons*. London: Macmillan.

Lang, S. (2017). Más allá del Ebro, ¿Los salvajes? La "España Africana" como impulso del regeneracionismo catalán hacia 1900. In Tschilschke & Witthaus (Eds.). *El otro colonialismo. España y África, entre imaginación e historia* (pp. 105–130). Madrid: Iberoamericana.

Lewis, M. (2009). *An Introduction to the Literature of Equatorial Guinea: Between Colonialism and Dictatorship*. Missouri: University of Missouri Press.

López, M.S. (Ed.) (2008). *Afroeurope@ns: Cultures and Identities*. Newcastle: Cambridge Scholars Publishing.

Maccormack, C.P. (1998). Nature, culture and gender: a critique. In MacCormack & Strathern (Eds). *Nature, culture and gender* (pp. 1–24). Cambridge: Cambridge University Press.

Madariaga, M.R. de (2002). *Los moros que trajo Franco… La intervención de tropas coloniales en la Guerra Civil*. Barcelona: Ediciones Martínez Roca.

Maldonado-Torres, N. (2008). La descolonización y el giro des-colonial. *Tabula Rasa*, 9, 61–72.

Marazziti, M. & Riccardi, R. (2005). *Euroáfrica: lo que no se dice sobre la inmigración: lo que se podría decir sobre Europa*. Barcelona: Icaria.

Marcus, G.E. (1995). Ethnography in/of the World System: The Emergence of Multi-Sited Ethnography. *Annual Review of Anthropology*, 24, 95–117.

Martín Corrales, E. (2002). Del neomudéjar a las carnicerías "halal": la visión de los magrebíes del siglo XX. In Fauria & Aixelà-Cabré (Eds.). *Barcelona, Mosaic de cultures* (pp. 195–210). Barcelona: Bellaterra/Museu Etnològic de Barcelona.

Martín del Molino, A. (1994). *La ciudad de Port Clarence 1827–1859*. Malabo: Centro Cultural Hispano-Guineano.

Martín Díaz, E., Cuberos, F.J. & Castellani, S. (2012). Latin American Immigration to Spain. *Cultural Studies*, 26(6), 814–841.

Martínez Antonio, F.J. (2009). Imperio enfermizo. La singular mirada mórbida del primer franquismo en los documentales médicos sobre Marruecos y Guinea. *Medicina & Historia*, 4, 1–15.

Martino, E. (2012). Clandestine Recruitment Networks in the Bight of Biafra: Fernando Pó's Answer to the Labour Question. 1926–1945. *IRSH*, 57, 39–72.

Matas, J. (1890). *Memoria de las Misiones de Fernando Póo y sus dependencias / escrita con las licencias oportunas por el Rdo. P. Procurador de los Misioneros Hijos del Inmaculado Corazón de María*. Madrid: Imprenta de A. Pérez Dubrull.

Mbare Ngom, F. (1996). *Diálogos con Guinea. Panorama de la literatura guineoecuatoriana de expresión castellana a través de sus protagonistas*. Madrid: Labrys.

Mbembe, A. (1999). Du government privé indirect. *Politique Africaine*, 73, 103–121.

Mbembe, A. (2007). Afropolitanism. In Njamy & Durán (Eds.). *Africa Remix: Contemporary Art of a Continent* (pp. 26–30). Johannesburg: Jacana Media.

Mbembe, A. (2021). *Salir de la gran noche. Ensayo sobre África descolonizada*. Barcelona: Edicions Bellaterra.

Mbomio, J. (2016). *El párroco de Niefang*. Vienna: Ediciones en auge.

Mbomio, L. (2017). *Las que se atrevieron*. Madrid: Sial.

Memba, L. & Villaverde, M. (2018). *Malabo: ciudad y arquitectura*. Madrid: AECID.

Meneses, M.P. & Bidaseca, K. (Eds.) (2018). *Epistemologías del Sur: epistemologias do Sul*. Buenos Aires: CLACSO. Retrieved from https://www.jstor.org/stable/j.ctvnpok5d

Mignolo, W.D. (2004). Os esplendores e as miserias da ciencia: colonialidade, geopolitica do conhecimento e pluriversalidade epistémica. In Santos (Ed.). *Conhecimento prudente para uma vida decente: "Um discurso sobre as ciências" revisitado* (pp. 667–709). Sao Paulo: Cortez Editora.

Mignolo, W.D. (2018). The Decolonial Option. In Mignolo & Walsh (Eds.). *On Decoloniality: Concepts, Analytics, Praxis* (pp. 105–245). Durham: Duke University Press.

Miranda Junco, A. (1945). *Leyes coloniales*. Madrid: Imprenta Sucesores de Rivadeneyra.

Moreras, J. (1998). *La Immigració estrangera a Barcelona. L'Observatori Permanent de la Immigració a Barcelona, 1994–1997*. Barcelona: Ajuntament de Barcelona/Fundació CIDOB.

Moreras, J. (2024). Precarious lives, invisible deaths. A history of community funeral management among Moroccans in Catalonia. *Ethnic and Racial Studies*, 47(7), 1495–1509.

Mudimbe, V.Y. (1988). *The Invention of Africa: Gnosis, Philosophy, and the Order of Knowledge*. London: James Currey.

Muñoz y Gaviria, J. (1871a). *África: islas de Fernando Póo, Corisco y Annobón*. Madrid: Eds. Rubio, Grillo y Vitturi.

Muñoz y Gaviria, J. (1871b). *Tres años en Fernando Póo: viaje a África*. Madrid: Urbano Manini.

Nash, M. (1983). *Mujer, familia y trabajo en España, 1875–1936*. Barcelona: Anthropos.

Ndongo, D. (1977). *Historia y tragedia de Guinea Ecuatorial*. Madrid: Editorial Cambio 16.

Ndongo, D. (1987). *Las tinieblas de mi memoria negra*. Madrid: Editorial Fundamentos.

Ndongo, D. (1997). *Los poderes de la tempestad*. Madrid: Proyectos y Producciones Editoriales Cyan.

Ndongo, D. (2015). *El metro*. Madrid: Editorial Assata.

Nerín, Gustau (1999). *Guinea Equatorial. Història en blanc i negre*. Barcelona: Empuries.

Nfubea, A. (2021). *Afrofeminismo. 50 años de lucha y activism de mujeres negras en España (1968–2018)*. Madrid: Ménades/Trincheras.

Northrup, D. (2006). Becoming African: Identity formation among liberated slaves in nineteenth-century Sierra Leone. *Slavery and Abolition*, 27(1), 1–21.

Okenve, E. (2014). They Never Finished Their Journey: The Territorial Limits of Fang Ethnicity in Equatorial Guinea, 1930–1963. *International Journal of African Historical Studies*, 47(2), 259–285.

Oloruntoba, S.O. (2016). History of Euro-African Relations: From Yaoundé Convention to Economic Partnership Agreements. In *Regionalism and Integration in Africa* (pp. 69–85). New York: Palgrave Macmillan.

Ortiz, F. (2002 [1940]). *Contrapunteo cubano del tabaco y el azúcar (Advertencia de sus contrastes agrarios, económicos, históricos y sociales, su etnografía y su transculturación)*. In Santí (Ed.). Madrid: Cátedra.

Otabela, J.-D. & Onomo-Abena, S. (2009). *Entre estética y compromiso. La obra de Donato Ndongo-Bidyogo*. Madrid: UNED.

Otele, O. (2020). *Afro-Europeans: A History*. London: Hurst.

Oualdi, M. (2020). *A Slave Between Empires*. New York: Columbia University Press.

Pardo-Tomás, J., Zarzoso, A. & Sánchez Menchero, M. (Eds.) (2019). *Cuerpos mostrados. Regímenes de exhibición de lo humano. Barcelona y Madrid, siglos XVII-XX*. Barcelona: Anthropos.

Pardue, J. (2020). Antislavery and Imperialism: The British Suppression of the Slave Trade and the Opening of Fernando Po, 1827–1829. *Itinerario, 44*(1), 178–195.

Pekarofski, M. (2021). *Racial liminality and American constructions of race: negotiating, imagining, and creating color lines in the 1890s*. PhD thesis in Philosophy, University of New Jersey, US.

Pélissier, R. (1963). La Guinée Espagnola. *Revue Française de Science Politique, 13*(3), 624–644.

Persánch, JM. (2020). Towards the end of the white guilt era? The rise of nostalgic whiteness and magical populism. *Kairos: A Journal of Critical Symposium, 5*(1), 1–17.

Persánch, JM. (2023). La piel que te habita, el espacio que te recuerda: Breve aproximación a la racialización del otro yo y del espacio en "La cabeza del cordero". In Aixelà-Cabré & Rizo (Eds.). *Afro-Iberia (1850–1975). Enfoques teóricos y huellas africanas y magrebíes en la península ibérica* (pp. 169–176). Barcelona: Bellaterra Edicions.

Persánch, J.M. (2024). Racial Rhetoric in Black and White: Situational Whiteness in Francoist Equatorial Guinea through *Misión blanca*. *Ethnic and Racial Studies, 47*(7), 1478–1494.

Persánch, JM. & Aixelà-Cabré, Y. (2022). Introducción al dosier sobre multiculturalismo y gestión de la diversidad cultural Multiculturalismo y gestión de la diversidad en el mundo del siglo XXI. *Procesos Históricos. Revista de Historia, 41*, 26–43.

Pich, J.; Rodrigo, M. & Arnabat, R. (Eds). (2024). *Història, memòria i patrimoni, Entre Clio i Mnemòsine*. Barcelona: Icaria editorial, Càtedra Josep Fontana.

Pitts, J. (2019). *Afropean*. London: Penguin Books.

Plasencia Camps, I. (2019). Desde la ansiedad y la incertidumbre: relaciones sociales y versiones sobre la colonización en las primeras fotografías de Fernando Poo y sus dependencias (1861–1864). *Journal of Spanish Cultural Studies, 20*(1–2), 115–134.

Porzio, L. (2014). To Be Black in Spain: Experiences and Perceptions of Youth of Equatoguinean Origin. In Martí (Ed.). *African Realities: Body, Culture and Social Tensions* (pp. 53–75). Newcastle upon Tyne: Cambridge Scholars Publishing.

Quijano, A. (2014). Colonialidad del poder, eurocentrismo y América Latina. In Quijano (Ed.). *Cuestiones y horizontes: de la dependencia histórico-estructural a la colonialidad/descolonialidad del poder* (pp. 777–832). Buenos Aires: Clacso.

Ramos Izquierdo y Vivar, L. & Navarro y Beltrán Del Rio, E. (1912). *Descripción geográfica y gobierno, administración y colonización de las colonias españolas del golfo de Guinea*. Madrid: Impr. de Felipe Peña Cruz.

Raposo, O. & Garrido Castellano, C. (2023). Batida and the Politics of Sonic Agency in Afro-Lisboa. *Ethnic and Racial Studies, 47*(7), 1438–1455.

Resina, J.R. (2009). *Del hispanismo a los estudios ibéricos. Una propuesta federativa para el ámbito cultural*. Madrid: Biblioteca Nueva.

Restrepo, E. & Rojas, A. (2010). *Inflexión decolonial: fuentes, conceptos y cuestionamientos*. Instituto de Estudios Sociales y Culturales Pensar. Popayán: Universidad del Cauca.

Resúmenes Estadísticos del Gobierno General de los Territorios Españoles del Golfo de Guinea (1943). *Resúmenes del Año 1941*. Madrid: Instituto de Estudios Africanos, Negociado de Estadística.

Resúmenes Estadísticos del Gobierno General de los Territorios Españoles del Golfo de Guinea (1945). *Resúmenes del Año 1942 y 1943*. Madrid: Instituto de Estudios Africanos, Negociado de Estadística.

Resúmenes Estadísticos del Gobierno General de los Territorios Españoles del Golfo de Guinea (1947). *Resúmenes del Año 1944 y 1945*. Madrid: Instituto de Estudios Africanos, Negociado de Estadística.

Resúmenes Estadísticos del Gobierno General de los Territorios Españoles del Golfo de Guinea (1949). *Resúmenes del Año 1946 y 1947*. Madrid: Instituto de Estudios Africanos, Negociado de Estadística.

Resúmenes Estadísticos del Gobierno General de los Territorios Españoles del Golfo de Guinea (1953). *Resúmenes del Año 1950 y 1951*. Madrid: Instituto de Estudios Africanos, Negociado de Estadística.

Ribas, N. (1999). *Las presencias de la inmigración femenina. Un recorrido por Filipinas, Gambia y Marruecos en Catalunya*. Barcelona: Icaria.

Riochí Siafá, J. (2018). *Nuevas voces de la literatura de Guinea Ecuatorial*. Madrid: Diwán.

Rizo, E.G. (2012). Equatorial Guinean Literature in a Context of State-Promoted Amnesia. *World Literature Today, 86*(5), 32–36.

Rizo, E.G. (2023). Leandro Mbomio y las trampas de la Materia Reservada. In Aixelà-Cabre y Rizo (Eds.). *Afro-Iberia (1850–1975). Enfoques teóricos y huellas africanas y magrebíes en la península ibérica* (pp. 127–136). Barcelona: Bellaterra Edicions.

Rizo, E.G. (2024). Leandro Mbomio, the "Black Picasso": Spanish State Propaganda, Blackness, and Neocolonialism in Equatorial Guinea. *Ethnic and Racial Studies, 47*(7), 1456–1477.

Robertson, R. (1997). Glocalization: Time-Space and Homogeneity-Heterogeneity. In Featherstone, Lash & Robertson (Eds.). *Global modernities* (pp. 25–44). London: Sage.

Rodrigo, M. (2000). *Los marqueses de Comillas 1817–1925*. Madrid: LID Editorial Empresarial.

Rodríguez, D. (2004). *Inmigración y mestizaje hoy: Formación de matrimonios mixtos y familias transnacionales de población africana en Cataluña*. Barcelona: Publicacions de la Universitat Autònoma de Barcelona.

Rodríguez Vera, J. (1900). Posesiones españolas de Fernando Poo, Elobey y la Costa. *Revista de Marina, XLVI*, 80–87.

Rosaldo, M.Z. (1979). Mujer, cultura y sociedad: una visión teórica. In Harris & Young (Eds.). *Antropología y Feminismo* (pp. 153–180). Barcelona: Anagrama.

Rosenhaft, E. & Aitken, R. (2013). Introduction. In Rosenhaft & Aitken (Eds.). *Africa in Europe. Studies in Transnational Practice in the Long Twentieth Century* (pp. 1–15). Liverpool: Liverpool University Press.

Rotger, A. (2017). *Elles! 65 dones oblidades de la historia*. Barcelona: Institut Català de les Dones.

Roudometof, V. (2021). The new conceptual vocabulary of the social sciences: the "globalization debates" in context. *Globalizations, 18*(5), 771–780.

Ruiaz [Father A. Ruíz] (1928). Fernandinos Ilustres. *La Guinea Española, 679*, 25 December, 83–88.

Rubiés, J.-P. (2001). *Històries de la Guinea Espanyola*. Barcelona: Acontravent.

Rubiés, J.-P. (2017). Were Early Modern Europeans Racist? In Morris-Reich & Rupnow (Eds.). *Ideas of Race in the Histoy of the Humanities* (pp. 33–87). London: Palgrave Macmillan.

Sá, A.L. (2015). La construcción de la imagen del "indígena" en los Territorios Españoles del Golfo de Guinea (1904–1912). In Aixelà-Cabré (Ed.). *Tras las huellas del colonialismo español en Marruecos y Guinea Ecuatorial* (pp. 195–220). Madrid: CSIC.

Saavedra y Magdalena, D. (1910). *España en el África Occidental (Río de Oro y Guinea)*. Madrid: Imprenta Artística Española.

Sánchez Gómez, L.Á. (2006). África en Sevilla: la exhibición colonial de la Exposición Iberoamericana de 1929. *Hispania, LXVI*(224), 1045–1082.

Sant, J. (2015). Entre Barcelona i Fernando Poo. Interessos catalans al golf de Guinea, 1900–1936. *Barcelona Quaderns d'Història*, 22, 197–212.

Sant, J. (2017). *El comerç de cacao entre l'illa de Bioko i Barcelona: La Unión de Agricultores de la Guinea Española (1880–1941)*. PhD thesis in History, Universitat Pompeu Fabra, Barcelona, Spain.

Santana, J.M. (2020). The formation of North African otherness in the Canary Islands from the 16th to 18th centuries. *Culture & History Digital Journal*, 9(2), e012.

Sassen, S. (2013). *Inmigrantes y ciudadanos. De las migraciones masivas a la Europa fortaleza*. Madrid: Siglo XXI.

Sawyer, L. & Habel, Y. (2014). Refracting African and Black diaspora through the Nordic region. *African and Black Diaspora: An International Journal*, 7(1), 1–6.

Schlumpf-Thurnherr, S. (2022). *Voces de una comunidad poco visible. Los guineoecuatorianos en Madrid*. Madrid: Diwán.

Segura, I. (2011). *Dones de Sarrià – Sant Gervasi. Itineraris històrics*. Barcelona: Ajuntament de Barcelona.

Selasi, T. (2005). Bye-bye Babar (Or: What is an Afropolitan?). *LIP Magazine*. Retrieved from https://thelip.robertsharp.co.uk/2005/03/03/bye-bye-barbar/

Sepa, E. (2011). *España en la isla de Fernando Poo (1843–1968)*. Barcelona: Icaria.

Sipi, R. (2004). *Inmigración y género. El caso de Guinea Ecuatorial*. Donostia: Gakoa.

Sipi, R. (2010). *Genealogies femenines: les dones immigrades a Catalunya. 20 anys d'associacionisme en femení*. Barcelona: Yemanjà.

Small, S. (2018). Theorizing visibility and vulnerability in Black Europe and the African diaspora. *Ethnic and Racial Studies*, 41(6), 1182–1197.

Small, S. (2019). Ethnicity, Race, and Black People in Europe. In Ratuva (Ed.). *The Palgrave Handbook of Ethnicity* (pp. 1–21). Singapore: Palgrave Macmillan.

Smith, C.S. (1895). *Glimpses of Africa, West and Southwest coast. Containing the Author's Impressions and Observations during a Voyage of Six Thousand Miles from Sierra Leone to St. Paul de Loanda, and Return*. Nashville: A.M.E. Church Sunday School Union.

Sousa Santos, B. de & Meneses, M.P. (2014). Introducción. In Sousa & Meneses (Eds.). *Epistemologías del Sur (Perspectivas)* (pp. 7–16). Madrid: Akal.

Sow, P. (2004). Individual and collective commercial strategies, international fashion and religion in South Mediterranea: The Móodu-Móodu Wolof in Catalonia (Spain). *Documents d'Anàlisi Geogràfica*, 45, 41–53.

Spivak, G.C. (1988). Can the subaltern speak? In Nelson & Grossberg (Eds.). *Marxism and the Interpretation of Culture* (pp. 271–313). London: Macmillan.

Stoler, A.L. (1991). Carnal Knowledge and Imperial Power: Gender, Race, and Morality in Colonial Asia. In Di Leonardo (Ed.). *Gender at the crossroads of knowledge. Feminist anthropology in the postmodern area* (pp. 51–101). Berkeley: University of California Press.

Stoler, A.L. (1995). *Race and the Education of Desire: Foucault's History of Sexuality and the colonial order of things*. Durham and London: Duke University Press.

Stolcke, V. (1995). *Racismo y sexualidad en la Cuba colonial*. Madrid: Alianza Editorial.

Stolcke, V. (1996). Antropología del género. El cómo y el porqué de las mujeres. In Prat & Martínez (Eds.). *Ensayos de antropología cultural. Homenaje a Claudio Esteva-Fabregat* (pp. 335–343). Barcelona: Ariel.

Stolcke, V. (2010). A propósito de fronteras y mestizajes. In Ventura (Ed.). *Fronteras y mestizaje: sistemas de clasificación social en Europa, América y África* (pp. 19–29). Barcelona: Servei de Publicacions de la UAB.

Stucki, A. (2016). ¿Españolizar desde la raíz? La formación de una élite femenina de cooperación en el pequeño imperio español, c. 1960-1975. *Journal of Spanish Cultural Studies*, 17(4), 343-360.

Stucki, A. (2019). *Violence and Gender in Africa's Iberian Colonies. Feminizing the Portuguese and Spanish Empire, 1950s-1970s*. Cham: Palgrave Macmillan.

Sundiata, I.K. (1974). Prelude to scandal: Liberia and Fernando Po, 1880-1930. *African History*, XV, 97-II.

Sundiata, I.K. (1976). Creolization on Fernando Po: the nature of society. In Kilson & Rotberg (Eds.). *The African Diaspora: Interpretive Essays* (pp. 391-413). Harvard: Harvard University Press.

Sundiata, I.K. (1996). *From Slaving to Neoslavery: The Bight of Biafra and Fernando Po in the era of abolition 1827-1930*. Wisconsin: University of Wisconsin Press.

Taguieff, P.-A. (1987). *La force du préjugé. Essai sur le racisme et ses doubles*, Vol. I. Paris: CRAAL/Unesco.

Tatjer, M. (2002). Demografia de la immigració i el seu assentament a Barcelona als segles XIX i XX. In Fauria & Aixelà-Cabré (Eds.). *Barcelona, Mosaic de cultures* (pp. 345-369). Barcelona: Edicions Bellaterra/Museu Etnològic de Barcelona.

Terradas, I. (1979). *Les colònies industrials. Un estudi entorn del cas de l'Ametlla de Merola*. Barcelona: Laia.

Tessmann, G. (2008 [1923]). *Los bubis de Fernando Poo*. Madrid: Casa de África, Ministerio de Asuntos Exteriores.

Thomas, D. (Ed.) (2014). *Afroeuropean cartographies*. Newcastle: Cambridge Scholar Publishing.

Tsianos, V.S. & Karakayali, S. (2010). Transnational Migration and the Emergence of the European Border Regime: An Ethnographic Analysis. *European Journal of Social Theory*, 13, 373-387.

Ugarte, M. (2009). *Africans in Europe: The Culture of Exile and Emigration from Equatorial Guinea to Spain*. Urbana, IL: University of Illinois Press.

Unzueta y Yuste, A. de (1947). *Geografía Historica Fernando Poo*. Madrid: Instituto de Estudios Africanos.

Usera y Alarcón, J.M. (1848). *Memoria de la Isla de Fernando Poo*. Madrid: Imprenta T. Aguado.

Valenciano-Mañé, A. (2022). Mujeres y colonialidad en la Guinea Española: Fotografía de Mariana Dougan (1890-1900). In Calvo Maturana et al. (Eds.). *Fuentes para el estudio de historia de las mujeres* (pp. 417-420). Granada: Editorial Comares.

Van Gennep, A. (2008). *Los ritos de paso*. Madrid: Alianza.

Ventura, M. (2010). Introducción. Sistemas de clasificación social, fronteras y mezclas. In Ventura (Ed.). *Fronteras y mestizaje: sistemas de clasificación social en Europa, América y África* (pp. 9-16). Barcelona: Servei de Publicacions de la UAB.

Vertovec, S. (1999). Conceiving and researching transnationalism. *Ethnic and Racial Studies*, 22(2), 447-462.

Vilaró, M. (2011). *La colonización de la cruz en la Guinea Española*. Barcelona: Ceiba.

Vi-Makome, I. (2000). *La emigración negroafricana: tragedia y esperanza. Culturas alternativas*. Barcelona: Carena.

Walsh, C.E. (2018). Decoloniality in/as Praxis. In Mignolo & Walsh. *On Decoloniality: Concepts, Analytics, Praxis* (pp. 15-102). Durham: Duke University Press.

Wasihun, B. (2016). Afropolitanism writing. In Straub (Ed.). *Handbook of Transatlantic North American Studies* (pp. 391-410). Berlin: De Gruyter.

Wellesley Cole, R. (1987). *An Innocent in Britain*. London: Campbell Matthews & Co. Ltd.

Yakpo, K. (2010). *Gramática de Pichi*. Vic: Ceiba.

Yañez, C. (2006). Los negocios ultramarinos de una burguesía cosmopolita. Los catalanes en las primeras fases de la globalización, 1750-1914. *Revista de Indias*, LXVI(238), 679-710.

Online media

Chiquillo, M.A. (2017). Conoce la gira africana del RCD Español en 1961. *La Contra Deportiva*, 25 March. Retrieved from https://www.lacontradeportiva.com/conoce-la-gira-africana-del-rcd-espanol-1961/.

Merino, O. (2011). Eddy Collins Jones: La esclavitud me duele intelectualmente. *El Periódico*, 4 August. Retrieved from https://www.elperiodico.com/es/opinion/20110804/eddy-collins-jones-esclavitud-duele-1105663.

Radio Macuto (2017). Ha fallecido la Excma Sra Dña Ana María Dougan Thomson. *Radio Macuto*, 28 November. Retrieved from https://www.radiomacuto.net/2017/11/28/ha-fallecido-la-excma-sra-dna-ana-maria-dougan-thomson/.

Articles in blogs

García Gimeno, F. (2013). Maximiliano Jones, *Blog Fernando el Africano*. Retrieved from http://fernandoelafricano.blogspot.com/2013/11/maximiliano-cipriano-jones-11_14.html

My Primitive Methodists, Barleycorn, William Napoleon (1848–1925). Retrieved from https://www.myprimitivemethodists.org.uk/content/people-2/primitive_methodist_ministers/b/william_napoleon_barleycorn

Wiki, Castle, 81 Holloway Road, Islington N7 (house of Amelia Barleycorn in London). Retrieved from https://pubshistory.com/LondonPubs///Islington/Castle.shtml

Index

A

Abdelkrim, Muhammad ibn 221
abuse 93, 99, 100, 103, 105, 115, 208, 213, 214, 217
    authority 98
    of Africans 147, 242, 245
    of foremen 116
    of labourers 59
    of minors 98
    of women 16, 94, 98, 100, 116, 207
    physical 214, 217
    reported 98, 100
    sexual 29, 31, 98, 99, 207, 214-217, 225
Africanism 35, 187
Africanity 76
Africans. Passim
    black 22, 75, 162, 233, 237, 239, 242
    elite 22
    exotisation of 170
    expulsion of 103, 105, 106
    in Europe 14, 21-23, 25-28, 34, 107, 133, 182, 243-245
    in Spain 13-15, 23, 32, 33
    legal status 57
    racialised 120
    rights of 27, 244
    Spanish 16, 80, 103, 106, 108, 110, 116, 123, 131, 143, 146, 158, 159, 165, 166, 179, 184, 185, 190, 192, 194, 199, 211, 214, 240
    stereotypes 120, 122
    women 13, 15, 21, 22, 24, 31, 41, 42, 45, 62, 94, 99, 100, 107, 133, 146, 147, 174-176, 201, 202, 207, 225, 243, 244, 246
African War 156
Afrocentrism 33
Afro-Europeans 25, 27, 243, 245
    affiliation 32
    collective 26
    concept 25
Afropolitanism 15, 18, 20, 23, 34, 116, 133, 150, 187, 226, 244, 246
    concept 15, 33, 119, 249, 250
    status 21, 50, 55, 76

women 15, 177
aggression 14, 99, 101, 183, 184, 205, 219. See also race
Akpan Akpan, Pius 143
Akpan, Peter 95
Almonte, Enrique d' 65, 219
Americas 25, 46, 112
amnesia 28, 180, 181
Añau, Adama 208
androcentrism 22, 24, 28, 30, 44, 45, 47, 55, 59-62, 66, 67, 114, 146, 147, 174, 176, 178, 189, 201, 206, 230, 239
Anglicisation 51, 54, 57
Annobon 49, 82, 197
Annobon people 49, 57, 88, 108, 124, 137, 158, 179, 181, 207
Aragón, Guillemar de 53, 54, 223, 226
Areñas, Rafael 157
Argentines 148, 149
aristocrats 37, 147
    women 168, 177, 223
Arkins Bruch, Isabel 168
Arkins (family) 111. See also Balboa
artisan 57, 76, 221
Asia 112
associationism 206
Atti (family). See also Barleycorn
Atti, Sally 139
authority 59, 63, 102, 103, 147, 187, 242
    abuse of 98
    female 17, 24, 28, 31, 35, 62, 175, 176, 189, 201, 205-207, 240, 246
    marital 194
    parental 193, 194
autonomy
    female 35, 39, 175, 179, 201, 202, 206, 207, 210, 244, 245
    government 69, 93, 110, 123, 146, 169

B

Balboa Arkins, Abilio 75, 139, 168, 229
Balboa Arkins, Armando 229

Balboa Arkins, Consuelo 168, 224
Balboa Arkins, Manuel 168
Balboa Arkins, Norberto 229
Balboa Boneke, Juan 161
Balboa, Consuelo 75, 164
Balboa Dougan, Abilio 69
Balboa Dougan, Armando 168
Balboa Dougan, Norberto 169
Balboa During, Manuel 75, 124, 168
Balboa (family) 16, 64, 73-75, 80, 116, 124, 134, 135, 137, 139, 166, 168, 176, 183, 184, 186, 225, 229, 232, 246. See also Arkins and Dougan
Balboa, Isabel 176
Balboa, Javier 169
Balboa, Manuel 63, 73-75, 134, 136, 159, 179
Banapá mission 70, 137, 143
Bank of British West Africa Limited 86
banks 86, 157
baptism 71, 163, 227
Baptists 55, 198
Barcelona. Passim
Barcelona Bar Association 69
Barleycorn, Amalia 43-45, 53, 61, 64, 93, 157, 159, 201, 205, 207, 229, 231, 238, 241, 249
Barleycorn, Amelia 13, 15, 16, 19, 21-23, 26, 30, 38, 39, 42-46, 50, 52, 53, 56, 59-68, 70, 86, 93, 104, 105, 108, 114, 116, 123, 124, 129, 131-136, 148, 154, 157-159, 167, 168, 175, 178, 186, 189-191, 197-201, 203-207, 209, 213, 216, 218, 219, 227, 229, 231, 238, 240-245, 249
Barleycorn Atti, Eduardo 139
Barleycorn Bioco, Celestina 138
Barleycorn Boricó, George Armando 109, 168, 179
Barleycorn Boricó, Ricardo Emilio 168
Barleycorn Boricó, Veracruz 138
Barleycorn Collins, Maria Raquel 227
Barleycorn Collins, Rolando 227
Barleycorn, Daniel Omonie 108, 109
Barleycorn, Domingo 134
Barleycorn, Dorcas Fanny de 60, 131, 204, 251
Barleycorn, Eduardo C. 135
Barleycorn, Edward 60, 61
Barleycorn, Emilio 60, 71, 134
Barleycorn, Eva 60, 61, 209
Barleycorn (family) 23, 43, 55, 59-61, 63, 64, 66, 80, 86, 108, 114-116, 131, 134, 137, 139, 157, 160, 168, 186, 207, 208, 217, 229, 232, 238, 249. See also Atti, Boricó, Collins, Jones and Macfoy

Barleycorn, George Armando 108
Barleycorn, Gertrudis 133
Barleycorn Inta, Eugenia 138
Barleycorn, Jeremías 60, 134, 138, 139, 204
Barleycorn, John 60, 61, 111
Barleycorn Jones, Juan Walterio 109, 138
Barleycorn, Juan. See Barleycorn, John
Barleycorn, Julia 61, 209
Barleycorn, Juliana 60, 93
Barleycorn, Mabel 133, 208
Barleycorn Macfoy, Isabel 61, 138
Barleycorn Macfoy, Ricardo 61, 160
Barleycorn Macfoy, Rolando 61, 227
Barleycorn, Mariana 60, 134
Barleycorn, María Raquel 61
Barleycorn, Napoleon 60, 131
Barleycorn Norman, Susana 138
Barleycorn, Roberto 124, 134
Barleycorn, Rolando 60, 61, 82, 159, 160, 208, 213, 215-217
Barleycorn, Sally. See Fenaux Barleycorn, Sally
Barleycorn, Susana 86, 204, 208
Barleycorn, William Napoleon 45, 59, 60, 64, 131, 132, 134, 160, 168, 204
Bata 35, 53, 109, 197, 239, 249
Battle of Annual 221
Bdyogo Owono, José Manuel 110
Beecroft, John 232, 233
Benin 126
Bilbao 66, 139, 181
Bilelo Lopez, Leoncio Paciencia 144
Bioko 50, 111, 181
birth certificate 27
birthright 130, 168, 194
Bissio people 49, 88, 108, 124, 158, 207, 239
Black Atlantic 33
blackness 28, 29, 31, 33, 175, 177, 212, 237, 243
black people 14, 39, 52, 53, 56, 63, 79, 102, 122, 123, 143, 177, 179, 183, 184, 211, 223, 226
   American 226
   colonised 19
   coloniser 243
   hypersexualisation 98
   in Europe 32
   women 15, 21, 22, 24, 67, 98, 100, 147, 174, 177, 200, 201, 223, 225, 232, 233, 252
bloodline 43, 62, 111
   Barleycorn 59
   Collins 73, 227

INDEX 269

Jones 65, 227
Kinson 70
Boleko Brown, Anselmo 111
Boleko Browne, Pedro 144
Boneque, Elena 209
Boricó (family) 225. See also Barleycorn
Boricó Toichoa, Román 69
Botala Ripelo, Laureana 144
bourgeoisie 37, 115, 147, 227
    African 15, 37
    Afropolitan 31
    Catalan 15, 18, 20, 34, 35, 75, 121, 122, 125, 135, 136, 148, 154, 165, 174, 176-179, 187, 213, 214, 236, 240, 242, 246
    European 55
    industrial 151
    Krio Fernandino 35, 176, 179, 186
braceros 46, 55, 66, 72, 74, 79, 83, 103, 115, 116, 134, 205-207, 235, 245
Braun, María 210
British people 22, 27, 44, 49-53, 56, 57, 69, 76, 78, 86, 94, 110, 111, 115, 116, 125, 131, 132, 148, 157, 176, 186, 201, 222, 233, 234, 239, 243
browns 46
Bruch (family). See Arkins Bruch
Buaki Botuy, Adelaida 143
Buapache Donson, Bernedeta 144
Bubi people 31, 49, 56, 57, 62, 66, 88, 108, 124, 137, 145, 158, 159, 170, 181, 187, 209, 222, 225, 230, 231, 233, 239, 242
    language 60
    women 62, 83, 89, 98, 100, 207
burial 132, 167, 168, 209

C

Cabré Enclusa, Evelina 18
Cámara Agrícola de Barcelona 36
Cámara Agrícola de Fernando Poo 65
Camblé (family). See Lolín Camblé
Cameroon 40, 60, 112, 145, 146, 233
Canary Islands 36, 114, 124, 130, 132, 136, 161
capitalism 29, 115
    black 35
    colonial 15
Castillo, Encarnación 136
Castillo (family) 73, 225, 229. See also Jones
Castillo, Francisca 136
Castillo, Manuel 150
Castillo, Pablo 229

Castillo, Susana 136, 229
Catalans. Passim
Catalonia. Passim
Catholicism 37, 54, 55, 73, 76, 114, 115, 175, 190, 192, 195, 196, 227, 239
    conversion to 50, 52, 66, 69, 91, 137, 162, 190, 202, 203, 239
    deaths 190, 204
    expansion of 202
    marriages 190, 191, 227
    rites 191
child 29, 45, 47, 54, 60, 63, 66, 67, 69, 99, 100, 126, 131, 151, 161, 166-169, 183, 191, 202, 203, 224, 227, 233
Chileans 148, 149
Christian Davis, Carlota 227
Christianisation 190, 234, 238
Christianity 28, 50, 120, 175, 190
    conversion to 63
citizen 21, 67, 104, 107, 110, 183, 184, 193
    black 32
    Bubi 145
    Catalan 178
    European 182
    expulsion of 105
    Krio Fernandino 22, 75, 99, 104, 156, 161, 162, 170, 221
    Spanish 98
    white 52
citizenry 81, 97
citizenship 32
    European 25
    full 26, 58, 182
    rights 26, 182, 245
    Spanish 113
Ciutat Vella 148, 149
Civil Code 191, 192, 194-196
civilisation 37, 224
    necessary 123
    rhetoric 87, 170
Civil Marriage Law 191-193, 195, 196
civil servant 46, 51, 98, 99, 151, 158
Claretians 45, 62, 88, 124, 154, 168, 169, 210, 237
class 16, 29-31, 52, 55, 58, 90, 97, 100, 115, 125, 132, 147, 151, 164, 165, 170, 174, 176-180, 187, 189, 210-214, 220, 241, 242, 244-246
    asymmetries of 30
    barriers 55
    divisions 17, 19

first 128, 129, 143, 212
lower 147, 175, 177
middle 21, 29, 129, 147, 151, 175
privileges 226
second 129
significance of 58
third 129, 212
upper 21, 29, 63, 146, 147, 165, 175, 177
variables 29, 31, 178, 180
classism 20, 226, 245
Club Fernandino 71, 90, 92, 93
cocoa 35, 51, 54, 59, 63, 66, 68, 94, 158, 159
coexistence 27, 79, 94, 101, 103, 116, 120, 125, 180, 182, 187, 211, 214
coffee 54, 94, 123
cohabitation 98, 233
    Africans-Spaniards 16, 38
Coker, Constancia 75
Coker (family) 232
Cole, Esicalla 210
Cole (family) 71
Cole, Lucy 215-217
Cole Vivour, Claudio 71, 90, 134, 227
Collins and Son, Widow 72, 159, 209
Collins, Beatriz 136
Collins, Carlos 136
Collins Edgerley, Eduardo 139
Collins, Edmundo 65, 71-73, 90, 101, 124, 134, 227
Collins (family) 16, 55, 64, 66, 70-74, 111, 116, 134, 136, 137, 139, 161, 166, 186, 205, 208, 219, 229, 232. See also Barleycorn and Jones
Collins, Fanny 136
Collins Jones, Eddy 73, 161
Collins Jones, Edmundo 73, 229
Collins Jones, Juana Elena 72, 227
Collins Jones, Trinidad 60, 112, 165, 227
Collins, José Luís 73
Collins, Manuela 134
Collins, Margarita 136
Collins, Pepe. See Collins, José Luís
Collins, Reina 134
Collins, Sara 73, 134, 135, 208
Collins, Williams 136
Colonial Guard 252
Colonial Guards 100, 207
    black 102
    indigenous 16, 94, 99, 101-103, 116, 244
    white 99

colonialism 35, 37, 175
    European 16, 243
    Spanish 16, 19, 35, 36, 55, 67, 233, 242
coloniality 14, 25, 27, 32
    European 247
    Iberian 34
    of power 24
    racial 13, 14, 21
    rejection of 27
    Spanish 234
    survival of 246
colonies 19, 78, 125, 174, 175, 186, 193, 239
    African 14, 24, 31
    Catalonia 250
    constitution of 25
    Dutch 29, 34
    English 80, 104
    European 13, 30, 80
    French 80
    Portuguese 80
    Spanish 17, 22, 124, 189, 234
colonisation 14, 20, 26, 27, 36, 49, 51, 57, 58, 79, 87, 98, 99, 103, 105, 109, 110, 119, 122-124, 131, 146, 166, 181, 182, 189, 241, 245, 247
    English 51
    European 19, 21
    Spanish 120, 172, 195, 198, 202, 203, 224, 234, 239, 240, 246
colonisers 19, 29, 36, 51, 90, 94, 98, 102
    African 21
    black 19, 115, 243
    European 20, 101, 241
    Spanish 20, 52, 54, 68, 70, 91, 235, 242, 247
coloureds 39, 44, 46, 52, 79, 151, 156, 232, 238, 250
    women 98
Comercial Frapejo SA 75
Comillas, Marqués de 133, 250
Compañía Trasatlántica 35, 54, 65, 127, 129, 133
Concepción 74, 135, 159
consciousness
    Afropolitan 244
    elite 245
Constancia (association) 61, 209
Cooperativa Annobonesa 82
cooperatives 83, 210
Corisco 49, 197
cosmopolitanism 23, 34, 55, 120, 121, 125, 242
    African 15, 33

Creole people 49, 56, 111, 249
criminalisation 183
Cuba 15, 20, 35, 83, 112, 176, 242, 252
Cubans 54, 56, 73, 75, 136, 150, 224, 225
    emancipated 73
    minority 76

D

Davies, Domingo 99-101
Davies, Juan-Manuel 161
Davis, Blandavo 210
Davis (family) 232. See also Christian Davis
debts
    colonial 182, 245
    European 26
    historical 28, 245
decolonisation 13, 14, 16, 18, 66, 181, 182, 189, 240, 245
    decolonial studies 22
    inflection 249
    turn 249
demonstrations 17, 105, 107, 183
    against colonial power 73, 208
Dependents Association 93
de-racialisation. See racialisation
desacralisation 91
diaspora 33
    African 32, 247
    black 33
    Krio Fernandino 16, 19, 31, 42, 115, 125, 126, 135, 136, 139, 148, 149, 156, 163, 166, 168, 181, 187, 246
diplomats 54, 92, 122
discrimination 14, 21, 29, 94, 182, 236, 246
    sexual 207
dis-encounter 123, 251
domestic service 17, 210, 211, 213, 214, 241
domination 14, 29, 34, 44, 162
Dougan (family) 16, 55, 64, 66, 68, 69, 71, 111, 116, 125, 134, 136, 147, 160, 165, 166, 168, 183, 184, 186, 202, 205, 208, 229, 232, 246. See also Balboa, Jones, Kinson, and Okori
Dougan, Jorge 150, 156
Dougan, José 82, 134, 160, 219
Dougan, Joseph 65, 168, 205, 209, 227
Dougan, José Walterio 68-70, 134, 136, 159, 162, 229
Dougan, Juliana 163
Dougan Kinson, Anita Sara 71
Dougan Kinson, Juliana 71, 227
Dougan Kinson, Lorenza 69, 75, 229
Dougan Kinson, Susana 136
Dougan Kinson, Teófilo 69, 160
Dougan Kinson, Teófilo Jorge 88, 160
Dougan, Lorenza 98, 168
Dougan, Mariana 150, 209
Dougan McCarthy, José Walterio 168
Dougan, Samuel 209, 227
Dougan, Sara W. 134, 135
Dougan, Susana 165, 168
Dougan, Teófilo 227
Dougan, Teófilo J. 229
Dougan, Theodora 227
Dougan, Theodore 227
Dougan, Theophilus 168
Dougan Thomson, Ana María 69
Dougan, Walter 134
dress 29, 34, 44, 125, 165, 175, 176, 218, 220-224, 233, 242
Dutch language 29
Dutch people 29, 34, 53

E

Early Modern period 14, 23, 29
Echenique, Góngora 222, 224
Edgerley, José 124
education 23, 29, 32, 39, 47, 49, 52, 53, 55, 57, 61, 63, 64, 67, 75, 87-89, 109, 119, 125, 131, 132, 137-139, 141, 143-145, 150, 151, 154-158, 160-163, 166, 167, 169-172, 174, 181, 186, 193, 202, 203, 218, 226, 234
ego 176
Egypt 112
Eixample 148, 149
Electrical Power Station 65
elite 15, 23, 24, 35, 50, 59, 120, 122, 164, 165, 178, 180, 189, 201, 206, 212, 214, 218, 225, 230, 234, 240, 241, 245, 246
    African 15, 20, 22, 98, 115, 200
    Afropolitan 21
    Cuban 20
    self-reliant 141
    white 20
elitism 23, 31, 200, 241
Elobey 49, 197
emancipation 27, 44, 54, 57, 58, 73, 98, 100, 108, 136, 187, 211, 240, 245
    African 243

full 94, 97, 103, 108, 116, 138, 193
letter of 19, 108, 109, 115, 158, 168, 180, 183, 200, 225, 244
limited 26, 57, 97, 108, 244
semi- 190
unemancipated. See status
emigrant 46
emotional geography 13, 22, 243
endogamy 56, 69, 135, 214, 225, 226, 229, 230, 242
England 23, 27, 40, 49, 51, 57, 62, 64, 86, 121, 131, 132, 134, 135, 160, 163, 176, 191, 198, 201, 203, 221, 233, 241
English language 44, 49, 51, 53, 75, 202, 233, 239
English people 51. See British people
enlightenment 37
equality 26, 53
    of rights 26
    racial 24
Equatorial Guinea Bar Association 69
Equatorial Guineans. Passim
ethnicity 24, 33, 88, 137, 158, 233, 249
ethnography 39, 249
Euro-Africans 15, 25-28, 245
    affiliation 32
    concept 25, 26, 28
    connection 33
    heritage 182
    hybridisation 42
    memory 185
    status 200
Eurocentrism 22, 23, 175, 176, 201
    colonial 44, 45
    racism 178, 244
Europe. Passim
    androcentrism 22
    black 32
    colonial 245
    Fortress 28
    male-focused logic 24
    treatment of women 24
Europeanised Africans 218
Europeanness 76, 224
Europeans 18, 19, 26, 27, 29, 31, 42, 45, 46, 54, 55, 58, 72, 75, 79, 80, 85, 86, 88, 90, 94-96, 99, 100, 116, 120, 125, 128, 175, 181, 190, 207, 211, 213, 214, 218, 221, 222, 224-226, 232, 235, 241, 246
    black African 19
    ego 176
    minority 28, 58
    white 210, 230
    women 21, 24, 99, 133, 175, 206
European Union 28, 32
Evinayong 145
exile 34, 50, 73, 110, 112, 117, 145, 233
    political 16, 146
exploitation 87, 120, 147
expulsion 15, 103-107, 183
    of Africans 105, 106
    of Spaniards 111
    of Spanish Africans 16, 103, 116

F

Fa d'Ambô people 49
Fang language 98
Fang people 49, 57, 88, 108, 124, 137, 158, 159, 181, 207, 230, 233, 239
fashion 221, 223
    English 53
    European 223
feminisation 44, 56
feminism 62
Fenaux Barleycorn, Sally 43
Fernando Poo 13, 16, 20, 22, 36, 45, 49-54, 56-58, 60, 62, 63, 65-68, 70, 73, 74, 76, 79, 86, 90, 93, 94, 106, 115, 120, 122, 126, 129, 131-135, 143, 144, 159, 160, 164, 167-169, 172, 175, 178, 181, 186, 191, 198, 202, 203, 207, 211, 212, 215, 218, 221, 224, 226, 230, 232, 234, 239, 246, 247, 249, 251
First World War 27, 83, 135
Fockne, Francisco 210
forefathers 62, 114
foreigners 33, 51, 76, 106, 107, 110, 148, 149, 176
    African 199
    arrival of 39
    eternal 20, 21, 200
    expulsion of 183
    rights of 183, 192, 194
    status 34, 149, 199
foremen 116, 204, 205
France 27, 138
    colonies 80
Franco, Francisco 27, 36, 61, 66, 79, 89, 125, 144, 168
freedom 101, 124, 217, 229
Freetown 51, 56, 223
French language 202
French people 125, 148, 149, 233

G

Gabon 112, 146
García Vivour, Carlos. See Vivour, Carlos G.
gender 14-16, 22, 24, 28-30, 45, 52, 177, 178, 180, 187, 189-191, 200, 239, 241, 243, 245, 246
    African women 62
    asymmetries of 30
    variables 29, 31, 174, 178
geography 139
    context 179
    emotional 13, 22, 243
    origin 31, 114, 122, 147, 176
    space 15
German language 233
Germanophilia 233
Germans 78, 125, 135, 148, 149, 238
Germany 86, 233
    East 112
Ghana 67, 226
glocalisation 23, 249
Gomán, Gaspar 172
Gotzens, Josefina 164
Government Police 46, 106, 109, 124, 138
Gràcia 148, 149
Granada 161
Great Britain 181. See England
guardianship 26, 57, 193, 194

H

health 87, 90, 119, 138, 144, 155, 158, 162, 171
healthcare 57, 90, 155, 157, 158, 186, 250
hegemony change 160
heritage 249
    Bubi 31
    Cuban 176
    Euro-African 182
herstory 13, 243, 244
hierarchy 32, 100, 103, 124, 143, 162, 214
    colonial 29, 183
    European 29
    sexual 24, 174
Hispanisation 16, 35, 51, 53, 54, 64, 67, 78, 104, 115, 169, 209, 234, 238, 239, 249
Hispanophone 35
homeland 23, 109, 157, 207
hotel 156, 163, 164, 167, 234
    Beausejour 154
    Inglaterra 163, 164
    Majestic 163
    Ritz 163, 165, 166, 182
humanitarianism 175
hybridism 37, 42
hypersexualisation 98

I

identity 25, 41, 189
    African 15, 22, 26, 76, 147, 226
    Afro-Spanish 27
    card 113
    cultural 25
    family 46, 62, 146
    Krio Fernandino 20, 33
    national 28
    political 25
    self-definition of 32
    Spanish colonial 42
    transcultural 42
    transnational 42
ignorance 23, 182, 184, 210, 237
immigration 31, 32, 79, 98, 105-107, 120, 149, 180, 181, 184, 199, 235. See also migration
Immigration Law (1985) 15
Immigration Regulation (1934) 106, 211
imperialism 37, 147, 180, 182
independence 16, 25, 26, 28, 45, 49, 50, 69, 81, 93, 110-112, 114, 117, 130, 137, 146, 161, 180, 181, 187, 212, 234, 238, 245
    female 61, 133, 201, 229, 245
    post- 14, 27, 119, 141, 200
    pro- 144, 145
indigenous Other 29
indigenous people 57, 58, 71, 85, 89, 90, 99, 100, 108, 121, 124, 134, 169, 171, 181, 182
    non- 94
    women 79, 99
industrialisation 121
industrial revolution 250
inequality 24, 27, 100, 125, 214
    legal 21, 194
    women 21
infantilisation 55, 94
inferiority 21, 115, 123, 176, 177, 222
influence 35, 61, 66, 83, 87, 92, 93, 100, 101, 108, 132, 139, 159, 179, 182, 202, 204, 229, 230, 239, 240
    African 13, 28, 65, 200, 237

British 51, 52, 54, 69, 76, 186, 191, 200
Catalan 36, 236, 246
European 13, 34, 44, 50, 62, 76, 90
female 21, 44, 45, 47, 59, 62, 64, 67, 73, 100, 104, 147, 159, 189, 200-202, 206, 210, 238, 240, 241, 244
Protestant 238
Spanish 45, 115
integration 37, 69, 79, 107, 162, 181, 183, 187, 227, 233, 234, 239, 242
of women 187
intersectionality 15, 16, 21, 29, 30, 35, 45, 52, 90, 91, 97, 103, 165, 187, 210, 245
concept of 147, 174
invisibility 32, 45, 64, 113, 247
African 19, 29, 32
of women 44, 69
Isuwu people 226
Ita, Gertrude 138
Italians 125, 148, 149
Italy 138

J

Jamaicans 56, 224
Jones, Alfredo 124, 165
Jones, Alfredo J. 135
Jones, Aurora 165
Jones, Bernardo J. 135
Jones Bishop, Eduardo 229
Jones, Caridad 66
Jones Castillo, Fernando 139
Jones Castillo, Miguel 66
Jones Castillo, Pablo 139
Jones Castillo, Wilbardo 139
Jones, Daniel 165
Jones Dougan, Lucrecia 69, 73, 229
Jones, Eduardo 72, 160
Jones (family) 16, 64, 66, 71, 72, 80, 111, 116, 124, 125, 134, 135, 137, 139, 159, 160, 164, 165, 176, 186, 202, 208, 229, 238. See also Castillo, Dougan, and Níger
Jones, Juana 72, 135, 159, 227
Jones, Mabel 67, 68, 135, 159, 163, 164
Jones Mathama, Daniel 44
Jones, Maximiliano 58, 65-69, 71, 101, 134, 159, 160, 162, 164, 165, 204, 227, 229, 238, 239
Jones Mehilo, Jeremías 235
Jones, Miguel 163
Jones, Mildred 136

Jones, Moisés Cornelio 66
Jones Mookava, Guillermo 163
Jones Níger, Alfredo 165, 166, 168, 182
Jones Níger, Wilbardo 66, 229
Jones, Raquel 135, 159, 176, 212
Jones Welah, Adolfo 160
jornaleros 46
Just Sant 154

K

king
black 126, 233, 234
Cameroonian 233
Spanish 157
King (family) 111
Kinson, Daniel 70, 74, 82, 229
Kinson de Dougan, María 136
Kinson de Dougan, Mariana 71, 231
Kinson (family) 16, 55, 64, 70, 71, 80, 116, 124, 134-136, 166, 216, 229, 232. See also Dougan
Kinson, María 209
Kinson, Mariana 69-71, 160, 209, 227, 229
Kinson, Samuel 65, 70, 71, 90, 124, 135, 136, 209, 210, 227, 229
Knox, Daniel 216, 217
Knox, Eva 70
Knox (family) 80, 217, 232
Knox, Francisco 70
Knox, J.W. 65
Krio Fernandino. Passim
krumanes 46, 223, 226

L

La Barcelonesa 65, 178
labourers 19, 46, 54, 57, 59, 61, 62, 66, 72, 74, 88, 94, 96, 101, 187, 205, 207. See also workers
Lagos 56, 63, 225
Las Palmas 129, 134, 136, 144
Late Modern period 14, 23, 29
Latin Americans 31, 56, 79
La Vigatana 61, 111, 126
Lawson Mecheba, Inocencio 144, 145
Lebu, Isabel 209
legitimacy 58, 99, 100, 167, 191, 194, 196, 197, 229
Liberia 22, 55-57, 61, 79, 133, 134, 139, 213, 221, 225, 226
liminality
racial 20, 28, 243, 249
Liverpool 23, 56, 63, 86, 131

Loeri Comba, José María 144, 145
Lolín Camblé, Luís 71, 75, 90, 227
Lolín (family) 75, 80. See also Camblé, and Vigour
Lolín, Luís 209
London 23, 56, 68, 74, 104, 131, 132, 150, 186, 223, 232, 251
Luddington, William B. 60
luxury 66, 82, 156, 157, 163, 187, 218-220, 223, 232, 234, 237
Lynsleger, James 222, 232

M

Macfoy, Adelaide 135
Macfoy, Benito 124, 217
Macfoy (family) 71, 134, 216. See also Barleycorn
Macfoy, Isabel 160, 215, 217
Macfoy, Susana 213, 215-217
Macías Nguema 73, 110-112, 117, 161, 182, 238
Macoli, Origiana 210
Maho Chuaham, Beatriz 143
Maho (family) 225
Maho, Luís 145, 169
Maho Sicachá, Luís José 174
maid 62, 212, 215-217
Malabo 13, 16, 49, 50, 53, 65, 110, 117, 161, 181, 230, 238, 249
Manchester 56, 63, 131
marginalisation 174
market 61, 208
marriage 62, 68-71, 73, 93, 125, 163-165, 167, 187, 189-191, 193, 195-198, 226, 227, 229-231, 233, 241
   African 215
   aristocratic 164
   Catholic 190, 191, 227
   civil 196
   endogamic 225, 226, 229, 230, 242
   exogamous 225
   interracial 225, 242
   isogamy 226
   mixed 20, 75, 169, 225
   polygynous 207
   Protestant 191, 194, 196, 198, 199, 203, 240
   with black woman 232
   with Bubi 56, 231
   with Cuban 56, 75
   with white man 232
master 126, 162, 211, 212
Materos, Enry 201

matrilineality 62, 207
Mba, Cirilo 144, 145
Mba Mba, Luciano 144
Mbela, Gustavo 109
Mbolo, Mercedes 99-101
McCarthy (family). See Dougan
Meaca Bubi, Eugenia 98
mediation 105
   Fernandino–European 234, 242
memory 32, 184, 185, 230
   and history 250
   collective 45, 111, 114, 243
   colonial 25, 180, 181
   lived 39, 40
   narrated 39, 249
   oral 42, 44, 249
   postcolonial 182
   Spanish colonial 114
Mentz, Gustavo 124
Methodists 55, 60, 64, 92, 187, 192, 195, 196, 203, 223, 251
   pastor 203
migration 13, 15, 25, 32, 36, 39, 40, 46, 52, 100, 111-114, 121, 125, 137, 141, 148, 183, 185, 249. See also immigration
   racialised 31, 32
   regulation 15, 94, 103, 107
   transnational 14, 111
military 28, 78, 85, 94, 98, 175, 218
minimisation 62, 212, 246
miningas 98
minoritisation 19, 30, 42
minority 28, 57, 139, 224, 225
   African 26, 125, 201
   black 125
   Cuban 76
   European 58
   Krio Fernandino 15, 27, 49, 58, 111, 133, 144, 200, 226
   white 54, 78
mission 27, 37, 55, 70, 76, 143, 170, 175, 203, 204
   Banapá 70, 137, 143
   Catholic 202, 237, 239
   Claretian 169
   Methodist 195, 223
   Protestant 237
   Spanish 24, 74, 171, 239
missionaries 51, 53, 74, 137, 139, 143, 154, 158, 169-171, 175, 190, 197, 204, 212, 213, 218, 242

Catalan 45, 52, 62, 88, 120, 124, 169, 237
Catholic 55, 62, 88, 120, 169, 175, 199, 206, 237
Claretian 45, 88, 168
Daughters of the Immaculate Conception 169
English 232
European 59
Sons of the Immaculate Heart of Mary 170
Spanish 44, 68, 203, 237
women 169
mobilisation 105, 183, 208, 210, 241
African 105
anti-colonial 146
social 103
mobility 18, 52, 119, 129, 130, 133, 158, 186, 243
Mboro 250
transcontinental 18, 50, 129, 130, 132, 133, 176, 246
transnational 23, 50, 129
Mochoma Soka, María 144
Momo, Pilar 89, 171, 172
Monrovia 56, 127, 134, 139, 250
Moreno (family) 73, 225
morenos 46, 78, 93, 97, 123, 134, 169, 172, 175, 179, 202, 205, 210, 213, 217, 223, 224
Morgades, Manuel 165, 172
Morgades, Trinidad 161
Moroccans 122, 148-150, 183
Morocco 156, 199, 221, 249
mortality 71, 169
causes 162
Mulato Godhech 207
mulatto 123, 201
multilocality 13, 15, 18, 21, 23, 29, 33, 50, 55, 56, 116, 129, 187, 246, 249
Muñoz y Gaviria, J. 53, 81, 126, 131, 201, 223, 225, 232
Munuera, José 95

N

Nanga, Luís 144
narrative 23, 39, 107, 162, 175, 202, 211, 249
nationalism 37
nationality 103, 114, 121, 138, 149, 150, 186, 189, 190, 194, 197, 199, 241, 244, 250
adoption of 199
African 25, 26, 202
de facto 26
dual 114
English 194
Equatorial Guinean 114
European 25, 26, 182, 245
legal 26, 28
obtaining 17
pseudo-European 245
Spanish 22, 52, 79, 106, 113, 114, 138, 139, 150, 182, 198-200, 241
naturalisation 79, 199
Ndowe people 49, 57, 88, 108, 124, 137, 158, 181, 207, 239
Negre de Banyoles 250
Negre, Gastón 164
Netherlands 34, 40
networks 25, 33, 187, 227
educational 158
family 112, 114, 141, 144, 207
health 158
missionary 143, 158
multi-local 33
transnational 33
Níger (family). See also Jones
Nigeria 22, 55, 56, 63, 109, 112, 133, 143, 213, 225, 227
Nigerians 57, 59, 95, 145
Níger, Isabel 135
Nou Barris 149
Núñez del Prado, Miguel 199

O

Obiang Nguema 110, 111, 182
oblivion 31, 43, 186, 187
Okara, Paulina 208
Okori Dougan, José 229
origin 46, 53, 56, 57, 60, 76, 91, 107, 108, 111, 120, 136, 150, 159, 166, 184, 205, 207, 227, 233
African 28, 33, 56, 58, 73, 106, 179, 200, 211, 212
black 52
English 64
geographical 31, 114, 122, 147, 176
multi-ethnic 13, 22, 224
transcontinental 214
otherness 29, 42, 121, 245
African 14, 18, 176

P

palm oil 51, 59, 131, 158
Pamu people 222, 233

Paris 74, 150
passenger list 23, 45, 46, 54, 111, 129, 132, 134, 136, 137, 211, 212, 250
passport 27, 47, 113, 138
patrilineality 146, 207
Patronato de Indígenas 57, 58, 108, 138
Peñalosa, Luís Gabriel 98
pension 151, 154, 171
    La Africana 154
Pérez Portabella, Francisco 150
Pérez Portabella, Francisco-Javier 165
Pérez Portabella, J. 75
Peruvians 148, 149
Peter, Paulina 73
Pichi language 49, 51, 53, 115, 150, 212, 239
Pidgin English. See Pichi language
Pilmont 131
plantation 36, 46, 57, 60, 61, 63-65, 68, 69, 71, 72, 74, 79, 83, 86, 94, 111, 126, 131, 134, 204, 205, 222
    cocoa 54, 63, 94, 159
    coffee 54, 94
    timber 94
police 46, 86, 88, 94, 99, 106, 109, 124, 138, 155, 177, 184, 208, 219
Port Clarence 51, 53, 56, 60
Portugal 50, 80, 138
Portuguese people 78, 125, 249
postcolonialism 14, 24-26, 28, 31, 89, 125, 181, 182
    decolonial studies 42
    postcolonial studies 22, 42
Premià de Mar 154
Presbyterians 60, 132
    conversion to 54
primitive people 122, 123, 223, 237, 242
primitivism 120, 193, 222
Prince (family) 80
privileges 15, 24, 25, 29, 37, 59, 94, 100, 110, 187, 200, 201, 204, 206, 225, 226, 230, 234, 235, 240-242, 246
Protestantism 17, 51, 53-55, 62, 73, 76, 109, 110, 115, 162, 175, 187, 191, 192, 195, 200, 210, 227, 238, 239
    conversion to 50, 204
    decline 202
    rites 192, 197
Protestants 55, 59, 60, 62, 64, 67, 114, 124, 190, 197-200, 202-204, 223, 238, 241
    African 239

marriage 191, 194, 198, 199, 203, 240
mission 237
pastor 109, 192, 193, 197-199
provincialisation 93, 109, 130, 146
pyramid 98
    colonial 57, 96
    racial 96, 243
    social 57

Q
Quinton 60, 131, 132

R
race 14, 16, 29, 30, 52, 58, 100, 119, 125, 165, 176, 177, 180, 187, 191, 193, 194, 211, 214, 226, 240-242, 245, 246
    African 184
    asymmetries of 30
    biases 165, 244
    black 183
    coloured 98
    concept of 29, 39, 249
    discourse 20, 102, 125
    Hispanic 31, 125
    ideology 31
    mixed 147, 226
    variables 29, 30, 174, 178, 187
    white 123, 213
racialisation 19, 20, 24, 29-34, 52, 58, 59, 79, 90, 97, 101, 120, 123, 125, 134, 164, 174, 177, 181, 186, 189, 211, 213, 239, 241, 243, 245, 246
    colonial 21
    de-racialisation 17, 28, 177, 210, 213, 214, 245
    European 42, 115
racism 29, 31, 34, 93, 102, 122, 147, 165, 182, 186, 201, 213, 214, 239, 245, 246
    aggression 14, 23, 34, 114, 183, 246
    Dutch 34
    effects 180
    Eurocentric 178
    European 30
    institutional 186
    reaction against 183
    rise 15, 16, 180, 181, 187, 246
Rebola 72, 143, 161
rhetoric 37
    benefits of colonisation 120
    civilisational 58, 87, 170
    colonial 24, 47, 55, 174, 176, 181, 242

278 INDEX

Eurocentric 23
Hispanic race 31, 125
male-focused 67
otherness 18, 245
racial 20
Spanish state 146
Spniash colonising 123
Rhodes, Esteban 68, 163, 164
Rhodes (family) 164, 165
Ricardo, Claudio 124
rights 17, 19, 26, 52, 57, 58, 88, 91, 97, 100, 114, 116, 124, 182, 186, 194, 200, 211
   absence of 99
   citizenship 26, 182, 245
   civic 24
   denial of 24
   domestic service 214
   equality of 26, 62, 115, 138, 179, 191, 201, 243
   improving 158
   inequality of 90, 100
   loss of 106, 115
   of Africans 19, 27, 99, 244
   of African Spaniards 108, 110, 240
   of African women 45, 99
   of foreigners 183, 192, 194
   of freedom 217
   of inheritance 191, 192
   of Spanish Africans 190, 192, 194
   of women 189, 194, 201, 207
   preservation of 146
   recognition of 244
   reduction of 21, 24, 31, 57, 62, 207, 244
   to travel 244
Robinson, Captain 202
Robinson, José 210
Roca, Joaquín Carlos 104, 231
Ruiaz, Father A. Ruíz 124, 168, 175, 210, 237, 239

S

Saavedra y Magdalena, D. 80, 221, 223
salaries 57, 83, 85, 89, 131, 151, 181
Salinas, José 73
San Carlos 49, 63, 65, 67, 71, 86, 87, 92, 95, 138, 144, 159, 160, 178, 186, 187, 197, 203, 218, 219, 241
Santa Coloma de Gramanet 154
Santa Cruz de Tenerife 131
Santa Isabel. Passim
Sant Andreu 149

Sant Martí 148, 149
Sants-Montjuïc 148, 149
Sarrià-San Gervasi 148, 149
Schengenisation 28
schooling. See education
Scott, Mrs 232
Second World War 83
secularism 37
segregation 35, 58, 79, 88, 91, 93, 115, 148, 186, 211, 239
segregationism 53, 119
self-affirmation 37
self-criticism 182
self-employment 23
self-reliance 133, 141, 176, 202, 206
self-rule 58
servant 76, 101, 135, 167, 176-178, 189, 202, 211-214, 216, 217, 221, 241, 245
settlers 20, 36, 105, 107, 182, 201, 210, 211, 219
   Spanish 20
   white 237, 243
sexes 24, 28, 29, 55, 62, 66, 112, 245
   biases 244
   variables 187
sexism 174, 175
sexual abuse 29, 31, 98, 99, 207, 214-217, 225
sexual relations 99, 174, 216, 239
sex work 32
Sierra Leone 22, 51, 55, 56, 63, 65, 67, 68, 70, 71, 112, 127, 133, 134, 167, 202, 210, 213, 224-227, 236, 249
skin colour 20, 21, 24, 31, 32, 52, 55, 58, 79, 91, 97, 102, 103, 123, 143, 150, 164, 165, 174, 176-178, 186, 211, 213, 214, 243, 245
   criminalisation 183
slave 14, 18, 120, 145, 215, 222
   arrival 22
   descendant of 44, 73
   freed 44, 56, 63
   recaptured 226
   ships 226
   trade 22, 133
slavery 56, 73, 222
   impact of 15
Slavery Abolition Law 56
Smint, Mercedes 210
Sociedad Caridad y Amor 210
Sociedad Hijas de África 209
Sociedad Mariana 209, 210

soldiers 85, 129, 213
   indigenous 27
Sorizo Becelebó, Bernabe 144
South Africa 40
Spain. Passim
   black 26, 37, 114, 119
Spaniards. Passim
   African 46, 80, 88, 103, 106, 108, 110, 115, 116, 123, 130, 131, 146, 147, 149, 158, 159, 165, 166, 179, 180, 184, 185, 190, 192, 194, 199, 211, 214, 240
   black 52, 123
   indigenous 27
   women 169, 206
Spanish Civil War 27, 36, 83, 89, 172
Spanishness 110
Spanish Post Office 219
status 20, 21, 39, 46, 53, 57, 60, 66, 67, 89, 97, 98, 101-104, 108, 110, 113, 116, 120, 132, 146, 154, 176, 187, 193, 202, 207, 218, 230, 231, 233, 237
   African 181
   African Spaniards 158
   Afropolitan 50, 55, 76
   Afro-Spanish 27
   black women 15, 21, 24, 75, 177
   colonist 94
   economic 141, 180, 246
   elite 59, 180, 189, 201, 212, 218, 225, 230, 241, 246
   emancipated 26, 27, 58, 97, 100, 103, 108, 136, 187, 190, 245
   Euro-African 200
   European 26, 29
   Europeanised 129, 147, 226
   foreigner 34, 149
   full citizen 58
   inferior 21, 123
   legal 245
   liminal 21
   marital 195
   mixed 129
   privileged 241, 242
   resident 199
   servant 218
   slave 14
   Spanish 52, 182
   Spanish African 199, 200
   Spanishness 110
   symbol 220

undefined 207
unemancipated 19, 57, 58, 97, 100, 115, 136, 245
women 200, 233
steamer 90, 128, 129, 131, 134-136, 138, 212, 215, 241
   Accra 217
   Cataluña 68, 135
   Ciudad de Cádiz 129, 135
   Fernando Poo 133
   San Francisco 134, 203
stereotypes 120, 122, 174, 182, 234
   of immigrants 107
   of women 62, 174
stigmatisation 183, 242
Stone, Pedro Juan 104
Stone, Peter John 103, 104
subalternisation 19, 30, 246
subjects 23, 27, 51, 52, 67, 74, 76, 79, 91, 101, 115, 189, 204, 233, 237
subordination 52, 57, 89, 93, 97, 129, 212
   of women 24
superiority 24, 94, 99, 123, 213
Switzerland 40

T
Tessmann, Günter 63, 238
trade 13, 35, 47, 51, 57, 63, 83, 86, 106, 115, 124, 127, 132, 135, 138, 157, 158, 186, 187, 225, 234, 240, 242, 246
   slave 22, 133
transcontinentalism 18, 21, 33, 50, 55, 56, 116, 119, 129-133, 176, 187, 214, 246
   women 15
transculturality 23, 42
translocality 187
transnationality 15, 18, 21, 23, 33, 50, 55, 116, 119, 125, 128, 129, 159, 187, 246
Tribunales de Raza 58

V
Valencia 111, 114, 121, 124, 130, 161, 181
Venezuela 112
Victoria 60, 215-217
Viñas, Juan Domènech 165
visas 27, 28, 46, 69, 108, 109, 112, 130, 137-139, 143, 144, 212
visibility 24, 26, 32, 34, 35, 57, 60, 62, 66, 91, 115, 116, 147, 176, 201, 205, 214, 221, 227, 239, 241, 243. See also invisibility

of women 73
Vivour, Amelia Barleycorn de. See Barleycorn, Amelia
Vivour Barleycorn, Julia 70, 227
Vivour, Carlos G. 104, 206, 231
Vivour de Kinson, Isabel 135
Vivour, Esteban 139
Vivour (family) 23, 60, 61, 63, 66, 70, 71, 114, 115, 134, 137, 186, 219, 229, 231, 232. See also Barleycorn, Cole, Kinson, and Lolín
Vivour, Isabel 46, 63
Vivour, Jacob 63
Vivour Lolín, Susana 139
Vivour, Sarah 104, 105, 231
Vivour, Valerina 184
Vivour, Valerina Diana 18
Vivour, William Allen 19, 22, 59, 62-64, 68, 114, 131, 159, 167, 168, 190-192, 198, 203, 227, 238

W
Wartron, Ana 227
Watson, Ana 209
wedding. See marriage
Welah, Adolfo. See Jones Welah
whiteness 123, 251
white people 19, 31, 39, 52, 63, 71, 76, 79, 90, 91, 94, 95, 97, 99, 101-103, 115, 126, 147, 162, 181, 210, 213, 223, 230, 232, 237, 243
  abuse 24, 103, 115, 147
  androcentrism 147
  elite 20
  impunity 94, 95, 102, 115
  majority 32, 103
  minority 54, 78
  non- 179
  nuns 143
  Spanish Africans 143
  women 100
Wilson (family) 134
Wilson, Francisco 135, 163
workers 20, 46, 66, 205, 206. See also labourers

X
xenophobia 114, 122, 147, 183